PRAISE FOR *THE DEBT RESISTERS' OPERATIONS MANUAL*

"That debt is neither inevitable nor ethical is one of the powerful assertions of Strike Debt, whose brilliant manual is both a practical handbook and a manifesto for a true debt jubilee: an economic rebirth in which the indebted are freed and financial institutions are reinvented. It's a stunning intersection of ferocity (against the debt industry) and compassion (for the people whose lives are broken by debt). In years to come, we may look back on it as a landmark in social transformation; right now it is both useful and exhilarating."

— **Rebecca Solnit**, author of *A Paradise Built in Hell: The Extraordinary Communities That Arise in Disaster* and *Wanderlust: A History of Walking*

"The impact of the neoliberal assault on the U.S. population in the past generation has rightly been designated a 'failure by design.' This failure is sharply class-based—for the designers it has been a grand success, and a failure for most of the rest. The same is true of debt. That sets two tasks for those who care about the health of the society: change the design, and find ways to cope as effectively with the failures it imposes. This valuable monograph by Strike Debt provides a good guide to undertake both."

— **Noam Chomsky**, author of *Hopes and Prospects* and *M̶a̶k̶i̶n̶g̶ ̶t̶h̶e̶ Future: The Unipolar Imperial Moment*

"This manual is a practical guide that w̶ gling with debt. But even more importan̶ illuminates the myriad kinds of debt re̶ society and helps us imagine how we can̶ ̶g̶i̶t̶ ̶t̶o̶ organize collectively against debt."

— **Michael Hardt**, coauthor of *Empire*, *Multitude: War and Democracy in the Age of Empire*, and *Commonwealth*

"*The Debt Resisters' Operations Manual* is a powerful tool for resistance and creation. It shows how we can say 'No!' to debt—resist and refuse—while at the same time opens the possibility of alternative ways of relating and creating real value together—based on solidarity and care."

— **Marina Sitrin**, author of *Everyday Revolutions: Horizontalism and Autonomy in Argentina*

"*The Debt Resisters' Operations Manual* is a sober, practical book that will save its readers much money and many sleepless nights. At the same time it is a visionary text that goes into the bowels of the debt machine to chart a collective way out of the state of debt-induced indentured servitude that millions of Americans face. It is the new debt resisters' movement's opening challenge to Wall Street that is making the bankers anxious. Get a copy and join the movement."

—**Silvia Federici**, author of *Revolution at Point Zero: Housework, Reproduction, and Feminist Struggle* and *Caliban and the Witch: Women, the Body, and Primitive Accumulation*

"*The Debt Resisters' Operations Manual* is a guide for every debtor living in the United States. Given that more than 75% of American households are in debt right now, its relevance cannot be overstated. The manual is ambitious in subject matter but grounded in tone: plain and clear English is the best weapon if we want to understand the deliberately over-complicated debt economy. Readers learn that personal debt— credit card, medical, student, and housing—is rarely just personal and an important section on municipal debt reclaims the conversation about debt from the Right, where it is used so often to justify austerity. It questions the received wisdom that an indebted city logically must pursue cuts by showing that the money that is now considered 'owed' did not magically disappear; it was transferred to the 1 percent and should be taken back. The authors undo the assumptions that prop up the debt economy and challenge the notion that repaying debts is a moral duty; in fact, they argue, debt resistance is the moral choice."

—**Natasha Lewis**, freelance journalist and Occupy reporter

THE
Debt
Resisters'
Operations
Manual

STRIKE DEBT

The Debt Resisters' Operations Manual
Strike Debt

ISBN: 978-1-60486-679-7

LCCN: 2013911518

Cover and interior design: Antumbra Design/antumbradesign.org

10 9 8 7 6 5 4 3 2 1

PM Press   Common Notions
PO Box 23912   131 8th St. #4
Oakland, CA 94623   Brooklyn, NY 11215
www.pmpress.org   www.commonnotions.org

Autonomedia
PO Box 568 Williamsburg Station
Brooklyn, NY 11211-0568
www.autonomedia.org

Printed in the USA by the Employee Owners of
Thomson-Shore in Dexter, Michigan. www.thomsonshore.com

COMMON NOTIONS is a publishing project that circulates both enduring and timely formulations of autonomy at the heart of movements beyond capitalism. The series traces a constellation of historical, critical, and visionary meditations on the organization of both domination and its refusal. Inspired by various traditions of autonomism in the United States and around the world, Common Notions aims to provide tools of militant research in our collective reading of struggles past, present, and to come.

Series Editor: Malav Kanuga
info@commonnotions.org | www.commonnotions.org

OTHER BOOKS FROM COMMON NOTIONS/PM PRESS

Selma James, *Sex, Race, and Class—The Perspective of Winning: A Selection of Writings 1952–2011*

Silvia Federici, *Revolution at Point Zero: Housework, Reproduction, and Feminist Struggle*

George Caffentzis, *In Letters of Blood and Fire: Work, Machines, and the Crisis of Capitalism*

CONTENTS

GLOSSARY

ACCOUNTS RECEIVABLE MANAGEMENT—A term used by insiders to describe the debt collection industry.

ACTIVE TRANSPORTATION—Transportation policy or choices that prioritize walking, biking, mopeds, scooters, trolleys, buses, shuttles, light rail, local, regional, and continental train systems over automobiles.

ADJUSTABLE RATE MORTGAGE (ARM)—A type of mortgage where the interest rate paid on the outstanding balance changes according to a specific indicator, often out of the control or knowledge of the borrower.

AFFIDAVIT—A voluntarily written statement made by a person under oath.

AFFIANT—A person who swears to an affidavit.

AFFORDABLE CARE ACT (ACA)—President Obama's health care reform law signed in 2010, most parts of which went into effect by 2014. The law has the stated intent of making health care more affordable, although at least 23 million people will remain uninsured. It has been criticized for widely expanding the role of private health insurance and for-profit care, rapidly transferring public money to private hands through the individual mandate. Also referred to as the Patient Protection and Affordable Care Act (PPACA) or Obamacare. See **INDIVIDUAL MANDATE**.

ALTERNATIVE FINANCIAL SERVICES (AFS)—See **FRINGE FINANCE**.

AMENABLE MORTALITY—A death that could have been prevented with access to effective health care.

ANNUAL PERCENTAGE RATE (APR)—The rate of a loan's interest, expressed as the amount that would be accrued over the course of a year.

ASSET—Anything of economic value owned by a person or company, the value of which may be expressed in cash.

AUSTERITY PROGRAMS—Cuts to government spending on social programs justified as a means of balancing municipal, state, and national budgets in times of financial distress.

AUTO DEBT—See **CAR DEBT**.

AUTO-TITLE LOAN—When a borrower exchanges their automobile's title for cash, generally for about one-quarter of the vehicle's value, with a high APR. The vehicle can still be driven, however, during the loan's duration.

BANKRUPTCY—A court-supervised legal process in which the debts of an individual or business in financial distress are restructured or dismissed.

BANKRUPTCY ABUSE PREVENTION AND CONSUMER PROTECTION ACT (BAP-CPA)—Passed in 2005 as the result of massive lobbying on behalf of the credit industry, BAPCPA is a harsh reform to the federal bankruptcy code that makes it significantly harder and more expensive for debtors to file.

CAPITAL GAINS—Profits obtained by selling assets, for example, a home, family business, stock, or bond.

CAPITALISM—An economic system, or mode of production, in which the bulk of the means of production are privately owned, products are exchanged in a market (i.e., the primary determinant of prices is competition among individual enterprises trying to make a profit), and most people work for others, who own the means of production in exchange for wages or a salary.

CAR DEBT—Debt incurred by the purchase, use, and maintenance of an automobile.

CARBON EMISSIONS—The release of carbon dioxide into the earth's atmosphere—primarily from the use of oil, natural gas, coal, and other fossil fuels—which results in an increase in the average global temperature.

CARD (CREDIT CARD ACCOUNTABILITY RESPONSIBILITY AND DISCLOSURE) ACT—The CARD Act of 2009 requires card issuers to determine a consumer's ability to pay prior to increasing a credit limit or opening a new credit card account.

CHAPTER 7 BANKRUPTCY—One of the two main chapters in the federal bankruptcy code under which individuals may file, Chapter 7 wipes away all consumer, medical, and other unsecured debts, but does not discharge certain tax debts, student loan debt, or debt from alimony and child support obligations.

CHAPTER 13 BANKRUPTCY—One of the two main chapters in the federal bankruptcy code under which individuals may file, Chapter 13 emphasizes the restructuring of an individual's debts as opposed to outright dismissal, allowing the debtor a chance to retain some important assets.

CHECK-CASHING OUTLET (CCO)—A store where people can cash checks for a fee, often used by people who don't have a checking account.

CHURNING—A process whereby lenders prolong the duration of debt in order to extract as many fees as possible.

CLIMATE CHANGE—Severe and sudden changes in the earth's atmosphere and weather patterns brought about by human activity. Although technically the earth's climate is constantly changing over vast periods of time, drastic increases in greenhouse gas emissions over the past two centuries have had unprecedented and profound impacts on the planet, and thus the term "climate change" primarily refers to human-induced changes.

CLIMATE DEBT—Originally known as "carbon debt," the term "climate debt" refers to a measureable ecological obligation from the world's wealthiest countries to the global South, calculated with the understanding that the former are responsible for most greenhouse gas emissions, while the latter tends to suffer the harshest consequences. Contrasted with the monetary debts imposed by the richest nations, the concept of climate debt challenges conventional assumptions regarding who owes what to whom.

COLLECTION AGENCY—A business that profits through the collection of debts and interest owed by individuals or businesses.

COMMONS—Natural, intellectual, and social resources for which access, use, and management are shared among members of a community.

CONSOLIDATION—Combining several loans into one larger loan from a single lender in order to pay off the balances on the others.

CONSUMER FINANCIAL PROTECTION BUREAU (CFPB)—An independent U.S. federal agency whose stated purpose is to regulate financial institutions such as banks, payday lenders, and collection agencies, and to protect consumers from fraudulent or misleading financial products and services. The CFPB was created in 2011 following the passage of the Dodd–Frank Wall Street Reform and Consumer Protection Act.

COPAY—The portion of payment for a medical service that is provided by a person with insurance. Higher copays often deter insured individuals from seeking care, resulting in them being effectively uninsured.

CORPORATE WELFARE—A term used to describe when a government gives tax breaks or other special treatment to corporations, in contrast to the characterization of poor people as undermining the system through use of social services.

CREDIT CARD RECEIVABLES—A projection of a credit card companies' future business income that consists of all the interest that could potentially be collected from cards issued.

CREDIT REPORT—A document produced by a credit reporting agency (CRA) summarizing a person's credit history. Information in credit reports factors critically in decisions to grant credit (e.g., mortgage loans, auto loans, credit cards, and private student loans) and in other financial spheres, including eligibility for rental housing, setting premiums for auto and homeowners insurance in some states, and employment. See **CREDIT REPORTING AGENCIES (CRAs)**.

CREDIT REPORTING AGENCIES (CRAs)—Companies that gather, organize, and standardize certain consumer financial information—such as credit card balances, payment history, and outstanding student loan debt—and then sell this information to banks and other creditors. Increasingly, this information is also being sold to employers, insurers, and consumers themselves. The largest CRAs—known as the "Big Three," or the "national" CRAs—are Equifax, TransUnion, and Experian.

CREDIT SCORE—A number produced by inputting a person's credit information from their credit report into a proprietary algorithm. Credit reporting agencies (CRAs) generate this number and provide it to banks or other financing companies, which use it to decide whether to lend to someone, and at what interest rate. Scores have different ranges, the most common one being 300 to 850, with a higher number signifying greater "creditworthiness." Increasingly, credit scores are used in other major decisions besides lending, such as employment and housing. See **CREDIT REPORT** and **CREDIT REPORTING AGENCIES (CRAs)**.

CREDITOR—A person or institution to whom money is owed, typically as the result of a legally binding loan agreement.

CURRENTLY NOT COLLECTIBLE—A program where the IRS voluntarily agrees not to collect on one's tax debts for approximately one year.

DATA-MINING—A process of analyzing large amounts of data to discover patterns, often used by businesses to determine sales trends and increase profit.

DEDUCTIBLE—The expenses—expressed as either a flat rate or a percentage of all costs—that must be paid out-of-pocket by the patient before an insurer will pay any remaining costs.

DEFAULT—Failure to make required payments on debt on time.

DEFERMENT—See **STUDENT LOAN DEFERMENT**.

DEPARTMENT OF THE TREASURY—The accounting arm of the U.S. federal government, responsible for the collection of all incoming revenue as well as the payment of all federal obligations. Where revenue falls short of covering operating expenses, the Treasury issues government debt in the form of bills, notes, and bonds. The Treasury is also responsible for printing currency.

DISASTER CAPITALISM—The exploitation of natural disasters to promote market-based redistribution from the poor to the wealthy, and the outsourcing of basic services like education, health care, and housing to private providers at the local level.

DISPOSABLE INCOME—The amount of one's income after legally required deductions are made, such as taxes and employee retirement systems.

ECOLOGICAL DEBT—See **CLIMATE DEBT**.

ELECTRONIC BENEFIT TRANSFER (EBT) CARD—A card issued by government agencies and used by cardholders to access benefits such as food stamps, unemployment compensation, veterans' benefits, etc.

EMINENT DOMAIN—The power of the government and quasi-public development corporations to seize privately owned land. Land seized through eminent domain must be used for the "public benefit," loosely defined. It may remain property of the state or may be immediately transferred to private developers with the often-vague mandate to foster economic development.

FAIR CREDIT REPORTING ACT (FCRA)—Passed in 1970 in response to the increasing concentration of personal consumer credit information in the hands of a few national credit reporting agencies, the FCRA sets out a number of requirements and rules for all agencies that compile consumer credit reports on individuals nationwide.

FAIR DEBT COLLECTIONS PRACTICES ACT (FDCPA)—A 1977 amendment to the Consumer Credit Protection Act (1968) that makes certain abusive debt collection practices illegal.

FANNIE MAE (FEDERAL NATIONAL MORTGAGE ASSOCIATION)—A U.S. federal program created in 1938 as part of the New Deal to expand the homeowner population by loaning money to people who previously didn't qualify. Fannie Mae was privatized in 1968.

FEDERAL HOUSING ADMINISTRATION (FHA)—A U.S. federal program created in 1934 with the express purpose of insuring mortgage loans from banks and other parties in the private sector.

FEDERAL RESERVE BANK—The national bank of the United States, which is a central banking system with twelve branches spread across the nation. It controls monetary policy and has supervisory and regulatory authority over the nation's private banking system.

FICO SCORE—The most common type of credit score. Credit reporting agencies (CRAs) calculate this score by taking financial data about a consumer and plugging it into an algorithm created by the Fair Isaac Corporation (hence the name "FICO score"). This algorithm is proprietary and secret. The score's range is 300 to 850, and the median score is about 720. If someone's score is above the median, they will likely have access to the best credit terms. About 20% of the U.S. population do not have a FICO score because there is not enough information in their credit report, which has a negative impact on their ability to get loans. The majority of lending decisions in the United States are made using the FICO score. See **CREDIT REPORTING AGENCIES (CRAs)** and **CREDIT SCORE**.

FINANCIALIZATION—A process whereby economic growth becomes increasingly dependent upon money earned through investment and speculation, and whereby financial institutions increasingly influence economic policy.

FORBEARANCE—See **STUDENT LOAN FORBEARANCE**.

FORECLOSURE—The process by which a lender secured by a mortgage or deed of trust engages in the eviction and subsequent sale of property to recover money unpaid by the borrower.

FREE SCHOOLS—Grassroots-organized schools emphasizing the exchange of knowledge without hierarchy or institutional structures.

FRINGE FINANCE—An array of predatory "alternative" financial services (AFS) usually offered by providers that operate outside of federally insured banks. Services include check cashing, remittances/money transfers, prepaid cards, payday loans, pawnshop loans, auto-title loans, and rent-to-own agreements.

G20—A group of finance ministers and central bank governors from nineteen countries plus the president of the European Council and Head of the European Central Bank, representing twenty major economies. The G20 has been meeting once or twice a year since November 2008 and has the stated goals of achieving "global economic stability" and "sustainable growth," although each summit has faced resistance due to a myriad of criticisms, including the group's lack of transparency and inherently undemocratic nature.

G8—Heads of governments of eight major national economies who meet annually to discuss international issues and are routinely criticized for reasons similar to the G20.

GARNISHMENT—The practice of deducting money from a debtor's income (typically the salary), sometimes as a result of a court order. Wage garnishment often continues until the full debt is paid off.

GENERAL PURPOSE RELOADABLE (GPR) CARD—A prepaid card set up with the user's own funds, used in place of a debit or credit card.

GLEANING—The act of gathering unharvested crops left behind by a landowner. Historically, gleaning has at times been sanctioned or even encouraged, at others forbidden or criminalized.

GLOBAL SOUTH—A term used to differentiate economically "developed" or rich nations like the United States and those in Western Europe from the "underdeveloped" or poor nations of Africa, Latin America, and most of Asia.

GREENHOUSE GASES—Gases—most notably carbon dioxide, methane, and nitrous oxide—that trap heat in the earth's atmosphere and affect changes in the climate.

GUARANTEE AGENCY—A company that insures private issuers of federal student loans. Only loans issued prior to June 30, 2010, may be serviced by a guarantee agency. On such loans, in the event of a default, the guarantee company reimburses the private lender—largely with funds provided by the government—and takes over the responsibility for collection.

HIPAA (HEALTH INSURANCE PORTABILITY AND ACCOUNTABILITY ACT)—A U.S. law that protect patients' privacy and requires providers to notify patients if a breach has occurred.

INDEPENDENT CONTRACTOR—Someone who is self-employed and determines their own schedule and mode of work. Examples include nurses, lawyers, barbers, cabdrivers, and accountants.

INDIGENT—An individual without enough income to afford basic needs like food, clothing, and shelter, or in a criminal case, someone who cannot afford their own attorney.

INDIVIDUAL MANDATE—When an individual is required to obtain private health insurance instead of, or in addition to, a national health insurance plan.

INDIVIDUAL TAX IDENTIFICATION NUMBER (ITIN)—An IRS-issued, nine-digit number for taxpayers who are not eligible for a Social Security number.

INSURANCE PREMIUM—The rate a patient pays for some portion of the expense of office visits, including prescription medications, surgical procedures, mental health services, ongoing treatment, and emergency services.

INTEREST—A fee for borrowing, calculated as a percentage of money owed.

INTEREST RATE SWAP (IRS)—A financial tool engineered by Wall Street banks and marketed to states, cities, and other issuers of municipal debt as a means of converting variable interest payments to stable fixed rates. In practice, swaps have locked many municipalities into artificially high interest payments from which banks profit greatly.

INTERNATIONAL MONETARY FUND (IMF)—An international organization with the mandate of expanding global trade which, in coordination with the World Bank, issues loans to countries in need under the guise of alleviating poverty, often while imposing structural adjustment programs. According to the IMF, it differs from the World Bank in that it is a "cooperative" institution tasked with overseeing the balance of accounts between countries. See **WORLD BANK** and **STRUCTURAL ADJUSTMENT PROGRAMS (SAPs)**.

JUBILEE—Historically, jubilee refers to the abolition of slavery, the cancellation of all debt, and a return of all lands to the common. In the late eighteenth century the term was used in the English countryside to demand an end to enclosures while African slaves used "jubilee" to demand liberation from slavery. The term was used more recently in the alter-globalization movement in the 1990s to demand an end to third world debt and by debt resistance groups after the financial crisis of 2008 to demand the cancellation of household debt.

LEGAL FINANCIAL OBLIGATIONS (LFOs)—Fines, fees, and other costs associated with a criminal sentence, for example, supervision fees if on probation, administrative fees, "pay to stay" fees, and prison fees.

LIBOR (LONDON INTERBANK OFFERED RATE)—Benchmark used to set interest rates for over $800 trillion in investments globally. Calculated daily based on data provided by eighteen of the world's largest banks. For several years following the financial crisis of 2008, banks committed massive fraud by reporting false data to intentionally manipulate interest rates around the world.

LIEN—In the event of non-payment, a lien is a creditor's right to take possession of and sell the debtor's asset that was used to secure a loan.

MEANS TEST—A set of criteria used to determine eligibility for financial assistance or debt relief based on an individual's perceived need.

MEDIAN WAGE—In a set of wages, the wage that falls between the highest-paid 50% of workers' wages and above that of the lowest 50%.

MEDICAID—A U.S. federal- and state-funded health insurance program available only to specific low-income populations, including children, pregnant women, and people living with disabilities.

MEDICAL LOSS RATIO—A term used by insurance companies to account for the money that is actually spent on care instead of profits.

MEDICARE—A U.S. federal social insurance program funded largely by a payroll tax on employers and workers, Medicare provides health insurance for U.S. citizens 65 and older and others with qualifying conditions.

MICROCREDIT—A particular practice of lending where loans are not given to isolated individuals, but to each person in a "solidarity group," often women, in order to finance a small business venture. The members of the group are collectively responsible to make the recipient pay the loan back to the bank. This use of social pressure to achieve high payback rates has been justified as an alternative to the usurious practices of moneylenders in poor communities all over the world.

MICROLOANS—See **MICROCREDIT**.

MILITARY-INDUSTRIAL COMPLEX—A term used to describe the strong ideological and material connections between a nation's armed forces, elected officials, and corporations. See **PRISON-INDUSTRIAL COMPLEX**.

MINI-MIRANDA—A legally required statement from a collector informing the lender that they are collecting a debt and that any information gathered during correspondence will be used to collect that debt.

MONETIZATION—A process of converting something into legal tender, for example, paper currency or coins.

MORTGAGE—An agreement in which a loan is obtained to buy property and in which the lender may take ownership in the event that the repayment does not occur according to the terms of the agreement.

MORTGAGE-BACKED SECURITY (MBS)—A tradable financial product whose value is based on the likelihood of repayment on a mortgage or collection of mortgages.

MORTGAGE-MODIFICATION—A process where the lender and borrower of a mortgage agree to modify terms of the original agreement often in service of helping the borrower avoid eviction and foreclosure.

MUNICIPAL BOND—Bonds issued to raise funds by state and local governments or publicly funded incorporated entities, such as school districts, development corporations, transportation authorities, or public utilities. Municipal bonds are explicitly or implicitly backed by future tax revenue or other revenue streams such as tolls and utility fees, and are often issued by government-formed authorities run by unelected boards of directors.

MUNICIPALITY—Any incorporated local governmental division, such as a county, city, town, or village.

MUTUAL AID—A practice of freely sharing or lending resources or labor based on the understanding that the betterment of a community member is ultimately beneficial to all. It has been observed everywhere in nature and throughout history.

NATIONAL DEBT—Debt created by selling government bonds and securities to banks and investors within the country issuing the bonds.

NEGATIVE EQUITY—When the market value of an asset or investment falls below its outstanding loan balance.

NEOLIBERALISM—A form of capitalism that claims that what had previously been done by the state or through cooperative social action would be better done by capitalist firms competing in the marketplace. It differs from "old" liberalism, which argued for tearing down tariff barriers and other "hindrances to trade." In neoliberalism, commodification extends into realms that previously resisted it—such as the human parts market—and whole new areas of property—such as the DNA of a species. Neoliberal economic policies generally include the push for privatization of public services, lower wages for the majority of workers, and loosening restrictions on businesses. See **CAPITALISM**.

NET WORTH—See **WEALTH**.

ODIOUS DEBT—Debt imposed on a government that should never have been taken on in the first place. Often incurred by undemocratic regimes in the interest of those in power, it is the country's population that is held responsible for repayment, typically at the cost of great suffering.

OFFER IN COMPROMISE—A way to settle one's tax debts for less than what one owes, based on ability to pay, income, expenses, and asset equity.

ORIGINAL CREDITOR (OC)—The company to which a debt was originally owed.

PARTICIPATORY BUDGETING—A process by which community members work together to determine priorities for public spending. Participatory budgeting has been shown to result in a more equitable distribution of public resources than budgets determined exclusively by representative governments.

PAWNSHOP LOAN—When a borrower gives property to a pawnbroker to secure a small, high-APR loan, generally for half of the item's value.

PAYDAY LOAN—Small-credit, high-APR loans deceptively marketed as a quick and easy way to tide borrowers over until the next payday.

POVERTY TAX—The surcharge people pay for not having savings or access to prime credit and are thus consigned to fringe finance.

PRECARIOUS LABOR—A trend in employment practices in which opportunities for long-term stable jobs with benefits are scarce.

PREDATORY LENDING—The practice of deceiving borrowers into entering abusive or unfair loan agreements.

PRISON-INDUSTRIAL COMPLEX—A concept used to draw parallels with the military-industrial complex, to highlight ways in which corporate profits incentivize a rapidly increasing prisoner population. See **MILITARY-INDUSTRIAL COMPLEX**.

PROGRESSIVE TAXATION—A tax system where people with higher incomes have a higher tax rate in order to better distribute wealth. See **REGRESSIVE TAXATION**.

PUBLIC BANKING—An alternative to standard state and local government banking and financing models. State or municipal revenues are held in a publicly owned an operated bank rather than a Wall Street financial institution. Bank funds are used to finance infrastructure, economic development and programs that provide long-term returns and benefit the public good, allowing governments to avoid the bond-financing trap. Bank dividends are returned to the public treasury.

REDLINING—A practice that makes loans or insurance inaccessible to people of color, historically used to enhance segregation. See **REVERSE REDLINING**.

REFUND ANTICIPATION CHECKS (RACs)—A financial product in which consumers who can't afford tax preparation costs agree to have a temporary bank account opened where the IRS deposits their tax refund. When the refund is deposited, the tax preparation company takes out the amount equal to the cost of their services as well as burdensome fees.

REFUND ANTICIPATION LOANS (RALs)—A financial product where consumers can receive the amount of their tax refund in advance in the form of a short-term, high-interest loan. This product has, as of 2013, been largely replaced by refund anticipation checks. See **REFUND ANTICIPATION CHECKS**.

REGRESSIVE TAXATION—A tax system in which people with lower incomes bear a disproportionately high tax burden. See **PROGRESSIVE TAXATION**.

REMITTANCE—A money transfer sent to an immigrant's home country.

RENT-TO-OWN LENDER—A store that rents appliances, electronics, and other items to people which they can, in theory, eventually own. This is different from credit purchases where the customer immediately gains the title to the product.

REPRODUCTIVE LABOR—Work done in and around the home, often without a wage, including but not limited to childrearing, housework, and procreation; traditionally done by women and unrecognized as "work."

RESERVE CURRENCY—The primary currency of exchange used by governments and institutions in global trade. The U.S. dollar has been the reserve currency for the past seven decades.

REVERSE REDLINING—Aggressively targeting communities of color with predatory services such as loans, insurance, for-profit education, etc. See **REDLINING**.

RISK POOLING—The subsidization of wealthy households' credit cards.

RISK PREMIUM—The cost increase required to compensate for credit risk.

ROBO-SIGNING—When an employee, agent, or software of a mortgage servicing company signs foreclosure documents without reviewing them, often resulting in fraudulent or faulty agreements.

SALLIE MAE (STUDENT LOAN MARKETING ASSOCIATION)—Created as a government-sponsored enterprise in 1972, Sallie Mae's initial purpose was to issue federally guaranteed student loans, financed by a mix of subsidies and private capital. Now it is a publicly traded multibillion-dollar company that issues private student loans and makes millions servicing loans originated by the government.

SECONDARY MARKET—A market where original investments (loans, mortgages, etc.) are pooled or split in order to be traded to other investors. The New York Stock Exchange and the NASDAQ are examples of secondary markets.

SECURED DEBT—A debt in which specified assets (collateral) become the property of the lender in the event that the borrower cannot repay. See **UNSECURED DEBT**.

SERVICE ECONOMY—A range of jobs that produce intangible goods, for example, retail, food, and education. Employees in this sector usually require specialized skill sets and are paid low wages.

SINGLE-PAYER HEALTH CARE—Health care in which a government pays for all expenses except copays and coinsurance, rather than private insurance companies.

SLABS (STUDENT LOAN ASSET-BACKED SECURITIES)—Tradable financial products whose value is based on the likelihood of repayment on private student loans that are collected in a pool.

SOCIALISM—An economic system in which the bulk of the means of production are held in common and production is democratically planned by the producers.

SOVEREIGN DEBT—Debt created by national governments borrowing from foreign sources like the World Bank, the International Monetary Fund (IMF), or nation-states like China.

SQUATTING—The common practice of taking up residence in an otherwise unoccupied property and making it one's home without permission from the legally recognized property owner.

STATED INCOME LOAN—A type of mortgage that allows the borrower to note their income and assets on the loan application without verification.

STATUTE OF LIMITATIONS (SOL)—A legal limit on the number of years a creditor may attempt to pursue payment.

STRUCTURAL ADJUSTMENT PROGRAMS (SAPs)—Conditions set by the International Monetary Fund and World Bank primarily for countries in the global South to repay debts or apply for new loans.

STUDENT LOAN DEFERMENT—An agreement between lender and financially distressed borrower to postpone repayment for a defined period during which interest does not accrue for subsidized loans.

STUDENT LOAN FORBEARANCE—An agreement between a lender and a financially distressed borrower to reduce or delay payments to avoid default. Interest continues to accrue during this period.

SUBPRIME—Loans that are characterized by high interest rates, designed for "high-risk" borrowers due to their low credit scores, inadequate documentation, or high debt loads.

TREASURY NOTES—See **DEPARTMENT OF THE TREASURY**.

UNBANKED—People without checking or savings accounts.

UNDERBANKED—People with checking or savings accounts but who at least partially rely on alternative financial products.

UNDERWATER HOME—A home in which the value of the mortgage is higher than the home's market value.

UNSECURED DEBT—Money borrowed that is not backed by collateral. See **SECURED DEBT**.

UPSIDE-DOWN CAR LOAN—A loan in which the purchaser owes more on a car than that car's current value.

USURY LAWS—Laws that establish legal maximum interest rates for loans regulated by states to protect borrowers.

WAGE STAGNATION—An economic trend in which average wages do not increase when adjusted for inflation.

WEALTH—The amount someone owns minus the amount that they owe. Also referred to as net worth.

WORLD BANK—An international organization with the mandate of expanding global trade which, in coordination with the International Monetary Fund, issues loans to countries in need under the guise of alleviating poverty, often while imposing structural adjustment programs. See **INTERNATIONAL MONETARY FUND (IMF)** and **STRUCTURAL ADJUSTMENT PROGRAMS (SAPs)**.

INTRODUCTION

DEBT RULES EVERYTHING AROUND ME

Everyone is affected by debt, from people taking out payday loans at 400% interest to cover basic living costs, to recent graduates paying hundreds of dollars in interest on their students loans every month, to working families bankrupted by medical bills, to elders living in "underwater" homes, to the teachers and firefighters forced to take pay cuts because their cities are broke, to people in the global South suffering due to their countries being pushed into austerity and poverty by structural adjustment programs.

Everyone seems to owe something, and most of us are in so deep it'll be years before we have any chance of getting out—if we have any chance at all. But few of us are asking, "Who do we all owe this money to, anyway?" and "Where did they get the money they lent?"

TO WHOM ARE WE INDEBTED?

Even among people drowning in debt, typical conversations around the subject are framed in terms of personal responsibility: the debtors have no one to blame but themselves for getting into this situation, and moreover, to not pay one's debts is an act of blasphemy, shame, and dishonor. To default is to expose one's callous disregard for all that is decent.

Today, morality is bound to debt—the two are inextricably linked. When we dispose of all the jargon attached to credit and debt, we can see that at its core, a loan is essentially a bet on whether or not that person—the debtor—will make good on their word. It is a risk, and that risk is higher or lower depending on that person's status in society (defined only in the most narrow economic terms). A debt represents the willingness and ability of one to keep their promise. But a person's actual ability to repay is often out of their hands. Frequently it depends on powers beyond their control. Debt further distorts our basic perceptions of ourselves and others; not only is a person's word on the line, but also their value as a human being. In a way, we invest the value we place on ourselves into that credit arrangement and into our relationship with debt. We measure how and who we are as a human being and then bet on our trustworthiness, our character.

The subprime mortgage crisis is a particularly egregious example of moralistic victim-blaming. Subprime mortgages were concentrated in areas with higher racial segregation and targeted people of color, yet some people blamed the victims of this financial disaster, often with racialized language, proclaiming that, "those people shouldn't have borrowed so much." Arguments such as these, however, ignore the whole history of the exclusion of people of color from mainstream financial opportunities that could have led to homeownership. In addition, when many people of color finally got access to credit through legislative reforms, the lending was often predatory in nature. The effects of the subprime mortgage crisis and the subsequent credit crisis resulted in the further degradation of debtors' social status. Edmund Andrews, the former economics correspondent at the *New York Times*, tied the issue together quite well when he reflected on his own credit troubles: "to see yourself plunged down to being a debtor, the likes of which are being made fun of all over the place—it's just an awful experience."[1] This statement makes clear what many already feel (and fear): the debtor is seen as *subordinate* or somehow *of less value* than a non-debtor. This is unfortunately held as a near-universal belief and many people are socially and economically excluded because of it. Debt warps the way we look at each other and encourages us to evaluate one another through a financial lens. Debt serves as a way to classify people, to put them into hierarchies, and to separate and isolate them in the process.

Most of us have been brought up in a society where we are conditioned to hold these beliefs dearly, and on the surface it all sounds reasonable. If you take out a loan, you are obligated to pay it back. Focusing on debt at the individual level is a common approach. However, it is insufficient for understanding debt *as a system* and understanding why one would be right in resisting it. We have to go deeper by examining the terrain on a structural level and explore the circumstances that have put people (and municipalities and entire countries) into debt.

DEBT AND INCOME INEQUALITY

Over three-quarters of us have some type of personal debt. At least 14% of people living in the United States are already being pursued by debt collectors, which is more than double from a decade ago.[2] Are so many people *really* so reckless, so irresponsible? Granted, total household debt has been on the decline since 2008, but it is neverthe-

---

[1] *The Flaw*, DVD, directed by David Sington (2011; London: Studio Lambert, 2012).

[2] "Quarterly Report on Household Debt and Credit," *Federal Reserve Bank of New York*, November 2012. http://tinyurl.com/DROMFedNY, 15.

less still sitting at a whopping $11.31 trillion.[3] Moreover, the median debt amount has risen substantially over the past decade and a half.[4]

Contrary to popular misconceptions, debt cannot simply be explained as the consequence of financially irresponsible individuals acquiring luxurious items beyond their means. Instead it is quite typically the outcome of people and families just trying to survive under capitalism. Forty percent of indebted U.S. households use credit cards to cover basic living costs such as rent, food, and utilities, and nearly half of indebted households have accrued debt due to medical costs.[5] Indeed, we are told to consume to stimulate the economy and are subsequently demonized for accruing debt. In the wake of any financial blip or disaster, politicians often implore people to spend money for the sake of economic growth (remember that then-mayor Giuliani's advice to New Yorkers after 9/11 was to go shopping). After the financial crash, however, we were told that we spent *too much*. According to a Consumer Reports survey in 2009, over half of the respondents paid off credit card bills each month. The remaining people accrued debt not by living large, but mostly by spending money on health costs, transportation, and other basic needs.[6] Many credit card-indebted households making under $10,000 per year spend over 40% of that meager income to pay off debt.[7] Dēmos and the Center for Responsible Lending have also debunked this myth of irresponsibility, stating, "the underlying reason behind some households having higher levels of credit card debt than other households was the occurrence of unforeseen events, such as job loss, medical expenses, or car breakdowns."[8]

There are myriad factors that explain these circumstances, but a good place to start is by looking at economic trends over the past four and a half decades. The actual value of the federal minimum wage reached its peak in 1968.[9] Since then, the real median hourly wage has basically stagnated, while labor productivity has increased con-

---

[3] "Quarterly Report," *Federal Reserve Bank of New York*, 1.

[4] Tim Mullaney, "More Americans Debt-Free, but the Rest Owe More," *USA Today*, March 21, 2013. http://tinyurl.com/DROMMullaney.

[5] Amy Traub and Catherine Ruetschlin, "The Plastic Safety Net: Findings from the 2012 National Survey on Credit Card Debt of Low- and Middle-Income Households," *Dēmos*, 2012. http://tinyurl.com/DROMTraub, 9.

[6] "Take Control of Your Credit Cards," *Consumer Reports*, November 2009. http://tinyurl.com/DROMCR.

[7] "The Racial Gap in Debt, Credit and Financial Services," *Insight Center for Community Economic Development*, June 2009. http://tinyurl.com/DROMICCED, 2.

[8] Tamara Draut et al., "The Plastic Safety Net: The Reality Behind Debt in America," *Dēmos and The Center for Responsible Lending*, October 2005. http://tinyurl.com/DROMDraut, 9.

[9] John Schmitt, "The Minimum Wage Is Too Damn Low," *Center for Economic and Policy Research*, March 2012. http://tinyurl.com/DROMSchmitt, 1.

siderably.[10] Notably, the average U.S. debt-income ratio doubled over this same period, with average household debt beginning to exceed income in the early 2000s.[11]

> **If wages were to increase with productivity over the past fifty years, the hourly minimum wage would be three times what it currently is,[12] and median hourly wages in the United States would be $27.87 instead of $16.07.[13]**

Of course, wage stagnation affects different populations with varying degrees of severity. Compared to 1966, the wage increase for an overwhelming majority of people in the United States averages only fifty-nine more dollars a year when adjusted for inflation. The increase since 1966 for the top 10% of income earners in our society, on the other hand, is over two thousand times this amount, and over *ten thousand* times this amount for the top 1%![14] Looking just at the years since the 2008 financial crisis, the top 1% of incomes rose considerably as the bottom 99% decreased.[15]

One-quarter of jobs in the United States pay below the poverty line for a household of four. To make matters worse, job security has diminished over the past few decades with many more jobs becoming casual, flexible, and temporary.[16] The shift from the manufacturing economy to the service economy has contributed to a steep rise in precarious work—insecure jobs with low wages and no benefits.[17]

As any wage laborer knows, the power exercised over them in the workplace is sometimes absolute. But in today's unstable economy, where it's common to hear of people working more than one part-time job without benefits, often just finding and keeping a job is a huge struggle. Today, even the ability to find a job can be determined

---

[10] Lawrence Mishel and Kar-Fai Gee, "Why Aren't Workers Benefiting from Labour Productivity Growth in the United States?" *International Productivity Monitor*, no. 23, 2012. http://tinyurl.com/DROMMishel, 42.

[11] J.W. Mason and Arjun Jayadev, "Fisher Dynamics in Household Debt: The Case of the United States, 1929–2011," *University of Massachusetts Boston, Economics Department Working Papers*, no. 13, 2012. http://tinyurl.com/DROMMason, 26.

[12] Schmitt, "Minimum Wage," 1.

[13] Mishel and Gee, "Why Aren't Workers Benefiting?" 31.

[14] David Cay Johnston, "Income Inequality: 1 Inch to 5 Miles," *Tax Analysts*, February 25, 2013. http://tinyurl.com/DROMJohnston2.

[15] Emmanuel Saez, "Striking It Richer: The Evolution of Top Incomes in the United States," January 2013. http://tinyurl.com/DROMSaez, 3–4.

[16] Erin Hatton, "The Rise of the Permanent Temp Economy," *New York Times*, January 26, 2013. http://tinyurl.com/DROMHatton3.

[17] Judy Fudge and Rosemary Owens, "Precarious Work, Women and the New Economy: The Challenge to Legal Norms," in *Precarious Work, Women and the New Economy: The Challenge to Legal Norms*, ed. Judy Fudge and Rosemary Owens (Portland, OR: Hart, 2006), 3–28.

by one's debt. Employers can view your credit reports to determine whether or not you are "responsible," and therefore "employable." In other words, prospective employers look to see whether or not your personal circumstances will affect your work or if you have a history of being "financially imprudent." Credit scores are often the determining factor, and more will be discussed about this in Chapter One.

The extent to which people are affected by precarity and wage stagnation is greatly informed by their gender, race, sexuality, and ability. Women across the globe continue to comprise the majority of precarious workers.[18] On average, in the United States, women are paid less than men, and women of color are paid even less. Median annual earnings for White men are $45,542, while the median for White women is 71% of this amount, 61% for Black women and only 51% for Latina women.[19] For transgender people, rampant discrimination often prevents hiring in the first place, and those who are hired receive significantly less pay.[20] They are much more likely than cisgender people (those who do not identify as transgender or genderqueer) to make under $10,000 per year.[21] Children of gay or lesbian parents are more likely than children with married straight parents to live in poverty,[22] and a disproportionate number of homeless youth are lesbian, gay, bisexual, transgender, or queer (LGBTQ).[23] Within the LGBTQ community, race and gender contribute to further widening income gaps.[24] Meanwhile, people with disabilities in the United States are twice as likely to live in or near poverty than able-bodied people. On average, they earn considerably less than what people without disabilities earn.[25] Compared to fifteen peer countries, the United States ranks second-to-last—only marginally better than Australia—when it comes to this particular income gap.[26]

---

[18] International Metalworkers' Federation, "Global Action against Precarious Work," *Metal World*, no. 1, 2007. http://tinyurl.com/DROMIMF, 20.

[19] "Who Is Affected by the Wage Gap?" *Women are Getting Even*, 2004. http://tinyurl.com/DROMWAGE.

[20] Crosby Burns, "The Gay and Transgender Wage Gap," *Center for American Progress*, April 16, 2012. http://tinyurl.com/DROMBurns.

[21] "All Children Matter: How Legal and Social Inequalities Hurt LGBT Families," *Movement Advancement Project, Family Equality Council*, and *Center for American Progress*, October 2011. http://tinyurl.com/DROMMAP, 9.

[22] "All Children Matter," 8.

[23] Joseph N. DeFilippis, Susan Raffo, and Kay Whitlock, "Tidal Wave: LGBT Poverty and Economic Hardship in a Time of Economic Crisis," *Queers for Economic Justice*, 2009. http://tinyurl.com/DROMDeFilippis2, 8.

[24] DeFilippis, Raffo, and Whitlock, "Tidal Wave," 4.

[25] "Sickness, Disability, and Work: Keeping on Track in the Economic Downturn," *Organisation for Economic Co-operation and Development*, May 2009. http://tinyurl.com/DROMOECD, 34–35.

[26] "How Canada Performs: Disabled Income," *The Conference Board of Canada*, January 2013. http://tinyurl.com/DROMCBC.

Wage stagnation means people in the United States are finding it harder and harder to afford basic necessities, so they turn to credit cards and end up paying even more through high interest rates. As Kelly Gates observes, "The consumer credit industry exploded at precisely the time when social welfare programs were being dismantled and wages were stagnating for large numbers of people, with consumer credit filling the widening gap between the wages people earned and the personal expenses they accumulated in the new economy."[27] As the evidence demonstrates, the situation is often even harder—due to income gaps and a host of other factors which are in turn a result of structural oppression—for people who are not White, male, able-bodied, cisgender, or straight.

Looking beyond income inequality

Income alone, however, does not illustrate the gravity of the situation. It is more accurate to discuss wealth, or net worth—the amount someone owns minus the amount that they owe. After all, the United States ranks 138th out of 141 countries in terms of wealth equality.[28] Here the disproportionate impact on Black and Latino/a people becomes even starker. The median household net worth is now *twenty-two times* greater for Whites than it is for Blacks.[29] One would hope that by now at least some progress is being made, that the wealth gap is slowly closing, but in reality the opposite is true. Wealth disparity is far greater now than it was about two decades ago, when the wealth differed "only" by a factor of seven between Whites and Blacks.[30] Compared to three decades ago, the wealth gap has quadrupled![31] Even when one looks at households with similar incomes, White households consistently have a higher median net worth than Black and Latino/a households.[32] It is also true that, compared to Whites, Black and Latino/a families are more likely to lose a home to foreclosure, a disproportion that becomes greater as income *increases*.[33] According to a recent study by the Institute on Assets and

---

[27] Kelly Gates, "The Securitization of Financial Identity and the Expansion of the Consumer Credit Industry," *Journal of Communication Inquiry* 34, no. 4, 2010, 427.

[28] Paul Buchheit, "America Split in Two: Five Ugly Extremes of Inequality," *Common Dreams*, March 25, 2013. http://tinyurl.com/DROMBuchheit.

[29] Robert Frank, "Wealth Gap Rises Between Whites, Non-Whites," *CNBC.com*, June 22, 2012. http://tinyurl.com/DROMFrank.

[30] Jeannette Wicks-Lim, "The Great Recession in Black Wealth," *Dollars & Sense*, February 2012. http://tinyurl.com/DROMWicks.

[31] Thomas Shapiro, Tatjana Meschede, and Laura Sullivan, "The Racial Wealth Gap Increases Fourfold," *Institute on Assets and Social Policy*, May 2010. http://tinyurl.com/DROMShapiro2, 1.

[32] Shawna Orzechowski and Peter Sepielli, "Net Worth and Asset Ownership of Households: 1998 and 2000," *U.S. Census Bureau*, 2003. http://tinyurl.com/DROMOrzechowski, 12.

[33] Debbie Gruenstein Bocian, Wei Li, and Keith S. Ernst, "Foreclosures by Race and Ethnicity: The Demographics of a Crisis," *Center for Responsible Lending*, June 18, 2010. http://tinyurl.com/

Social Policy, "half the collective wealth of African-American families was stripped away during the Great Recession due to the dominant role of home equity in their wealth portfolios and the prevalence of predatory high-risk loans in communities of color. The Latino community lost an astounding 67% of its total wealth during the housing collapse."[34] The particularly severe impact of economic inequality on Black and Latino/a people can be attributed to a long history of structural racism that continues to exist in the form of, among other things, redlining (the denial of loans or insurance to people of color) and reverse redlining (aggressively targeting communities of color with predatory services).

Discussing income exclusively is also insufficient when talking about debt as it relates to age. Recently, a new type of loan targeting the elderly known as pension advances has emerged. People sign over their pension checks to companies in exchange for cash, but with interest rates that can exceed 100%.[35] People with a fixed income, such as those on Social Security, can barely keep up with skyrocketing costs of living, but they're still viewed as a golden goose by creditors.

The problem goes deeper than stagnant wages. While stagnation has contributed greatly to people's inability to get by and caused them to accrue debt, simply raising wages would not prove to be an adequate solution. Namely, this would ignore those *without* wages in the first place, including the millions of unemployed people in the United States.[36] And it's worth pausing here to consider what work gets identified as worthy of a wage, and the many kinds of vital labor that have long been unpaid—labor that is done to create and maintain our lives and to produce and sustain a workforce for profit-seeking enterprises. This work, *when performed for one's own family* and which includes child bearing and rearing, cooking, cleaning, and elder care, is often referred to as "housework."[37] Some feminists call it "reproductive labor."[38] It's the invisible work that makes "traditional work"—that is, waged labor—possible. Caring for others has traditionally been deemed "women's work"—something which women

---

DROMBocian, 10.

[34] Thomas Shapiro, Tatjana Meschede, and Sam Osoro, "The Roots of the Widening Racial Wealth Gap: Explaining the Black-White Economic Divide," *Institute on Assets and Social Policy*, February 2013. http://tinyurl.com/DROMShapiro, 4.

[35] Jessica Silver-Greenburg, "Loans Borrowed Against Pensions Squeeze Retirees," *New York Times*, April 27, 2013. http://tinyurl.com/DROMSilver10.

[36] "The Employment Situation—January 2013," *Bureau of Labor Statistics*, January 2013. http://tinyurl.com/DROMBLS5, 2.

[37] As women in wealthier countries enter the paid workforce in larger numbers, others, primarily immigrant women, are paid a measly sum to perform this domestic work—either in addition to or at the expense of performing housework for their own families.

[38] Silvia Federici and Nicole Cox, "Counterplanning from the Kitchen," in *Revolution at Point Zero: Housework, Reproduction, and Feminist Struggle* (Oakland: PM Press/Common Notions, 2012), 36.

are supposedly naturally inclined to do for their own fulfillment. This, it could be argued, has a lot to do with why this labor remains largely unwaged and undervalued. The fact that some men perform reproductive labor doesn't change the fact that it's still dismissed as "women's work" and valued accordingly. If the contribution of this work to the economy sounds negligible, imagine what would happen if those performing reproductive labor went on strike.[39] Any conversations about the relationship between wages and debt need to take into account the very nature of waged labor itself.

There are other forms of unwaged labor as well, including modern day slavery. The issue of unfree prison labor also requires our attention. Global capitalism "thrives on the unwaged labor of millions of women and men in the fields, kitchens, and prisons of the United States and throughout the world."[40] To demand an increase in the minimum wage would benefit a large segment of the U.S. population, but the situation would be unchanged for most wageless workers.

DEBT AND CAPITALISM

Livable wages for *all* workers—including those who do not conform to conventional notions of "workers"—would be a necessary first step toward freeing ourselves from the debt system. But this approach, too, appears insufficient. We have to ask ourselves: is our economic system adequately meeting people's needs and desires, or do we need to consider other ways of structuring a society? It is under capitalism, after all, that corporations are obligated *by law* to maximize profits. Unsurprisingly, then, corporate profits as a percentage of national income are the highest since 1950, while workers' incomes are at the lowest percentage since 1966.[41] Wall Street isn't stealing workers' wages and trammeling our ability to lead dignified lives all on their own, though; legislators and politicians are complicit. Only recently did it surface that taxpayers subsidize big banks around *$83 billion per year*, a perk for which the financial industry has vigorously lobbied.[42] Since 2008 and also before, people have said that Wall Street ignored "systemic risk," or the interconnectedness of the financial system. This muddles the central problem: the problem is systemic because the problem *is* the system. We know that those who plan and profit from capitalism need us, but do we need them?

[39] Sarah Jaffe, "A Day without Care," *Jacobin*, April 2013. http://tinyurl.com/DROMJaffe3.

[40] Federici and Cox, "Counterplanning From the Kitchen," 31.

[41] Nelson D. Schwartz, "Recovery in U.S. Is Lifting Profits, but Not Adding Jobs," *New York Times*, March 3, 2013. http://tinyurl.com/DROMSchwartz.

[42] "Why Should Taxpayers Give Big Banks $83 Billion a Year?" *Bloomberg*, February 20, 2013. http://tinyurl.com/DROMBloomberg.

An analysis of debt is becoming increasingly relevant in the fight for justice. Economic exploitation and oppression exist not only in the workplace. Through debt we feel this exploitation in nearly all facets of our lives, from the houses we live in to the schools we attend to the hospitals we rely upon. Yet the exploitation is often subtler, and therefore debt requires more careful attention. As will be demonstrated throughout this book, all aspects of the debt system maintain and exacerbate already existing social inequalities, in the United States and internationally.

Credit scores (*see Chapter One*) are not only used in determining access to credit, but these quite arbitrary numbers are impacting decisions regarding utilities, apartment rentals, car costs, insurance rates, and even employment, among other things.[43] Meanwhile in places where credit is hard to come by—particularly in communities of color—a deregulated lending market has set up shop with exorbitantly expensive products and services like payday loans and check-cashing outlets (*see Chapters Seven and Eight*), ensuring that the poor continue to get even poorer. And in the global South, the World Bank and International Monetary Fund impose structural adjustment programs under the guise of helping governments pay their debts (*see Chapter Thirteen*). It is against this backdrop that Jamaica spends more than twice on debt repayment than what it does on education and health combined.[44] Among many African countries, the result of structural adjustment is the privatization of land, the displacement of subsistence farmers, the depletion of social services, a decline in life expectancy, an increase in refugee populations, and the death of millions of people, to name just a few horrific consequences of living under a global system that dictates paying one's debts is more important than life itself.[45]

Debt as a social relationship, a weapon, and a form of control

People may feel like most kinds of debt—sometimes *including* their own personal debts—are far removed from their lives or that they are too abstract to understand. More often than not, technical terms surrounding debt serve to confuse and scare people rather than educate and empower them. In the past, debt and the language employed in its discussion have been used not only as a way to divide those "in the know" from the rest, but also as tools of control and discipline in order to limit and direct people's life choices.

---

[43] Chi Chi Wu and Birny Birnbaum, "Credit Scoring and Insurance: Costing Consumers Billions and Perpetuating the Economic Racial Divide," *National Consumer Law Center* and *Center for Economic Justice*, June 2007. http://tinyurl.com/DROMWu, 3–4.

[44] Nick Dearden, "Jamaica's Decades of Debt Are Damaging Its Future," *The Guardian*, April 16, 2013. http://tinyurl.com/DROMDearden.

[45] Silvia Federici, "War, Globalization, and Reproduction," in *Revolution at Point Zero: Housework, Reproduction, and Feminist Struggle* (Oakland: PM Press/Common Notions, 2012), 84.

Debt is a profoundly effective form of social control, and, as many have argued, it has become the primary form of extracting and accumulating wealth for the rich.[46] Debt affects nearly every part of our lives. Not only does it determine the material possessions in our lives, but it also shapes our psyches. Debt is not something that exists outside of us, but rather something that is central in forming our identities, characters, and our relationships.

As demonstrated earlier, debt is used as an oppressive financial tool that entangles class, race, gender, sexuality, age, and ability. It exploits members of marginalized groups, plunging them further into hardship. It is a strategy that impoverishes people and serves as a stark reminder of the power differences in our society. Though the effects of debt are felt across the social spectrum, debt does not "equalize" or make oppression uniform. But as a form of control, it does force us to have similar, sometimes shared, experiences, all of which define our self-perceptions and our relationships with our neighbors.

Perhaps the most notable aspect of debt is the asymmetry in power. Creditors and Wall Street banks use financial markets, the power of the legal system, and the power that comes with having political and economic clout to accumulate staggering amounts of money. Preserving these privileged positions demands that they issue credit and create vast populations of debtors, from whom they gain commission, interest, and ultimately profit. This profit, like all profit, comes at a cost. Not only is our labor the source of much, if not all, of their revenue, but they also rob us of our future by demanding we work *more* to pay for ever-increasing interest rates that balloon if we miss payment. Beholden to these financial institutions, debtors are pushed to become complacent laborers. Of course, no one should begrudge people for trying to make ends meet or provide for their families, but what this relationship also deprives us of is an imagination of a world outside the creditor-debtor relationship. The ideas and experiences that fuel our imagination diminish, and it becomes harder to fight for a better, more just world.

As a weapon, debt determines where we live, where and how we work, as well as our mental health. From a young age, we are conditioned to feel that being in debt is shameful and worthy of punishment. To offer a particularly poignant example, recently students at a middle school in Massachusetts were deprived of eating cafeteria food for having as little as five cents of debt on their prepaid cards.[47] The lesson

---

[46] Steve Fraser, "The Politics of Debt in America," *Jacobin*, February 4, 2013. http://tinyurl.com/DROMFraser.

[47] Kristen Gwynne, "Middle School Forces Hungry Students to Throw Out Their Lunches When They Couldn't Pay," *AlterNet*, April 5, 2013. http://tinyurl.com/DROMGwynne.

is clear: debtors, no matter their age or circumstances, don't deserve to have their basic needs met.

In addition to being socially ostracized, debtors suffer from psychological problems that often go unnoticed. Although there is strikingly little research in the United States about debt's impact on mental health, there are whole message boards filled with people citing their debt as a source of their depression. We also see an increasing number of people in the United States contemplating or committing suicide because of debt.[48] Deteriorating mental health and personal relationships are common among debtors, as well as insomnia, anxiety, and a slew of physical and psychological illnesses.[49] These harmful effects can be amplified in an unstable economic climate such as today's.

As if ushering us from one point in our lives to another, debt acts as both a deterrent and catalyst. As a tool of capitalism that is used intentionally to extract wealth from people, debt forces us to take more than one job and to quit school or the things that give us an identity outside of work. Low-income students are more likely to rely on loans to afford college. Faced with skyrocketing tuition, these same students sometimes have to work many jobs to cover the costs. This forces students to compromise their studies in order to work, which affects their achievements and ultimately perpetuates class divisions.[50] Debt is also used to shape certain attitudes, behaviors, ideas, and actions. For instance, the criminal justice system is seeing a dramatic rise in the number of indigent, or poor, individuals who are incarcerated because of their debt. Once in prison, harsh measures dictate prisoners' entire lives, while simultaneously their forced manual labor floods our economy with cheap goods and commodities. Although debtors' prisons were outlawed in the United States long ago, people are still imprisoned because they can't afford to pay fines for what are sometimes minor infractions. Once in the criminal justice system, people are burdened with more fees that they cannot pay, driving them further into debt. Prisons are continually filled with impoverished people, giving life to a cycle of poverty and imprisonment that is hard to escape (*see Chapter Nine*).

• • •

[48] C. Cryn Johannsen, "The Ones We've Lost: The Student Loan Debt Suicides," *Huffington Post*, July 2, 2012. http://tinyurl.com/DROMJohannsen.

[49] "Debt Stress Causing Health Problems, Poll Finds," *NBC News* and *Associated Press*, June 9, 2008. http://tinyurl.com/DROMNBC.

[50] Jason DeParle, "For Poor, Leap to College Often Ends in a Hard Fall," *New York Times*, December 22, 2012. http://tinyurl.com/DROMDeParle.

ABOUT STRIKE DEBT

This operations manual is written by an anonymous collective from Strike Debt. For over a year now, Strike Debt has been part of an international debt resistance movement—developing tactics, resources, and frameworks for expanding the fight against the debt system while developing alternative systems based on mutual aid.

Strike Debt emerged in New York City as an offshoot of Occupy Wall Street in the wake of May Day 2012, receiving a great deal of inspiration from the student strikes in Québec happening at the time. We soon expanded to organize around *all* forms of debt. Chapters began popping up all over the country, including in Philadelphia, Denver, Boston, the Bay Area, Chicago, and Raleigh. The group operates under many principles that were adopted by Occupy participants from other nonhierarchical movements across the world. These principles include political autonomy, direct democracy, direct action, a culture of solidarity, and a commitment to combating all forms of oppression. As we intend to demonstrate in this book, Strike Debt believes that debt binds us all—though it binds some people (people of color, queer and trans people, women, people with disabilities, and the poor) more tightly than others.

In addition to the creation of this manual, Strike Debt has organized a number of initiatives and actions, such as the Rolling Jubilee. The Rolling Jubilee purchases debt on the secondary market for approximately 1–5% of the original principal and subsequently abolishes it. Other Strike Debt projects involve debt education, hosting debtors' assemblies, offering free health care, and protesting hospital closings.

About this manual

The Debt Resisters' Operations Manual (DROM) seeks to provide widely applicable yet detailed information about debt as well as strategies for resistance. It highlights our commonalities—namely, that people are not alone in their struggles against debt—as well as our different relationships to debt. We strive to analyze debt from many different angles, always maintaining a nuanced, critical analysis that is conscious of race, gender, class, sexuality, age, ability, and their intersections. We strive to write in simple language and will work to translate the manual into languages other than English.

A 120-page pamphlet version of the manual was collectively researched and written in August 2012 as a contribution to strengthening and expanding the debt resistance movement. Following its release in September 2012, over twelve thousand copies were printed and distributed for free within two months, from New York to Portland to Chicago to New Orleans. Digital versions were read by tens of thousands more people. In order to reach out to a wider audience and encourage more acts of debt resistance (and to avoid accruing more debt ourselves through printing and distribution costs!), we decided to expand the breadth of issues we covered in the pamphlet and publish this book with Common Notions and PM Press. Although this edition is sold online and in bookstores, we are committed to making the contents of the DROM available for free to anyone who might need them.

In both the earlier pamphlet and this book, a decision was made to not attach any individual names to this manual. This decision is rooted in our principle of collectivity. A large collective of people from all over the country were directly involved in the researching, writing and editing of this book, but moreover, this manual is an attempt to reflect, and explore further, the endless conversations that have happened within Strike Debt over the past year. Whether it's collectively developing an analysis of debt as a form of social control or contemplating particular strategies to resisting various forms of debt at meetings, countless people have made essential contributions to the content of this manual in both direct and indirect ways.

People in and out of Strike Debt were invited to participate in creating this book as much as they desired in various capacities—as a researcher, writer, editor, coordinator, or various other roles. We also relied on input from the larger Strike Debt group in determining what concepts and tactics should be included in this manual. To ensure the group remained democratic, contributors of the manual reached consensus on decisions that affected the overall tone or structure of the book, such as the table of contents, the book description, and a style guide to inform each chapter. Meanwhile, researchers and writers of a particular chapter coordinated among themselves, while taking into consideration concerns raised by other members.

As stated in the original preface, the DROM is a collective, living document; it remains open to revision, and we invite constructive, critical dialogue. From the original preface:

> We don't claim to have all or even most of the answers regarding debt. To produce this manual, we have reached out to our networks to the best of our ability. Some sections barely scratch the surface and in fact deserve their own book-length treatment. Researching debt has uncovered many connections we didn't expect, and we know there are types of debt we haven't addressed. It is our hope that readers will have their own strategies to contribute to future versions of this manual. . . . Any ideas, plans, tips, corrections, resources, schemes—legal or otherwise—should be sent to DROM@riseup.net.

Since September 2012, we have received a tremendous amount of feedback from fellow debt resisters as well as lawyers, accountants, and other experts, and we have done our best to incorporate those suggestions into this edition. We have expanded upon each of the original chapters and have written four new ones (*Chapters Six, Eleven, Thirteen,* and *Fourteen*). We have endeavored to place greater emphasis on strategies for collective action and alternatives to relying on the debt system for meeting basic needs.

A GENERAL OUTLINE, CHAPTER BY CHAPTER

Talking about debt is difficult not only because it elicits raw, emotional responses, but also because it's a complex and intricate subject. On top of this, each chapter of this book tries to provide you with pragmatic ways to fight back. This can be anything from going through strategic bankruptcy to legal action to living off the financial grid entirely. So, in order to avoid confusing the reader any more than they already have been confused by credit card companies or student loan servicers, we have tried to make this manual as accessible as possible. We guide the reader from the "micro" forms of debt to the "macro," or in other words, the types of debt people directly experience everyday to the more abstract forms of debt that people think about less, but nonetheless affect their everyday life.

This manual begins, then, with one of the manifestations of debt, of which many people are aware: credit reporting agencies and credit scores (*Chapter One*). In the first chapter we explain the role of credit reporting agencies (CRAs) and credit scores in people's lives. In Chapter Two we move on to credit card debt and automobile debt—two of the most common forms of consumer debt. In this chapter we briefly explain the history and role of credit cards, as well as provide a wider explanation as to why so many people are reliant on credit to survive. Cars are the primary means by which most people travel, yet most households cannot purchase and maintain them without incurring debt. We then go on to medical debt (*Chapter Three*) and student debt (*Chapter Four*)—two forms of debt that have become increasingly common in the United States. Chapter Three lays out the current state of health care in the United States and offers strategies for challenging medical bills. Chapter Four explains the ins and outs of student debt, who profits from it, how you can survive with student debt, and the fight for free higher education. In Chapter Five we take on housing debt—the history and development of the housing bubble to its crash in 2008, as well as the shady tactics employed by mortgagees to profit from low-income individuals' misfortunes.

We discuss our taxation system in Chapter Six, including an analysis of who benefits and who loses out, as well as the financial distress taxes bring to some of the more vulnerable people in society. We also, of course, discuss the IRS and how it can affect you if you don't pay your taxes. The next two chapters (*Seven* and *Eight*) delve into the fringe finance industry: prepaid cards, cash checking outlets, and various forms of predatory lending geared toward the "unbanked" and "underbanked"—those who live without mainstream bank accounts and those who utilize both traditional and "alternative" financial services. In Chapter Nine, with debt collection, we get into the more "abstract" ideas surrounding debt. This chapter will not only teach you about the debt collection industry, its dirty practices, and its legal limits, but also how to fight back against harassment and intimidation from collectors. If you are thinking about declaring bankruptcy, Chapter Ten might prove useful. We discuss the different chapters of bankruptcy as well as the historical development of debt forgiveness through bankruptcy. We also highlight the circumstances under which bankruptcy is a wise or unwise strategy. Chapter Eleven goes through some of the many ways you can live without necessarily being on the "financial grid." Recognizing that some people do or want to live without using any of the financial services mentioned in the rest of the manual, we have provided some strategies to living in the margins of this exploitative system. Municipal and State Debt (*Chapter Twelve*) and National Debt (*Chapter Thirteen*) are affected by each other and each affects individuals. In these chapters you will see how the effects of sovereign debt crises and municipal budget cuts interrelate and penetrate our individual lives. Chapter Fourteen, Climate Debt, discusses and analyzes how climate change, industrial growth, and capitalism relate to one another, causing a strict divide in the balance of wealth and power.

This all paints a pretty bleak picture, but it is not one without hope. The final chapter, Prospects for Change (*Chapter Fifteen*), envisions a more mass-based approach to the individual and collective problems this manual addresses and invites you, the reader, to critically engage with the questions we ask in order build a grassroots debtors' movement. Prospects for Change features just some examples of successful debt resistance throughout the world, and there are more to come. We try, and will keep trying, to imagine a world free of exploitation, white supremacy, patriarchy, and all other forms of oppression that set so many of us against each other. We encourage you to pass this book on to your friends, neighbors, members of your community, and coworkers. We see this book and the knowledge it collects as a tool that can be used to resist the debt system that oppresses us.

To come back to the original question of "To whom are we indebted?" we should say that not all debt is bad. We are indebted to our friends and communities who raise us, support us, and give us strength and a sense of belonging and identity. Some debts keep up relations—important relations that help us survive and make us human. There are many factors that make certain debts immoral, however, like exploitation, force, violence, or profiteering.

To the financial establishment of the world, we have only one thing to say: we owe you nothing. To our friends, our families, our communities, to humanity and to the natural world that makes our lives possible: we owe you everything. Every dollar we take from a fraudulent subprime mortgage speculator, every dollar we withhold from the collection agency is a tiny piece of our own lives and freedom that we can give back to our communities, to those we love and respect. These are acts of debt resistance, which come in many other forms as well: fighting for free education and health care, defending foreclosed homes against eviction, demanding higher wages, and practicing mutual aid.

The late (and not-so-great) British Prime Minister Margaret Thatcher offered the world a stubborn acronym in defense of global capitalism and the free market: TINA, there is no alternative. There are ceaseless attempts to force us to believe this, to distrust others and keep our heads down, to discredit our collective visions of another society, and to keep our dreams at bay. Witness the ongoing militarization of society, the increase in police and state repression, and the controlling of dissent in this country and others around the world. Meanwhile, defenses of free market capitalism continue to be made with straight faces by pundits and sycophants as our economic system seems to be on the brink of collapse. Through the lens of debt, this book humbly offers a challenge to the logic of TINA, to this assault on the radical imagination. Another world is not only possible, but necessary.

REFERENCES

Associated Press. "Debt Stress Causing Health Problems, Poll Finds," *NBC News*, June 9, 2008. http://tinyurl.com/DROMNBC.

Bloomberg View Editorial Board. "Why Should Taxpayers Give Big Banks $83 Billion a Year?" *Bloomberg*, February 20, 2013. http://tinyurl.com/DROMBloomberg.

Bocian, Debbie Gruenstein, Wei Li, and Keith S. Ernst. "Foreclosures by Race and Ethnicity: The Demographics of a Crisis." *Center for Responsible Lending*, June 18, 2010. http://tinyurl.com/DROMBocian.

Burns, Crosby. "The Gay and Transgender Wage Gap." *Center for American Progress*, April 16, 2012. http://tinyurl.com/DROMBurns.

Buchheit, Paul. "America Split in Two: Five Ugly Extremes of Inequality." *Common Dreams*, March 25, 2013. http://tinyurl.com/DROMBuchheit.

Bureau of Labor Statistics. "The Employment Situation—January 2013." *U.S. Department of Labor*, January 2013. http://tinyurl.com/DROMBLS5.

Conference Board of Canada. "How Canada Performs: Disabled Income." January 2013. http://tinyurl.com/DROMCBC.

Consumer Reports. "Take Control of Your Credit Cards." November 2009. http://tinyurl.com/DROMCR.

Dearden, Nick. "Jamaica's Decades of Debt are Damaging Its Future." *The Guardian*, April 16, 2013. http://tinyurl.com/DROMDearden.

DeFilippis, Joseph N., Susan Raffo, and Kay Whitlock. "Tidal Wave: LGBT Poverty and Economic Hardship in a Time of Economic Crisis." *Queers for Economic Justice*, 2009. http://tinyurl.com/DROMDeFilippis2.

DeParle, Jason. "For Poor, Leap to College Often Ends in a Hard Fall." *New York Times*, December 22, 2012. http://tinyurl.com/DROMDeParle.

Draut, Tamara, Ansel Brown, Lisa James, Kathleen Keest, Jabrina Robinson, and Ellen Schloemer. "The Plastic Safety Net: The Reality Behind Debt in America." *Dēmos and The Center for Responsible Lending*, October 2005. http://tinyurl.com/DROMDraut.

Federal Reserve Bank of New York. "Quarterly Report on Household Debt and Credit." November 2012. http://tinyurl.com/DROMFedNY.

Federici, Silvia. "War, Globalization, and Reproduction." In *Revolution at Point Zero: Housework, Reproduction, and Feminist Struggle*, 76–84. Oakland: PM Press/Common Notions, 2012.

Federici, Silvia, and Nicole Cox. "Counterplanning From the Kitchen." In *Revolution at Point Zero: Housework, Reproduction, and Feminist Struggle*, 28–40. Oakland: PM Press/Common Notions, 2012.

The Flaw. DVD. Directed by David Sington. 2011; London, UK: Studio Lambert, 2012.

Frank, Robert. "Wealth Gap Rises between Whites, Non-Whites." *CNBC.com*, June 22, 2012. http://tinyurl.com/DROMFrank.

Fraser, Steve. "The Politics of Debt in America." *Jacobin*, February 4, 2013. http://tinyurl.com/DROMFraser.

Fudge, Judy, and Rosemary Owens. "Precarious Work, Women and the New Economy: The Challenge to Legal Norms." In *Precarious Work, Women and the New Economy: The Challenge to Legal Norms*, edited by Judy Fudge and Rosemary Owens, 3–28. Portland, OR: Hart, 2006.

Gates, Kelly. "The Securitization of Financial Identity and the Expansion of the Consumer Credit Industry." *Journal of Communication Inquiry* 34, no. 4 (2010): 417–431.

Gwynne, Kristen. "Middle School Forces Hungry Students to Throw Out Their Lunches When They Couldn't Pay." *AlterNet*, April 5, 2013. http://tinyurl.com/DROMGwynne.

Hatton, Erin. "The Rise of the Permanent Temp Economy." *New York Times*, January 26, 2013. http://tinyurl.com/DROMHatton3.

Insight Center for Community Economic Development. "The Racial Gap in Debt, Credit and Financial Services." June 2009. http://tinyurl.com/DROMICCED.

International Metalworkers' Federation. "Global Action Against Precarious Work." *Metal World* 1 (2007): 18–21. http://tinyurl.com/DROMIMF.

Jaffe, Sarah. "A Day Without Care." *Jacobin*, April 2013. http://tinyurl.com/DROMJaffe3.

Johannsen, C. Cryn. "The Ones We've Lost: The Student Loan Debt Suicides." *Huffington Post*, July 2, 2012. http://tinyurl.com/DROMJohannsen.

Johnston, David Cay. "Income Inequality: 1 Inch to 5 Miles." *Tax Analysts*, February 25, 2013. http://tinyurl.com/DROMJohnston2.

Mason, J. W., and Arjun Jayadev. "Fisher Dynamics in Household Debt: The Case of the United States, 1929–2011." *University of Massachusetts Boston, Economics Department Working Papers*, no. 13 (2012). http://tinyurl.com/DROMMason.

Mishel, Lawrence, and Kar-Fai Gee. "Why Aren't Workers Benefiting from Labour Productivity Growth in the United States?" *International Productivity Monitor* 23 (2012): 31–43. http://tinyurl.com/DROMMishel.

Movement Advancement Project, Family Equality Council, and Center for American Progress. "All Children Matter: How Legal and Social Inequalities Hurt LGBT Families." October 2011. http://tinyurl.com/DROMMAP.

Mullaney, Tim. "More Americans Debt-Free, but the Rest Owe More." *USA Today*, March 21, 2013. http://tinyurl.com/DROMMullaney.

Organisation for Economic Co-operation and Development. "Sickness, Disability, and Work: Keeping on Track in the Economic Downturn." May 2009. http://tinyurl.com/DROMOECD.

Orzechowski, Shawna, and Peter Sepielli. "Net Worth and Asset Ownership of Households: 1998 and 2000." *U.S. Census Bureau*, 2003. http://tinyurl.com/DROMOrzechowski.

Saez, Emmanuel. "Striking it Richer: The Evolution of Top Incomes in the United States." January 2013. http://tinyurl.com/DROMSaez.

Schmitt, John. "The Minimum Wage Is Too Damn Low." *Center for Economic and Policy Research*, March 2012. http://tinyurl.com/DROMSchmitt.

Schwartz, Nelson D. "Recovery in U.S. Is Lifting Profits, but Not Adding Jobs." *New York Times*, March 3, 2013. http://tinyurl.com/DROMSchwartz.

Shapiro, Thomas, Tatjana Meschede, and Sam Osoro. "The Roots of the Widening Racial Wealth Gap: Explaining the Black-White Economic Divide." *Institute on Assets and Social Policy*, February 2013. http://tinyurl.com/DROMShapiro.

Shapiro, Thomas, Tatjana Meschede, and Laura Sullivan. "The Racial Wealth Gap Increases Fourfold." *Institute on Assets and Social Policy*, May 2010. http://tinyurl.com/DROMShapiro2.

Silver-Greenburg, Jessica. "Loans Borrowed against Pensions Squeeze Retirees." *New York Times*, April 27, 2013. http://tinyurl.com/DROMSilver10.

Traub, Amy, and Catherine Ruetschlin. "The Plastic Safety Net: Findings from the 2012 National Survey on Credit Card Debt of Low- and Middle-Income Households." *Dēmos*, 2012. http://tinyurl.com/DROMTraub.

Wicks-Lim, Jeannette. "The Great Recession in Black Wealth." *Dollars & Sense*, February 2012. http://tinyurl.com/DROMWicks.

Women Are Getting Even. "Who Is Affected by the Wage Gap?" 2004. http://tinyurl.com/DROMWAGE.

Wu, Chi Chi, and Birny Birnbaum. "Credit Scoring and Insurance: Costing Consumers Billions and Perpetuating the Economic Racial Divide." *National Consumer Law Center* and *Center for Economic Justice*, June 2007. http://tinyurl.com/DROMWu.

ONE

CREDIT SCORES AND CONSUMER REPORTING AGENCIES

SURVEILLANCE AND THE VICIOUS CYCLE OF DEBT

Imagine being tracked 24/7 by an invisible network, then classified and ranked according to a secret formula. Imagine your "file" was full of inaccurate and discrediting information, yet it was being sold to critical decision-makers and used to compute a numerical ranking which determined your ability to access the basic necessities of life—a roof over your head, basic utilities, even a job. Imagine this (low-ball) number turned out to be a *self-fulfilling prophecy*, sealing your fate in a financial caste system.

These are the basic dynamics of the system of surveillance and control known as "consumer reporting." Over 90% of the adult population is somehow entangled in the "dragnet," yet few know precisely how—it's hard to keep track. Consumer reporting agencies (CRAs, or simply "bureaus") gather, organize, and standardize consumer data—how we pay bills, how much money we owe, where we work and live, whether we've been sued, arrested, or filed for bankruptcy—then sell the information to creditors, as well as employers, insurers, and increasingly to consumers themselves. The "Big Three"—Equifax, TransUnion, and Experian—have long dominated the consumer reporting industry. Often labeled the "national credit bureaus," they are actually *global* corporate conglomerates, which source labor and operate in markets around the world. (Experian isn't even based in the United States, but in Ireland.)

CRAs play a crucial role in our ability to access even the basic requirements of life in our society. A survey by the Society for Human Resource Management found that almost 60% of its member employers used credit reports to screen applicants for at least some of their positions.[1] Credit scores also frequently factor into insurance rates—approximately 92% of auto and home insurers rely on them, according to a survey in 2001.[2] Alarmingly, hospitals have begun using credit scores to determine access to health care and to set costs.[3] This chapter guides you through the consumer-reporting matrix, but also questions many of its basic assumptions and standard operating procedures. Decades of industry surveillance and control—often with government assistance or approval—have steadily transformed our culture, altering our values and behavior and generally instilling financial obedience.

Today, credit scores are treated as a measure not just of our creditworthiness but of our all-around personal integrity. Low scores virtually guarantee punishing credit terms and ruinous cycles of debt. And because someone won't have a credit score unless they use credit, it penalizes people who do not use credit products. Hence, it gives a boon to the widespread use of credit and propagates debt relations. People no longer have a choice of whether to use credit or not. But even "good" behavior cannot guarantee high scores in our systematically flawed consumer reporting system. Financial surveillance is a corrupt and impersonal machine, not a system that genuinely determines people's trustworthiness. Can't make a credit card payment because of health costs this month? It's recorded. Got laid off and couldn't pay tuition? It's recorded. Tried to pay a mortgage fee with an already-low checking account? It's recorded.

The fact that the credit reporting and scoring system is set up to maximize profits for the corporations involved instead of helping consumers is leading more and more people to consider alternatives. Thus, in addition to suggestions for individual "self-defense" and collective "harm reduction" in the context of the current credit regime, the chapter also offers ideas for moving outside or beyond it.

THE CRA INDUSTRY

Operating much like a typical oligopoly, credit reporting in the United States has long been dominated by the Big Three of Equifax, TransUnion, and Experian—with combined revenue of more than

---

[1] "SHRM Research Spotlight: Credit Background Checks," *Society for Human Resource Management*, September 2010. http://tinyurl.com/DROMSHRM, 1.

[2] Brian Grow and Pallavi Gogoi, "Insurance: A New Way to Squeeze the Weak?" *Business Week*, January 27, 2002. http://tinyurl.com/DROMGrow2.

[3] Robert Berner and Chad Terhune, "Hospitals X-Ray Patient Credit Scores," *Business Week*, November 19, 2008. http://tinyurl.com/DROMBerner.

$6.7 billion in 2009.[4] More recently, two different firms—Innovis and CoreLogic—have been given the distinction of the "fourth" CRA. Collecting "supplementary credit information," they represent the biggest "specialty" CRAs, companies which compile reports about much more than credit history, for example, medical history, employment history, rental history, checking account history, auto and property insurance claims, and utility bill accounts.[5] These other *non*-credit reports are proving to be just as influential as credit reports; yet, even less is known about specialty CRAs than about the notoriously obscure Big Three, not to mention the shadowy connections between them.

CRAs started in the 1950s as regionally based companies that would track the publicly available details of your life—when you got married, if you got a speeding ticket, or if you committed a crime. CRAs have persistently drawn criticism for mishandling data and violating privacy; protest grew more intense and organized over the course of the 1960s. There was mounting evidence that credit files were riddled with errors and that they were being sold indiscriminately, to practically anyone who requested them. Columbia University professor Alan Westin became a vocal critic of industry practices after reviewing a sample of files from Equifax, which at the time went by the name Retail Credit Company. According to an article he wrote in 1970, Westin discovered "'facts, statistics, inaccuracies and rumors' . . . about virtually every phase of a person's life; his [*sic*] marital troubles, jobs, school history, childhood, sex life, and political activities."[6] The looming computerization of credit files, which were increasingly concentrated in the databases of a few newly "national" CRAs (or NCRAs), led to the 1970 passage of the Fair Credit Reporting Act (FCRA). Setting regulations on the collection, dissemination, and use of consumer data, the FCRA was the first federal law to implement privacy protections in the private sector in the United States.[7]

The expansion of retail credit and major innovations in informational technology led to a consolidation of the industry in the early 1970s, which meant data became shared across industries.[8] (Up

---

[4] Gale Group, "Credit Reporting Services Market Report," *Highbeam Business*, 2012. http://tinyurl.com/DROMGale.

[5] "'Other' Consumer Reports: What You Should Know about 'Specialty' Reports," *Privacy Rights Clearinghouse*, June 2013. http://tinyurl.com/DROMPRC.

[6] Cited in Simson Garfinkel, "Separating Equifax from Fiction," *Wired*, September 1995. http://tinyurl.com/DROMGarfinkel.

[7] Nicola Jentzsch, *Financial Privacy: An International Comparison of Credit Reporting Systems* (New York: Springer, 2007), 122.

[8] "Key Dimensions and Processes in the U.S. Credit Reporting System: A Review of How the Nation's Largest Credit Bureaus Manage Consumer Data," *Consumer Financial Protection Bureau*,

to that point, companies could only compile information about a particular type of credit, like your regional banking history or your mortgage.) CRAs saw rapid growth in the 1970s and 1980s with the proliferation of bank credit cards, and in the 1990s with the automation of mortgage underwriting.

Today, each of the Big Three has credit files on over 200 million adults and receives information from approximately ten thousand furnishers of data, including banks and finance companies. Every month, furnishers report on over one billion consumer credit accounts and other types of accounts.

The informational structure generated by consumer reporting is the basis of today's credit-oriented consumer economy and a primary means of statistically defining and differentiating the population. Its networks span across financial service providers, retailers, insurers, telecom and utility providers, and transportation companies. This data is increasingly used to determine our access to the basic necessities of life. Landlords use credit reports and scores for screening rental applicants, as do employers for job applicants.

A tremendous amount of power over the daily lives of people is given to profit-driven entities that, until recently, operated almost entirely outside of public oversight. In July 2012, the Consumer Financial Protection Bureau announced that it would become the sole federal regulator for thirty credit reporting agencies that account for 94% of the credit reporting market.[9] (Previously, the industry was only subject to occasional congressional oversight and the restrictions of the FCRA.) But CRAs have already amassed huge amounts of sensitive data and their business is selling it as widely as possible.

CREDIT REPORTS AND CREDIT FILES

Credit reports are reports provided by CRAs to lenders and other users. They factor critically in decisions to grant credit—for example, mortgage loans, auto loans, credit cards, and private student loans—and in other financial spheres, including eligibility for rental housing, setting premiums for auto and homeowners insurance in some states, and job hiring. Consumer reports, which include other information in addition to credit activity, are reports by a CRA "bearing on a consumer's credit worthiness, credit standing, credit capacity, character, general reputation, personal characteristics, or mode of living."[10] They are used to determine a consumer's eligibility

---

December 2012. http://tinyurl.com/DROMCFPB3, 7.

[9] Vickie Elmer, "U.S. Consumer Watchdog to Oversee Credit Bureaus," *New York Times*, July 16, 2012. http://tinyurl.com/DROMElmer.

[10] "Credit Reporting Agencies," Title 15 *U.S. Code*, Sec. 1681, 2010. http://tinyurl.com/DROMUSC, 1349.

for credit or insurance, for employment purposes, or other purposes specified in the FCRA.

Credit reports are based on "credit files," information about a consumer contained in the databases of the NCRAs. Credit files have some or all of the following components:

1. *identifying information* such as name (and other names previously used), current and former addresses, Social Security number, date of birth, and phone numbers;

2. *trade lines* (accounts) in a consumer's name reported by creditors, including type of credit, credit limit or loan amount, account balance, payment history, delinquencies, collections, and dates of activity;

3. *public record information* of a financial nature, including bankruptcies, judgments, and state and federal tax liens;

4. *third-party collections* by debt buyers or collections agencies; and

5. *inquiries* in the last two years for employment-related uses and for at least the last year for credit uses and most non-employment uses (e.g., tenant screening, insurance, government benefits).[11]

Examples of important information *not* contained in credit files include: income or asset data, credit terms such as interest rates, records of arrests and convictions (but specialty CRAs such as employment screening agencies include them), marriage records, adoptions, and records of civil suits that have not resulted in judgments.[12]

CREDIT SCORES

Credit scores are mathematical models that input a consumer's bureau credit report and output a number that is called a "credit score." The most common scores range from 300 to 850. The higher the number, the less likely a consumer is to default, and hence makes a better credit risk for the lender.

A credit score is used by a bank or financing company to decide whether to lend to someone, and at what interest rate. Because banks say that interest is charged partly to make up for the chance of default, people with lower credit scores end up paying higher interest rates. Usually, scores below 660 are considered "subprime," and consumers with such scores will be denied credit or given credit on bad terms. Consumers with scores above 720 will get the best interest rates.

Banks use credit scores to make their lending decisions because the CRAs have a consumer's *entire* credit report, including accounts from other banks. This gives more information than just the bank's

---

[11] "Key Dimensions and Processes," 8–9.

[12] "Key Dimensions and Processes," 8.

internal data. Banks also use credit scores because the ease of using the algorithm, or mathematical formula, allows banks to implement strategies quickly. The fact that a consumer is reduced to a three-digit number allows them to pull large batches of credit scores and treat people based on that factor alone. However, for major lending decisions with high potential losses, such as a mortgage, banks will use additional factors, such as income verification, down payment amount, and an assessment of other debt obligations.

Types of credit scores

There are many variants of credit scores, making it difficult for a consumer to navigate through them. Credit scores have two main components: the data that goes into the score, and the scoring algorithm itself. Equifax, TransUnion, and Experian are the three main providers of data. There are many different providers for the scoring algorithm, the most famous being FICO, and the credit bureaus themselves. When you encounter a "credit score," it is important to denote which bureau the data in the score came from and what algorithm is used. Different algorithms use different score ranges, which can further confuse consumers. Below, some common examples of scores are noted and explained.

FICO score

The FICO score's range is 300–850, and the median score is about 720. Experts agree that if your score is above the median, you will have access to the best rates.[13]

The FICO score is created by a publicly traded company called FICO (formerly known as Fair Isaac Corporation) founded in 1956. Because they have been around for so long and have patented their algorithms, FICO enjoys a near monopoly in credit scoring, boasting that an overwhelming majority of lending decisions in the United States are made using the FICO score.

FICO, as a company, does not own any data from which it creates the credit score. FICO is not a CRA; they only create statistical algorithms. FICO "borrows" data (through complicated contracts) from the bureaus for the sole purpose of creating the algorithm. This algorithm is then encoded into a black box and placed at each of the Big Three bureaus, none of which know the contents. When lending entities, such as banks or cell phone companies, want a FICO score, they ping an inquiry to the bureau with which they have a relationship. The bureau runs the person's Social Security number to retrieve information from their database. That information goes through the

---

[13] Dana Dratch, "Taking a Look at 'Good' Credit," *Bankrate*, June 9, 2008. http://tinyurl.com/DROMDratch2.

black box algorithm, and out comes a score which the entity receives. The money made from that transaction is split between FICO and the bureau that provided the information.

Because there are three different bureaus that can provide information, there are three FICO scores. Because different banks use different bureaus, and some banks use all three, all the three scores can affect lending decisions. What compounds the confusion is that FICO uses different branding with different bureaus, so the score names can vary. If you see that you received a BEACON score, it means that you received a score with a FICO algorithm and Equifax underlying data. "Classic" refers to TransUnion, and "Experian/FICO Risk Model" to Experian.

For each bureau, FICO creates other scores specially calibrated for different purposes, such as the Auto Industry Option FICO score. The algorithm in that score is customized to predict only default in autos, instead of default in any line of credit. When someone gets a car loan, they think they received a FICO score, but it most likely isn't the one that would be used to give them a credit card or mortgage. Also, there is no way for the public to get these custom industry score options; only auto dealers with special contractual relationships can get these scores. Other specialty industry option scores include mortgage and bank card.

Finally, because FICO has been making scores for decades, there are many different versions of the same type of algorithm. The newest algorithm is called FICO8, but many banks still use an older version. Consequently, two different banks may pull the same FICO score type from the same bureau, and still get different scores.

There are approximately fifty different FICO branded scores a consumer can have.[14] FICO allows you to check your general FICO8 score for all three bureaus on myFICO.com for an extremely hefty fee of approximately $60. The only other option is to get the score is from your lender.

VantageScore

Experian, Equifax, and TransUnion got together and developed the VantageScore algorithm as a response to the FICO score. Its current range is 300–850, although it used to be 501–990. They own their own data and don't have to share revenue with FICO for the score. FICO still dominates the space of scores that are used for lending decisions, but the VantageScore is used often in companies—such as Fitch and Standard & Poor's—to assess portfolio risk, since this

[14] John Ulzheimer, "Scores, Scores, and More Scores: How Many FICO Scores Do You Have?" *Credit Sesame*, August 27, 2012. http://tinyurl.com/DROMUlzheimer5.

score is cheaper. Due to differences in algorithms, VantageScore and the FICO score can differ quite dramatically for certain people.

TransUnion and Experian offer their VantageScore to consumers through their websites for a fee. Credit Karma also offers the TransUnion VantageScore for a fee, but it doesn't have to be paid if subscription is canceled within seven days. There is no way for a consumer to get the Equifax VantageScore.

Credit scores marketed to consumers

Although savvy consumers can find their FICO scores and VantageScores, they are not marketed to consumers. Because FICO's primary focus has been on servicing banks and maintaining their monopoly position in the lending space, they have not spent the time or money necessary to market their scores to consumers. FICO's consumer-facing site, myFICO.com, is rarely advertised.

That hole was filled by dubious consumer-facing offerings that came from the credit bureaus themselves, and later by other entrepreneurs. These offerings profit from confusing people about credit scores and propagating the myth of a "*single* credit score," so that the public will buy the score from them. *Almost all of the scores marketed to consumers are not used in lending decisions.* Lending decisions are almost exclusively made using the FICO algorithm, and perhaps some are made using the VantageScore. Rent decisions, however, are often made with the scores outlined below.

If you read the fine print in these consumer offerings, you will find excerpts such as, "the PLUS score is derived from information based on a credit report, using a similar formula to those used by lenders." These made-for-consumer scores are called "educational" credit scores, meaning that they aren't actually the algorithms used in credit decisions, but instead are meant to just "educate" people. These "educational" scores are often created and distributed by the bureaus themselves—like Experian's freecreditreport.com—or sold to other companies like creditkarma.com or creditsesame.com. It makes financial sense for these companies to buy data from the bureaus and give it away for free to consumers because they make money from credit card companies who pay for credit card leads obtained from their site. There are also many affiliate sites that give a "free" score only to monetize it in credit card offers.

Some common "educational" credit scores include:

PLUS score
Range: 330–830
Created by Experian on Experian data
Found on freecreditreport.com

TransRisk score
Range: 300–850
Created by TransUnion on TransUnion data
Found on creditkarma.com

National Equivalency Score
Range: 360–840
Created by Experian on Experian data
Found on creditsesame.com

CE score
Range: 350–850
Created by CE Analytics on Experian data
Found on quizzle.com

Factors in scoring algorithm[15]

Only information that can be found in a bureau credit report or in public records can go into the scoring algorithm. Even though we can't control how the algorithms are constructed, we can take steps to make sure that the underlying information is correct by reviewing all three bureaus' reports.

Characteristics that are *not* allowed to be used in the scoring algorithm include age, geographical location, race, and income or any other employment information. Interest rates that you are currently charged also can't be used in the algorithm. Even though these factors don't come in directly, they can be correlated with other factors that do. For example, age doesn't go into the score, but credit history length does. Since many people get their first credit card around eighteen years of age, this statistic is highly correlated with age.

Below are the factors that make up most scoring algorithms. The percentages indicate the weight to that attribute given by the FICO scoring algorithm. VantageScore uses similar attributes and weights. The scoring algorithms reward behavior that uses a lot of credit "responsibly" (e.g., making all scheduled minimum payments), and penalize people for not using credit or using credit but missing payments.

Length of credit history (15%)

Your credit history is usually calculated as beginning with your oldest loan or credit card. Hence, many websites say that it is better if you refrain from closing the oldest cards you have. How long it's been since you last used your accounts is also factored into this portion of the score. Also, the average age of your accounts is considered, so opening new accounts can lower the score.

---

[15] Fair Isaac Corporation, "Understanding Your FICO Score," *myFICO*, 2011. http://tinyurl.com/DROMFICO2.

Payment history (35%)

Payment history information includes details on how payments were made on existing accounts. Late or missed payments (delinquencies) and collection items will severely hurt your score. The more "good" accounts with no late or delinquent payments there are, the better the score. To have a good payment history, you only need to have made the minimum payments on time. There isn't a negative impact on *this portion* of the score from just paying the minimum, although there may be adverse effects if you retain a high utilization (see below). Also, if you only pay the minimum, there are negative effects from paying a lot to the credit card companies in interest and fees.

Utilization (30%)

Utilization is how much of your credit limit you are using.[16] For example, if your credit limit is $10,000 and your balance is $3,000, your utilization is $3,000 / $10,000 = 30%. Utilization can be calculated for each card and over all cards. As a rule of thumb, it's best to use less than 25% of your overall limit, and less than 25% *each card's* limit. Many people have a few cards, but use only one; it's better to use all your cards a little bit. Asking for an increase in limit while spending the same amount on the card would help your score as well.

The scoring algorithms usually don't take into account whether the balance is "transacted" (paid off in full) or "revolved" (interest paid on a balance that remains). The credit scoring algorithms only take into account the balance and the credit limit, but it is better to transact balances because less fees are paid to the predatory credit card issuers. If you have a $5,000 credit limit and you spend $5,000 on your card and pay it off every month, it will be just as detrimental to your score as having a $5,000 balance the entire time on which you pay off only the interest every month. If you pay off your card every time you spend $1,000, and never leave a balance over $1,000, you will dramatically increase your score.

Although lower utilization is generally better, there is one exception: 0% utilization. One way to boost your score is to take any credit cards that aren't being used and putting a monthly bill and an automatic payment on them. If you set up an automatic withdrawal for the bill from your bank account, instead set it to automatically withdraw from your card, and then have your card automatically paid from your bank account. This way, it'll look like the card is being used, and used "responsibly." Utilization of installment loans, which is how much of the loan has been paid off, may also be considered in this portion of the score.

---

[16] "Credit Card Utilization and Average Credit Scores," *Credit Karma*, January 2, 2009. http://tinyurl.com/DROMCK2.

Mix of credit (10%)

From the viewpoint of credit scoring algorithms, having both installment loans (a fixed loan such as a car, student, or mortgage loan) and revolving loans (a credit card or retail card) is best. People with the best credit scores have at least a couple of credit cards and at least one installment loan that is being regularly paid off.

This is yet another part of the credit score that benefits the use of credit and thus promotes debt. Someone who doesn't have student loans or a mortgage and pays for their car with cash will have a lower score than had they financed the car and paid it off every month. Also, if someone doesn't use credit cards, they will have a lower score.

Inquiries (10%)

Inquiries are recorded as "credit pulls" when a bank or other institution looks up the borrower's score or credit report. There are "soft" and "hard" credit pulls. When you are seeking a loan for a car, mortgage, student loan, home equity line of credit, a credit card, or other credit products, it counts as a "hard" credit pull and will affect your score. Personal pulls on credit websites or for rental purposes count as a "soft" inquiry and will not affect your score at all. Another example of a "soft" inquiry is one done by lenders in order to pre-approve credit card offers or use for portfolio risk evaluations. However, once you fill out a credit application from the offer you received in the mail, you will get a "hard" inquiry on your credit report.

Inquiries remain on the record for twenty-four months, but the FICO score algorithm only considers the last twelve months of inquiries. Large amounts of inquiries will hurt your score a lot more than just one. However, FICO counts several inquiries for the same type of loan as one inquiry, as long as they were all made in a small time. This is not the case for credit cards, where every inquiry counts.

Unscoreable populations

People who don't have a score are referred to in the industry as "unscoreable." Estimates put the unscoreable U.S. population at twenty-seven to thirty million.[17] There are two primary reasons why someone would be unscoreable. The first is that they have never used a credit product and hence do not have a credit report. The second is that they have a credit report, but there is not enough information in the report to make a score, such as someone who has only one credit card and no other credit. Unscoreable people are often young, recent immigrants, people who have declared bankruptcy, and "unbanked"

---

[17] Cheryl Wilson, "VantageScore 3.0 Promises a Better Picture of Previously 'Unscoreable' Individuals," *PR Web*, April 11, 2013. http://tinyurl.com/DROMWilson2.

people (*see Chapters Seven and Eight*). There are many businesses springing up to create scores for these populations based on information other than credit history—like rental information or cell phone payments—but there is no standard yet used by lenders. Being "unscoreable" puts many people in a catch-22 situation, where they are denied credit and hence can't build credit.

PROBLEMS WITH CREDIT SCORES

Credit scores are created by for-profit institutions whose mission is to maximize profits. The data and the algorithm that go into the score are managed by opaque unwieldy institutions. A 2004 study revealed that 79% of credit reports contained errors; 25% of these mistakes were serious enough to result in a credit denial. More than half of all credit reports contained outdated information or information belonging to someone else.[18] You might think that because the rich use credit so much more, they'd be the ones mainly affected by these errors. In actuality, the poorer you are, the more likely your credit agency is to make a mistake that influences your rating. There is no accountability or transparency for the CRAs and no incentive for them to provide accurate information.

There are also problems with FICO, a for-profit institution, creating algorithms. Because an algorithm is just a mathematical formula, they have to use restrictive patents so that they can make money from it. No one can know the formula, lest they replicate it and FICO would lose their profits. Hence, it is in their best interest to keep it secret. When individuals are told "their scores," they are usually not the FICO scores which are used in most lending decisions. It's in the score providers' interest to obfuscate that fact so that consumers continue to buy their scores.

Besides the fact that it's created for a profit, there are methodological issues. First, the model omits variables that are critical to repaying debts on time, such as income, assets, and credit terms. The model also assumes that borrowers are "statistically independent" of one another, meaning that one's default depends only on one's individual characteristics and is unaffected by the defaults of others. However, defaults are often strongly correlated (e.g., a foreclosure depresses housing values across a neighborhood, making property owners de facto poorer, which increases the probability of further foreclosures).[19] Finally, the model assumes that consumers' riskiness

---

[18] Malgorzata Wozniacka and Snigdha Sen, "Credit Scores: What You Should Know About Your Own," *PBS Frontline*, November 23, 2004. http://tinyurl.com/DROMWozniacka.

[19] See Akos Rona-Tas and Stefanie Hiß, "Consumer and Corporate Credit Ratings and the Subprime Crisis in the U.S. with Some Lessons for Germany," *SCHUFA*, September 2008. http://

or creditworthiness determines their credit scores. But in practice, low scores result in worse loan conditions that in turn increase their riskiness. Thus, the credit score functions more like a self-fulfilling prophecy than an "objective" prediction.

As with other components of the debt system, credit scoring negatively impacts people of color at a disproportionate rate. About 42% of Latino/as and nearly half of Black people in the United States have credit scores under 660, compared to just under 20% for Whites. While the median credit score for Whites rose from 727 to 738 during the 1990s, it decreased for Blacks from 693 to 676, and for Latino/as from 695 to 670. Just like the racial wealth gap (*see Introduction*), the racial gap in credit scores has worsened, not improved, over recent decades.[20]

Finally, misuse of the credit score is now rampant. Using it for access to housing, employment opportunities, or health care is absolutely erroneous, even more misguided and harmful than when used for simple access to credit. These decisions have grave consequences to people's lives; housing, health care, and the means of subsistence are fundamental human needs that should be available to all, not granted or withheld based on a person's credit history.

> Recent studies suggest that more than twenty million people could have errors on their credit reports.[21]
>
> Much of this process remains unregulated, including who can send information to the agencies that compile your score and who can access the information once it's compiled.
>
> Those in communities with higher concentrations of people of color are twice as likely to have low credit scores as those in other areas. Higher fees and interest rates are imposed on those with low credit scores, ensuring that class divisions along racial lines remain unchallenged.[22]

tinyurl.com/DROMRonaTas, 19; Paul S. Calem and Michael LaCour-Little, "Risk-Based Capital Requirements for Mortgage Loans," *Federal Reserve Board*, November 2001. http://tinyurl.com/DROMCalem; Gunter Löffler, "The Effects of Estimation Error on Measures of Portfolio Credit Risk," *Journal of Banking and Finance* 27, no. 8, 2003. http://tinyurl.com/DROMLoffler.

[20] Wu and Birnbaum, "Credit Scoring and Insurance: Costing Consumers Billions and Perpetuating the Economic Racial Divide," *National Consumer Law Center* and *Center for Economic Justice*, June 2007. http://tinyurl.com/DROMWu, 13.

[21] Shawn Fremstad and Amy Traub, "Discrediting America: The Urgent Need to Reform the Nation's Credit Reporting Industry," *Dēmos*, 2011. http://tinyurl.com/DROMFremstad, 10.

[22] Board of Governors of the Federal Reserve System, *Report to Congress on Credit Scoring and Its Effect on the Availability and Affordability of Credit* (Washington, DC: GPO, 2007). http://tinyurl.com/DROMFed, 54.

Some things we can do

1. *Check our reports.* We can change this system, but we have to know it first. This is how to do it:

> Go to: Annualcreditreport.com
>
> Call 877-322-8228 or
>
> Complete the Annual Credit Report Request Form
> and mail it to:
>
>> Annual Credit Report Service
>>
>> P.O. Box 105281
>>
>> Atlanta, GA 30348-5281

In order to receive your free report, you'll need to provide your name, address, Social Security number, and date of birth. You may need to give your previous address if you've moved in the past two years. For security reasons, you may also have to give additional information like an account or a monthly payment you make.

Beware of those charging you to get your report or signing you up for "free" services in order to access it. And beware of those offering to help your credit score; there is nothing they can do that you can't do more effectively for free.

2. *Demand accuracy.* There are laws that protect debtors from unfair and inaccurate credit score practices: the Truth in Lending Act, Fair Credit Reporting Act, Fair Credit Billing Act, and Equal Credit Opportunity Act. All guarantee protection and the possibility for citizen-directed credit scoring and reporting.

3. *Demand accountability.* The Consumer Financial Protection Bureau is now an operating governmental body. We should ask if it's doing its job when it comes to regulating credit scoring, and if it can do more.

4. *Demand regulation.* Seven EU countries and seventeen Latin American countries have public credit scoring agencies. Why don't we? Ultimately we would prefer to get rid of credit scores altogether, but in the meantime we must at the very least remove the profit motive from a system that plays such a vital role in determining our access to the means to live.

5. *Reject the system.* It is possible to live without a good credit score. If you can muster the time and energy to make some life changes, you can go totally "off-grid" (*see Chapter Eleven*). Below are some recommendations on how to live without the benefits of a good credit score:

- Prepaid cell phones are always an option.
- For housing utilities, if you have a roommate, you can ask them to put the accounts in their name. If you live alone, ask a relative or friend.
- Opt for services that don't require credit checks. If a company requires a check, try to talk them out of it. Build up an old-fashioned trusting relationship by spending time talking with the person. They may choose to bypass the credit check.
- Create your own credit report. Put together a portfolio showing you are a trustworthy person (reference letters, job history, life narrative).
- Check listings for housing, cars, and other necessities that are informal and don't go through brokers or other formal agencies.
- Offer to put down larger deposits in lieu of a credit check.
- Build networks of mutual support in your community so you rely less on outside services.

DIY credit repair

To repair an error on your credit report, it is best to do it yourself. This helps you avoid scams and fly under the radar of the CRAs who are looking to block credit repair companies from gaming their system. There are many books, websites, articles, and other resources dealing with this issue. Below are the steps we recommend:

1. Get a copy of all three of your credit reports.

2. Review your credit reports and note every single error. Note incorrect spellings of your name, inaccurate data, and any "derogatory" information.

3. Write letters disputing negative information and errors to the corresponding agencies.

4. Describe in your letter how you found out your credit was bad and how shocked you were at all of the errors the agencies have been reporting. Then ask them "per the Fair Credit Reporting Act (FCRA) enacted by Congress in 1970," to either provide physical proof of their claims or delete the mistakes immediately.

Include your name, current address, and Social Security number on your letter. You should not include any additional information.

Simply list the entry that you are challenging and briefly explain why you are challenging it. You only need to write a couple of words to do this—less is more. Say things like, "This is not mine" or "This record is inaccurate." Be sure to make the letter sound unique to you. If you do not, you may find that the CRA responds by saying that your claim is "frivolous." This is how they typically respond to credit repair companies, and is why you should not use them. There are competing theories on whether or not you should challenge everything on your report all at once. You are legally entitled to have each item you challenge verified at any point in time.

When sending your letter, request a "return receipt" or "delivery confirmation." The CRA has thirty days to respond to your dispute. If they do not respond within that time frame, you will have evidence that they are in violation of the Fair Credit Reporting Act.

5. Don't give up after the first round. Within a month, you will likely receive a response from the CRAs. Typically, they will only state whether or not they were able to verify an item. For any items they claim to have verified, you should contact the creditor directly and demand that they provide proof that the debt is yours. You can also continue to challenge the entry with the CRA. (*See Appendix A for sample letters.*)

If you play this game, there's a good chance you can eventually win. Keep pressing on and hammering them with letters demanding they correct their mistakes and they may eventually get sick of your letters and start deleting negative trade lines from your report. You will likely be writing letters for six months to a year, but you should see a substantial improvement to your credit report and score within three months. As usual, the person who yells the loudest for the longest wins. And don't forget, repairing your credit score isn't about regaining validity in the eyes of the system: it's about challenging an exclusionary and unjust surveillance machine.

CONSUMER REPORTING AGENCIES FOR CHECKING ACCOUNTS

The credit score is an essential piece of economic surveillance, but it's not the only one. There are other ways of watching us and keeping us in line. Many people, for example, have a checking account. Just as a series of private corporations monitor your borrowing activity in the economy, a different group of private corporations monitors your checking account. And just as credit score companies make a profit from calculating your score, consumer reporting agencies that monitor checking accounts make a killing when you overdraft or miss a payment.

ChexSystems and TeleCheck are two examples. Usually banks are very private about their own information, especially checking accounts, but in the interest of "preventing fraudulent activity" financial institutions report instances of "account mishandling" to these agencies. TeleCheck primarily deals with bad check-writing while ChexSystems, used by over 80% of banks in the United States, deals with that and more: "non-sufficient funds" (NSF), overdrafts, fraud, suspected fraud, and account abuse. Retailers report bad checks to Shared Check Authorization Networks (SCAN), which in turn report to ChexSystems. When someone tries to open an account elsewhere, the agency notifies the institution about that applicant's history.

ChexSystems, unlike credit bureaus, only provides *negative* information in their reports. Therefore, a single banking error can result in losing an account and could mean immense difficulty trying to open one elsewhere. Once in their systems, it is extremely difficult to get out, even if you ended up there in error. Something as inconsequential as failing to rectify a deliberately confusing overdraft fee may be enough to negate decades' worth of "responsible" banking.

There are some steps that can be taken to avoid triggering a ChexSystems or TeleCheck report in the first place. Know your balance before writing checks to make sure they won't bounce. And if your checkbook ever gets stolen, report it to your bank or credit union immediately. When you are closing an account, be sure to discontinue all automatic payments, wait until you're certain that all checks you've written have cleared, and *formally* close the account instead of simply taking all of your money out.[23]

Regardless of your checking account history, you are entitled to a free copy of your ChexSystems or TeleCheck report every twelve months. If you are denied a checking account because of your report, you are entitled to a free copy within sixty days from the CRA that is responsible. To request a copy of your report, go to consumerdebit.com for ChexSystems or firstdata.com for TeleCheck.

If the agency refuses to provide you with a copy of your report or you fail to receive it within sixty days of being denied an account, you can submit a complaint to the Federal Trade Commission (FTC) at ftccomplaintassistant.gov. Then send a letter via certified mail to ChexSystems or TeleCheck notifying them that they are in violation of the Fair Credit Reporting Act and that they have fifteen days to send you a copy of your report. Let them know that you are willing to pursue legal action and that you have already contacted the FTC. (*See Appendix B for sample letters.*)

If you are unable to open a checking account because of a negative report from one of these agencies, there are several possible courses of action. You can dispute your checking account report. For information on doing this, visit the website chexsystemsvictims. com. Another approach is to open an account at a financial institution that does not use ChexSystems or TeleCheck. A state-by-state

[23] Rob Berger, "ChexSystems: The Banks' Secret Watch Dog Is Watching You," *Dough Roller*, June 18, 2011. http://tinyurl.com/DROMBerger.

directory is available at nochexbanks.org. In addition, in some states you can take a six-hour "Get Checking" course, upon completion of which you can open an account at a participating financial institution. But there is a $50 course fee, and guess who sponsors the program—a parent corporation of ChexSystems by the name of eFunds.[24] The final option is to try to live without an account. As Chapter Eleven will illustrate, this can be difficult, but many people have no option but to survive "unbanked."

RESOURCES
Websites
• ChexSystems Victims (chexsystemsvictims.com)
• National Consumer Law Center: Credit Reports (nclc.org/issues/credit-reports.html)
• Privacy Rights Clearinghouse: Credit and Credit Reports (privacyrights.org)

Articles
• Kelly Gates, "The Securitization of Financial Identity and the Expansion of the Consumer Credit Industry," *Journal of Communication Inquiry* 34, no. 4 (2010), 417–431.
• "Information on Free Credit Reports," *NEDAP*, http://tinyurl.com/DROMNEDAP05.
• Mark Kantrowitz, "Credit Scores," *FinAid!*, 2012, http://tinyurl.com/DROMKantrowitz.
• Chi Chi Wu, "Automated Injustice: How a Mechanized Dispute System Frustrates Consumers Seeking to Fix Errors in Their Credit Reports," *National Consumer Law Center*, January 2009, http://tinyurl.com/DROMWu4.

REFERENCES
Berger, Rob. "ChexSystems: The Banks' Secret Watch Dog Is Watching You." *Dough Roller*, June 18, 2011. http://tinyurl.com/DROMBerger.

Berner, Robert, and Chad Terhune. "Hospitals X-Ray Patient Credit Scores." *Business Week*, November 19, 2008. http://tinyurl.com/DROMBerner.

Board of Governors of the Federal Reserve System. *Report to Congress on Credit Scoring and Its Effect on the Availability and Affordability of Credit.* Washington, DC: GPO, 2007. http://tinyurl.com/DROMFed.

Calem, Paul S., and Michael LaCour-Little. "Risk-Based Capital Requirements for Mortgage Loans." *Federal Reserve Board*, November 2001. http://tinyurl.com/DROMCalem.

Consumer Financial Protection Bureau. "Key Dimensions and Processes in the

---

[24] Don Taylor, "Negative ChexSystems Report Nixes Account," *Bankrate*, March 8, 2006. http://tinyurl.com/DROMTaylor.

U.S. Credit Reporting System: A Review of How the Nation's Largest Credit Bureaus Manage Consumer Data." December 2012. http://tinyurl.com/DROMCFPB3.

Credit Karma. "Credit Card Utilization and Average Credit Scores." January 2, 2009. http://tinyurl.com/DROMCK2.

"Credit Reporting Agencies." Title 15 *U.S. Code*, Sec. 1681. 2010. http://tinyurl.com/DROMUSC.

Dratch, Dana. "Taking a Look at 'Good' Credit." *Bankrate*, June 9, 2008. http://tinyurl.com/DROMDratch.

Elmer, Vickie. "U.S. Consumer Watchdog to Oversee Credit Bureaus." *New York Times*, July 16, 2012. http://tinyurl.com/DROMElmer.

Fair Isaac Corporation. "Understanding Your FICO Score." *myFICO*, 2011. http://tinyurl.com/DROMFICO2.

Fremstad, Shawn, and Amy Traub. "Discrediting America: The Urgent Need to Reform the Nation's Credit Reporting Industry." *Dēmos*, 2011. http://tinyurl.com/DROMFremstad.

Gale Group. "Credit Reporting Services Market Report." *Highbeam Business*. Accessed July 12, 2013. http://tinyurl.com/DROMGale.

Garfinkel, Simson. "Separating Equifax from Fiction." *Wired*, September 1995. http://tinyurl.com/DROMGarfinkel.

Grow, Brian, and Pallavi Gogoi. "Insurance: A New Way to Squeeze the Weak?" *Business Week*, January 27, 2002. http://tinyurl.com/DROMGrow2.

Jentzsch, Nicola. *Financial Privacy: An International Comparison of Credit Reporting Systems*. New York: Springer, 2007.

Löffler, Gunter. "The Effects of Estimation Error on Measures of Portfolio Credit Risk." *Journal of Banking and Finance* 27, no. 8, 2003: 1427–1453. http://tinyurl.com/DROMLoffler.

Privacy Rights Clearinghouse. "'Other' Consumer Reports: What You Should Know about 'Specialty' Reports." June 2013. http://tinyurl.com/DROMPRC.

Rona-Tas, Akos, and Stefanie Hiß. "Consumer and Corporate Credit Ratings and the Subprime Crisis in the U.S. with Some Lessons for Germany." *SCHUFA*, September 2008. http://tinyurl.com/DROMRonaTas.

Society for Human Resource Management. "SHRM Research Spotlight: Credit Background Checks." September 2010. http://tinyurl.com/DROMSHRM.

Taylor, Don. "Negative ChexSystems Report Nixes Account." *Bankrate*, March 8, 2006. http://tinyurl.com/DROMTaylor.

Ulzheimer, John. "Scores, Scores, and More Scores: How Many FICO Scores Do You Have?" *Credit Sesame*, August 27, 2012. http://tinyurl.com/DROMUlzheimer5.

Wilson, Cheryl. "VantageScore 3.0 Promises a Better Picture of Previously 'Unscore-able' Individuals." *PR Web*, April 11, 2013. http://tinyurl.com/DROMWilson2.

Wozniacka, Malgorzata, and Snigdha Sen. "Credit Scores: What You Should Know about Your Own." *PBS Frontline*, November 23, 2004. http://tinyurl.com/DROMWozniacka.

Wu, Chi Chi, and Birny Birnbaum. "Credit Scoring and Insurance: Costing Consumers Billions and Perpetuating the Economic Racial Divide." *National Consumer Law Center* and *Center for Economic Justice*, June 2007. http://tinyurl.com/DROMWu.

TWO

CREDIT CARD AND AUTOMOBILE DEBT

ON THE ROAD TO NOWHERE

Workers in the United States continue to be among the most productive in the world, yet median wages have barely increased over the past four decades. We've been working longer and harder, trying to keep up with the rising costs of living—housing, health care, education—yet we haven't actually managed to keep up without plastic. In the early 1980s, U.S. household debt as a share of income was around 60%. By the time of the 2008 financial crisis, that share had grown to exceed 100%, and today it's hovering around 112%.[1] So despite the fact that productivity has gone up, we have relied more and more on credit as a means of subsistence. This, in turn, intricately weaves people into the complex debt system at the heart of modern capitalism. This process essentially ensures that we will be dependent on Wall Street to provide us with a "lifeline" of credit. These "lifelines" of credit don't really solve our problems, though. Instead, they only make things worse in the long run.

The credit card industry is notorious for its lack of transparency, which makes credit cards some of the most hazardous and confusing financial tools out there. At their core, they embody the deceptive and bottomline-driven processes that are the engine of mafia capitalism. Many credit cards feature a fluctuating interest rate and a multiplicity of complicated and hidden fees.

Like credit card debt, car debt—money borrowed to purchase an automobile—is a form of consumer debt that enmeshes individuals, perhaps unwittingly, in the debt system. For many who live outside the public transportation infrastructure of a major city, owning a car is a necessity, not a luxury. (How else will they get to their job so they can earn money to pay off their auto loan?) But maintaining a car—buy-

[1] "Despite Recent Declines, U.S. Household Debt Is Still Very High Relative to Disposable Income," *Peter G. Peterson Foundation*, February 1, 2013. http://tinyurl.com/DROMPGPF.

ing gas, paying for repairs, paying for parking tickets—is an expensive undertaking. Sometimes, these payments are made with a credit card, thus compounding the consumer's debt and further entangling them into our predatory financial system.

Today in the United States, credit cards and automobiles are inescapable parts of daily life for many people. Throughout this chapter, we analyze the different ways the credit card and auto loan industries profit off people through duplicitous means. In doing so, we explain the history of the credit card industry, in particular what economic and political conditions allowed for the rise and proliferation of credit, and how credit has affected different communities. For both forms of consumer debt, we introduce strategies for practical alternatives, while hoping to open up avenues that allow for other, more creative individual and collective resistance strategies. We also explore the different ways you—the worker and consumer—can fight back to regain some of your economic independence.

CREDIT CARD DEBT: THE PLASTIC SAFETY NET

Although fewer people hold credit cards than before the 2008 financial crisis, most still do. Some fifty million households have credit card debt,[2] with about 75% of individuals having at least one credit card.[3] With nearly 383 million open credit card accounts and 700 million credit cards in circulation, it's fair to say that having a wallet full of plastic has now become one of the defining features of life in the United States—our plastic safety net. In all, credit card debt in the United States stands at about $670 billion.[4] This means the average U.S. household owes nearly $15,000 in credit card debt, which is actually down from 2010. However, the number of indebted households has increased by 3.5%. Basically, more people are in debt now than a few years ago, even if they have less of it.[5]

History in reverse

When credit cards were first introduced in the 1960s, the credit card industry would make its money on interest rates, but this never amounted to much. Universal credit cards such as Visa and Master-Card were offered then as loyalty rewards only to banks' "best" custom-

---

[2] Ray Martin, "Should You Ditch Your Credit Cards?" *CBS News.com*, June 22, 2012. http://tinyurl.com/DROMMartin3.

[3] Lisa Stark, "Your Debt May Raise Your Credit Card Rates," *ABCNews.com*, June 2, 2009. http://tinyurl.com/DROMStark.

[4] "Quarterly Report on Household Debt and Credit," *Federal Reserve Bank of New York*, August 2013. http://tinyurl.com/DROMFedNY2, 3.

[5] Tim Chen, "Bad News: Credit Card Debt Is Down," *Forbes.com*, May 30, 2012. http://tinyurl.com/DROMChen2.

ers who paid off their monthly balances—that is, affluent White men. The appeal of the cards was convenience and prestige, not a need for credit. Banks lost money on the product, but the idea was to build loyalty in order to do even bigger business down the road. The banks got something in return as well: the wealthiest, most powerful men served as walking advertisements for the cards every time they used one. In contrast, today, cardholders who never carry balances on their cards are known inside the industry as "deadbeats," or "money-losers."

A series of legal changes—effectively eliminating usury laws by allowing all lenders to register in South Dakota, where no such laws existed—along with the growth of computer networks that could trace credit ratings led to an explosion of credit card use in the 1980s. Interest rate deregulation helped transform credit cards from banks' loss leaders into profit engines. As more people acquired credit cards throughout the '80s and '90s, the wealthiest households' credit cards were subsidized by the least wealthiest households. This is sometimes called "risk pooling," although typically pooling involves those with more, subsidizing those with less; here it's the reverse. Through the use of so-called "risk-based pricing," credit card companies actually charge financially distressed households more to use their cards. Card companies claim that interest rate charges are based on "risk," but there is abundant evidence that the risk ratings are largely determined by where you live, a practice known as "redlining." Redlining was historically used to deny residents and businesses access to credit in predominantly Black neighborhoods—without using explicitly racial/ethnic criteria. However, now high-risk ratings are used to charge more for credit—a practice often referred to as "reverse redlining"—and this condition sets up a self-fulfilling prophecy. Being designated financially "risky" actually further exposes one to unfair and abusive financial practices. According to Robert D. Manning, founder of the Responsible Debt Relief Institute and author of *Credit Card Nation*, "[a] carefully guarded secret of the industry is that about a quarter of cardholders have accounted for almost two-thirds of interest and penalty-fee revenues. Nearly half of all credit card accounts do not generate finance and fee revenues."[6]

As mentioned above, U.S. household debt as a share of income has risen from 60% to over 100% in the past thirty years. So, despite all our exertions as workers over this period, the majority of us have only gone deeper into debt. The prime reason is clear: we're in debt because we're not paid enough in the first place. In the United States, there's minimal or non-existent social protection available to support us as we struggle to provide for our own basic needs and our dependents. Consolidated

---

[6] Robert D. Manning, "Five Myths about America's Credit Card Debt," *Washington Post*, January 31, 2010. http://tinyurl.com/DROMManning.

corporate greed, with its never-ending appetite for profit above all, continues to trump our basic rights. In a financial system characterized by a lack of transparency, credit cards are a complicated and risky product upon which too many of us depend. Additionally, credit cards feature a number of complicated, disguised fees; according to Professor Adam Levitin of Georgetown University Law Center, these "gotcha" fees cost families in the United States over $12 billion a year.[7]

Although total national credit card debt is small in comparison with mortgage debt, effective APRs (annual percentage rates) are at least five times as high as mortgage loans. The moment consumers get into trouble, card companies pounce, imposing penalties, even retroactively. These practices are unfair and abusive. In an attempt to address them, in 2009 Congress passed the Credit Card Accountability Responsibility and Disclosure (CARD) Act, which aimed to "establish fair and transparent practices relating to the extension of credit."[8]

Today, there are more than five thousand credit cards issuers; a majority of these (and the debt they manage) is owned by the big banks. The top three—Citigroup, Bank of America, and JPMorgan Chase—control more than 60% of outstanding credit card debt.[9] From 1993 to 2007, the amount charged to U.S. credit card carriers went from $475 billion to more than $1.9 trillion. Late fees have risen an average of 160% and over-limit fees have risen an average of 115% over a similar period (1990–2005).[10]

After the crash of 2008, families scrambled to get out of debt. Some were helped by the useful, if limited, regulatory reforms prescribed by the CARD Act. Credit card debt is down by 15% overall as regulations take effect and cardholders wise up to the industry's old tricks.[11] The problem is that, meanwhile, card companies have been devising new tricks, household expenses have risen, and incomes have either remained stagnant or have fallen. The total amount of credit card debt remains staggeringly high, and card issuers are still free to charge whatever rates of interest they like. (Only nonprofit credit unions are required by Congress to abide by an interest-rate ceiling of 15%.)

---

[7] Senate Committee on Banking, Housing and Urban Affairs, *Enhanced Consumer Financial Protection After the Financial Crisis*, testimony of Adam J. Levitin before the Committee on Banking, Housing and Urban Affairs, July 19, 2011. http://tinyurl.com/DROMLevitin.

[8] "H.R. 627—111th Congress: Credit Card Accountability Responsibility and Disclosure Act of 2009," *111th Congress*, 2009. http://tinyurl.com/DROMCARD, 1.

[9] Manning, "Five Myths."

[10] U.S. Government Accountability Office, "Credit Cards: Increased Complexity in Rates and Fees Heightens Need for More Effective Disclosures to Consumers," October 11, 2006. http://tinyurl.com/DROMGAO.

[11] "Credit Card Debt Decreases 15 Percent Nationally," *Credit Karma*, March 10, 2011. http://tinyurl.com/DROMKarma.

In the nine months between the passage and implementation of the CARD Act, credit card issuers did their best to hike interest rates, reduce lines of credit, increase fees, and water down rewards programs. For the millions with poor credit scores and borrowing costs that are through the roof, it may already be too late. Now, as credit scores are widely used as a screening tool for job applicants, workers face even greater challenges in finding employment, much less entering the increasingly mythological U.S. middle class.

The tricks of the trade

From risk-rating to pricing to credit limit determination, credit industry policies are extremely opaque and seem designed to keep cardholders in the dark. Analysts at Credit Karma, however, were able to study a sample of over two hundred thousand credit cards; the relationship between credit scores, income, and credit limits indicated that higher credit scores get you higher credit limits, regardless of income. Low credit scores, no matter your income, keep credit limits low.[12]

A history of compliance with minimum payments is more important to issuers than current ability to repay. Credit card companies don't mind late payments if you maintain a balance, as long as you pay your monthly minimum. Remember us "deadbeats"? Since almost all of the issuers' profits come from late fees and interest rate penalties, they depend on our slip-ups. This is why monthly statements are intentionally designed to be confusing. If they change the design of your statement—say, by moving a box to the left, or making the print a little smaller—in such a way as to cause even one cardholder out of a thousand to misunderstand and miss a payment, that's millions of dollars in additional profit for the credit card company. In the past, companies would trip up consumers by making the due date fall on a Sunday or a holiday, creating more "deadbeats" from which to profit.

The CARD Act outlawed several of the most predominant predatory lending practices. For instance, in the past, companies needed to provide only fifteen days notice before raising rates or making other changes to your contract, leaving little time to negotiate. Now, companies are required to notify customers forty-five days in advance.[13] However, this notification will most likely be sent by mail, so be sure to read everything your credit card company sends. Since the 1990s, credit card pricing has been a game of "three-card monte," according to Levitin. "Pricing has been shifted away from the upfront, atten-

[12] "How a Credit Card Limit Is Determined," *Credit Karma*, September 23, 2008. http://tinyurl.com/DROMCK.

[13] Leslie McFadden, "8 Major Benefits of New Credit Card Law," *Bankrate*, August 20, 2009. http://tinyurl.com/DROMMcFadden.

tion grabbing price points, like annual fees and base interest rates, and shifted to back-end fees that consumers are likely to ignore or underestimate."[14] If we are unable to gauge the true cost of products, how can we be expected to use them and be financially responsible?

For a credit card company, the perfect customer is one who charges up a large amount of debt impulsively, sits on it for a year or two so as to build up maximum high-rate interest charges, finally feels guilty, and pays it all back without asking any questions. That's why companies used to besiege high school and college students with free card offers: they calculated that students were likely to spend impulsively, attempt to avoid the problem, and eventually call their parents to foot the bill. The CARD Act restricts extensions of credit to those under twenty-one unless they have a cosigner or a proven means of income. Credit card companies are no longer allowed to hand out free gifts at or near colleges or college-sponsored events.[15]

The overwhelming bulk of credit card debt isn't driven by impulse spending at all, but by the predicaments of people trying to make ends meet. Even when jobless or unemployed, we remain consumers; our basic needs still include education, groceries, housing, doctor's visits, medicine, and transportation. One survey found that 86% of people who lose their jobs report having to live, to some degree, off of their credit cards until they find new jobs.[16] According to another survey, medical bills are a leading contributor to credit card debt, affecting nearly half of low- to middle-income households; the average amount of medical debt on credit cards is $1,678 per household.[17]

What can we do?

Obviously, no one wants to sit on a huge pile of "revolving" credit card debt accruing interest at usurious rates every month. Unfortunately, credit cards are the double-edged sword of the credit score world. If we have cards with high balances, our scores go down. If we have *no* credit card, our scores go down. Having low credit scores can keep us from getting the things we need, like an affordable mortgage, apartment, or job.

---

[14] Senate Committee on Banking, Housing, and Urban Affairs, *Modernizing Consumer Protection in the Financial Regulatory System: Strengthening Credit Card Protections*, testimony of Adam J. Levitin before the Committee on Banking, Housing and Urban Affairs, February 12, 2009. http://tinyurl.com/DROMLevitin2, 11.

[15] Connie Prater, "What the Credit Card Reform Law Means to You," *Creditcards.com*, June 13, 2012. http://tinyurl.com/DROMPrater.

[16] Amy Traub and Catherine Ruetschlin, "The Plastic Safety Net: Findings from the 2012 National Survey on Credit Card Debt of Low- and Middle-Income Households," *Dēmos*, May 22, 2012. http://tinyurl.com/DROMTraub, 22.

[17] Ann Carrns, "Medical Costs Contribute to Credit Card Debt," *New York Times*, May 22, 2012. http://tinyurl.com/DROMCarrns.

If we don't buy on credit, then banks will see us as "risky," and will not loan. On the other hand, if we have a credit card but spend too much, then we will also be denied a loan.

If you can't avoid having the cards, you can sidestep the traps by understanding the fine print. Card Hub (cardhub.com) offers free tools to help us understand and navigate credit reports and scores, compare cards, and even provides customized credit card recommendations. Credit Karma (creditkarma.com) is another great option.

Think about how important credit scores are, and how strongly some people are committed to preserving them. Consider the risks. This involves looking into the future, which always makes things more complicated and multiplies the "unknowns." Start by finding out where you currently stand. Get your free credit report (*see Chapter One*) and make sure it's accurate.

Whether you're drowning in credit card debt or simply have too many cards, the most appropriate tactics for fighting back against the credit card trap will depend on your individual needs and circumstances. Below we suggest a few options, including legal action, bankruptcy, or simply refusing to pay.

Going to court

You may have seen those lawyers who appear on late-night TV promising they can get us out of debt. Surprise—in a world is full of scam artists—some of them actually can! This is how the honest ones do it:

What most people don't realize is that, legally, there's nothing special about owing money. A debt is just a promise and, contractually, no promise is more or less sacrosanct than any other. If one signs with a credit card company, both the signer and the company are agreeing to abide by a contract that is equally binding. The fine print applies to both sides, so if American Express has failed to fulfill any of its contractual obligations—for instance, its obligation to alert us promptly of a change of policy—that's just as much a violation of contract as our failure to pay the agreed-upon sum. Knowing how this industry works, any skilled lawyer with a copy of the contract and access to all relevant correspondence is likely to discover half a dozen ways the company has violated its contractual obligations. In the eyes of the law, both parties are guilty, so we may have the power to renegotiate the terms of the relationship. This usually means the judge can knock off half or even three-quarters of the total sum owed.

The credit card industry is riddled with fraud on a scale that is only now beginning to be revealed. "The same problems that plagued the foreclosure process—and prompted a multibillion-dollar settlement with big banks—are now emerging in the debt collection practices of credit card companies," the *New York Times* reported in 2012. "As they work through a glut of bad loans, companies like American Express, Citigroup, and Discover Financial are going to court to recoup their money. But many of the lawsuits rely on erroneous robo-signed [i.e., automatically computer generated] documents, incomplete records, and generic testimony from witnesses, according to judges who oversee the cases." Lenders are "churning out lawsuits without regard for accuracy, and improperly collecting debts from consumers." One judge told the paper that he suspected a full 90% of lawsuits brought by credit card companies were "flawed and can't prove the person owes the debt."[18]

In some cases, banks have sold credit card receivables known to be inaccurate or already paid. In a series of transactions in 2009 and 2010, Bank of America sold credit card receivables to an outfit called CACH, LLC, based in Denver, Colorado. Each month CACH bought debts with a face value of as much as $65 million for 1.8 cents on the dollar.[19] The cut-rate pricing suggests the accounts' questionable quality, but what is remarkable is that the bank would even try to sell them and that it could make money from them. Over the last two years, Bank of America has charged off $20 billion in delinquent card debt. An undisclosed portion of the delinquent debt gets passed along to collectors. Once sold, rights to such accounts are often resold within the industry multiple times over several years. Other banks have also admitted that their debt sale contracts may be riddled with inaccuracies.

The lesson is, always keep copies of everything. Always keep the option of legal action open (small claims or otherwise), and make sure the credit card companies know that you're doing so.

What happens if you just don't pay?

After ninety days of non-payment, your account goes into default and the credit card company has the option of sending it off to a debt collection agency. They don't really like this option, because they will be taking a huge loss. Debt collection agencies make their money by buying up your debt at pennies on the dollar, often through brokers, and then trying to collect the whole thing, plus fees for the cost of collection. The original lender takes a loss. No doubt they can get some of it back through tax accounting and no doubt they figure a certain

---

[18] Jessica Silver-Greenberg, "Problems Riddle Moves to Collect Credit Card Debt," *New York Times*, August 12, 2012. http://tinyurl.com/DROMSilver5.

[19] Jeff Horwitz, "Bank of America Sold Card Debts to Collectors Despite Faulty Records," *American Banker*, March 29, 2012. http://tinyurl.com/DROMHorwitz.

percentage of that loss into their business model, but ultimately they would rather this didn't happen.

Obviously this is a bad thing for us as well; it means we will be hounded by a collection agency and our credit scores will take a major hit. If we want to borrow in the future, it might not be possible. If we *are* able to borrow, we will be charged much higher interest rates. If that isn't a concern, then go ahead, default: it's free money! But for most of us, it is a problem, so we must turn to other measures.

Negotiating with the credit card company

Since credit card companies don't want us to default, we can often negotiate. They may offer a substantial reduction on what we owe them if they think defaulting is our only other option. Remember: even if we offer them ten cents on the dollar, that's more than they would be getting if they sold it to a collection agency. On the other hand, they may not want to set a precedent—they know that if everyone just held out and negotiated a 90% reduction their business would be ruined. So they are being pulled in two different directions. This is important to bear in mind when negotiating. If you're seriously thinking about negotiating, see carreonandassociates.com for the exact sequence of procedures for how to do it.

Default versus bankruptcy

When you fail to make payments on your credit card, it falls into default. When this happens, your credit card company usually "closes" the card, meaning that no further charges will be allowed on the account. But that doesn't mean that the balance goes away—far from it. Interest and late fees will continue to accrue until you pay the balance. If you don't, the credit card company will most likely hire a collection agency to hound you for the money.

Declaring bankruptcy is an alternative to going into default. When you declare bankruptcy, credit card debts may be wiped out or lessened. However, it is a complex process that can backfire in many cases. In addition, bankruptcy will affect your credit rating for the next seven to ten years. If you are thinking of declaring bankruptcy, refer to Chapter Ten of this manual. The statute of limitations on defaults—the amount of time creditors or collectors have after you default to try to get it back legally—differs from state to state, from as little as three years to as many as ten. But after it's over, you're entirely off the hook and it's easy to wipe the default off your record. Which option to choose will vary according to your individual circumstances. Try to get all information about the different possibilities in your state of residence before you decide.

*What about those people who use one credit card
to pay interest on another?*

There definitely are people who have figured out the ropes—the way that one's credit score interacts with multiple credit card accounts, and so forth—so well that they can live off their credit cards for years before defaulting. It can be done. The major proviso is that making a living this way is not all that much easier than making a living in a more conventional way and it has the disadvantage of being extremely risky and time-consuming. If you, along with figuring out all the possible legal ramifications, deem this acceptable, then go ahead. Consider that for some, going "off the financial grid" is an easier way to live (*see Chapter Eleven*).

Resisting the credit card industry actions

Unlike student debt, a movement against credit card debt has yet to form. Launching such a movement is one of the aims of this manual and of Strike Debt. In the meantime, here are some examples of individual resistance actions that some people have taken. They tend toward the playful and absurd. As always, beware of the risks before you engage in such behavior. Dimitry Agarkov, a forty-two-year-old from Russia, turning the tables, has mischievously inspired others to do the same. Agarkov, discontent with unsolicited credit card offers from his country's leading online bank, Tinkoff Credit Systems, scanned, amended, and returned the contract on his terms. In their rush to capitalize on the contract, the bank signed off on the agreement without reading it. Two years later, due to overdue payments on a balance of $575 in Ruples, Agarkov's card was terminated. Agarkov later decided to sue Tinkoff Credit Systems for $727,000 in Ruples.[20]

Until we can organize and mount genuine collective resistance against credit card debt, registering your displeasure with a symbolic gesture might help let off some steam. Gathering with friends to stuff credit card companies' *own* prepaid envelopes that they've sent to you along with their offers is one such gesture. Stuff each envelope with wooden shims or roofing shingles to increase the postage costs and send them back to the company at their own expense. This is an example of an action that transforms debtors from passive victims to active rejecters of financialization tools. Also, as the proceeds of this action go to the U.S. Postal Service, we can help slow down this country's fast track toward mail delivery privatization.

---

[20] "700k Windfall: Russian Man Outwits Bank with Handwritten Credit Contract," *RT*, August 8, 2013. http://tinyurl.com/DROMRT.

CAR DEBT: GOING NOWHERE FAST

Debt incurred as a result of car ownership, upkeep, and repair represents the single most onerous form of consumer debt, according to a recent Consumer Federation of America complaint survey.[21] And at roughly $783 billion, auto loan debt is the third largest source of consumer debt after mortgages and student loans. Those who suffer most from automobile debt are those who depend on cars most— working people. It's not unusual for a person to take out a loan to buy a car in order to commute to work, only to discover that monthly loan payments, replacement parts, garage payments, and gas quickly eat into one's take-home pay:

> Even with a generous allowance for housing, Navy Electronics Techni- cian Riley Butler cannot feed his family of three without assistance from a local non-profit in his home city of San Diego, California. Butler's monthly take-home pay is $1,800, and because he receives a housing stipend, car costs are his biggest expense at $450 each month, followed by groceries at $300.[22]

Cars are the most common non-financial asset held by families in the country,[23] and as an asset they are a natural candidate for creat- ing *secured debt*. This means that unlike credit card agreements, which have no collateral, if you don't repay the auto loan, the car—as the underlying asset securing the loan—can be repossessed and sold by the creditor to cover its losses. Given how dependent many of us are on cars, repossession can be devastating. Costs associated with cars can also add to credit card debt, so if you are not of the more well-to- do, sliding further into debt is nearly impossible to avoid.

Monthly payments for cars tend to last for more than four years. As reported by Experian, the average new car payment is $452 per month,[24] and used car loans cost about $351 per month.[25] In 2011, the average total annual cost of a four-door car was almost $9,000 ($750 per month), according to the American Automobile Association.[26]

---

[21] "2011 Consumer Complaint Survey Report," *Consumer Federation of America* and *North American Consumer Protection Investigators*, July 31, 2012. http://tinyurl.com/DROMCFA, 6.

[22] Alicia Dennis, "Proud, Patriotic—and Hungry," *People*, December 24, 2012. http://tinyurl. com/DROMDennis.

[23] "Auto Financing: Practices to Avoid in Your Next Auto Loan," *Center for Responsible Lending*, accessed September 30, 2013. http://tinyurl.com/DROMCRL4.

[24] Philip LeBeau, "New Car Buyers Stretching Out Payments," *CNBC.com*, September 24, 2012. http://tinyurl.com/DROMLeBeau.

[25] Finn Lane, "How to Escape an Upside Down Car Loan," *The Digerati Life*, October 22, 2012. http://tinyurl.com/DROMLane.

[26] "Your Driving Costs: 2012 Edition," *American Automobile Association*, April 2012. http://tinyurl. com/DROMAAA, 6.

Cars—new or used—don't make sense as investments because they lose their value quickly after being purchased. If you buy a new car, this dramatic net loss occurs literally as you drive away from the seller's lot.[27] Even if you lease, by the time you finish paying it off, you have most likely paid more for your car than its original cost—you are "upside down" on your loan.[28] Often, just after your last car payment, it's time again to decide to look for a reliable car. Bottom line: if you need to finance a car—a necessity for many—through debt, it can easily lead to a net loss in your wealth. But it doesn't have to be that way.

Framing alternatives:
Transportation infrastructure as commons

One of the root causes of the scourge of car debt is the absence of affordable and reliable public transit. This lack of reliable transportation options tends to fall upon poor households and households of color the hardest. The troubles that come with insufficient access to safe and clean transportation for work or schooling in struggling communities are further compounded by advanced age, disability, illness, and whether one has dependents to transport. Although many see the purchase of an automobile as a ticket to prosperity and happiness, creating more car owners is not a solution to our collective transportation woes. Rather, the solution is to create infrastructure and practices around transportation that make transportation a collective good, rather than a private asset that must be financed by debt. Doing so will not only hopefully reduce the effects of car debt but also of climate change,[29] staggering public health costs,[30] the destruction of our precious wild areas for fossil fuel extraction and burning, resource wars in the Middle East,[31] and our rapid military expansion all over the world to feed our dependence on oil.[32] And of course, car accidents are responsible for well over thirty thousand deaths a year in the United States.[33]

---

[27] Joshua Kennon, "The Opportunity Cost of the Car You Drive Is One of the Biggest Financial Decisions You'll Ever Make," *JoshuaKennon.com*, April 20, 2012. http://tinyurl.com/DROMKennon.

[28] Lane, "How to Escape."

[29] Nadine Unger et al., "Attribution of Climate Forcing to Economic Sectors," *Proceedings of the National Academy of Sciences of the United States of America* 107, no. 8, 2010. http://tinyurl.com/DROMUnger, 3384.

[30] "The Hidden Health Costs of Transportation," *American Public Health Association*, February 2010. http://tinyurl.com/DROMAPHA.

[31] Rex Weyler, "Oil Wars," *Greenpeace International*, October 19, 2012. http://tinyurl.com/DROMWeyler.

[32] Chris Mansur, "Oil, Guns, and Military Bases: The U.S. in Africa," *Geopolitical Monitor*, November 19, 2012. http://tinyurl.com/DROMMansur.

[33] National Highway Traffic Safety Administration, "Traffic Safety Facts: 2010 Data," *U.S. Department of Transportation*, June 2012. http://tinyurl.com/DROMNHTSA, 1.

One thing we can do is to demand at the local, state, regional, and national levels transportation infrastructure and policies that are not centered on private automobiles, such as walking, biking, moped and scooter use, and transit such as trains (from local light rail to high-speed regional and transcontinental services), buses, and trolleys. One such example at the local level is families organizing non-car transportation arrangements for their children to get to school through the nationally funded program Safe Routes to Schools (saferoutesinfo.org).

While agitating for policy changes that bring multiple and safe transport options to our communities, we also must find ways *now* to envision—then to act upon—our needs to deliver ourselves from car debt. One example is the Build a Better Block project (betterblock.org), a model that interested members of your community can follow to create walkable, safe blocks in your neighborhood. There are countless creative ways to bring attention to problems with our current transportation culture, including interventions in public spaces (see my.parkingday.org and visiblecity.ca).

RESOURCES
Websites
Credit cards
- Card Hub (cardhub.com)
- Carreon and Associates (carreonandassociates.com)
- Credit Karma (creditkarma.com)
- Credit Slips (creditslips.org)

Cars and alternatives
- Build a Better Block project (betterblock.org)
- Park(ing) Day (my.parkingday.org)
- Safe Routes to Schools (saferoutesinfo.org)
- Visible City (visiblecity.ca)

Articles and books
Credit cards
- Kimberly Amadeo, "Consumer Debt Statistics: Consumer Debt's Role in the U.S. Economy," *About.com*, July 19, 2012. http://tinyurl.com/DROMAmadeo.
- "Landmines in the Credit Card Landscape: Hazards for Latino Families," *National Council of La Raza*, February 20, 2009, http://tinyurl.com/DROMNCLR2.
- Robert D. Manning, *Credit Card Nation: The Consequences of America's Addiction to Credit* (New York: Basic Books, 2001).

REFERENCES

American Automobile Association. "Your Driving Costs: 2012 Edition." April 2012. http://tinyurl.com/DROMAAA.

American Public Health Association. "The Hidden Health Costs of Transportation." February 2010. http://tinyurl.com/DROMAPHA.

Carrns, Ann. "Medical Costs Contribute to Credit Card Debt." *New York Times*, May 22, 2012. http://tinyurl.com/DROMCarrns.

Chen, Tim. "Bad News: Credit Card Debt Is Down." *Forbes*, May 30, 2012. http://tinyurl.com/DROMChen2.

Center for Responsible Lending. "Auto Financing: Practices to Avoid in Your Next Auto Loan." Accessed September 30, 2013. http://tinyurl.com/DROMCRL4.

Consumer Federation of America and North American Consumer Protection Investigators. "2011 Consumer Complaint Survey Report." July 31, 2012. http://tinyurl.com/DROMCFA.

Credit Karma. "Credit Card Debt Decreases 15 Percent Nationally." March 10, 2011. http://tinyurl.com/DROMKarma.

Credit Karma. "How a Credit Card Limit Is Determined." September 23, 2008. http://tinyurl.com/DROMCK.

Dennis, Alicia. "Proud, Patriotic—and Hungry." *People*, December 24, 2012. http://tinyurl.com/DROMDennis.

Federal Reserve Bank of New York. "Quarterly Report on Household Debt and Credit." August 2013. http://tinyurl.com/DROMFedNY2.

Horwitz, Jeff. "Bank of America Sold Card Debts to Collectors Despite Faulty Records." *American Banker*, March 29, 2012. http://tinyurl.com/DROMHorwitz.

Kennon, Joshua. "The Opportunity Cost of the Car You Drive Is One of the Biggest Financial Decisions You'll Ever Make." *JoshuaKennon.com*, April 20, 2012. http://tinyurl.com/DROMKennon.

Lane, Finn. "How to Escape an Upside Down Car Loan." *The Digerati Life*, October 22, 2012. http://tinyurl.com/DROMLane.

LeBeau, Philip. "New Car Buyers Stretching Out Payments." *CNBC.com*, September 24, 2012. http://tinyurl.com/DROMLeBeau.

Levitin, Adam J. "Enhanced Consumer Financial Protection after the Financial Crisis." Testimony before the Senate Committee on Banking, Housing, and Urban Affairs, Washington, DC, July 19, 2011. http://tinyurl.com/DROMLevitin.

Levitin, Adam J. "Modernizing Consumer Protection in the Financial Regulatory System: Strengthening Credit Card Protections." Testimony before the Senate Committee on Banking, Housing, and Urban Affairs, Washington, DC, February 12, 2009. http://tinyurl.com/DROMLevitin2.

Manning, Robert D. "Five Myths about America's Credit Card Debt." *Washington Post*, January 31, 2010. http://tinyurl.com/DROMManning.

Mansur, Chris. "Oil, Guns, and Military Bases: The U.S. in Africa." *Geopolitical Monitor*, November 19, 2012. http://tinyurl.com/DROMMansur.

Martin, Ray. "Should You Ditch Your Credit Cards?" *CBSNews.com*, June 22, 2012.

http://tinyurl.com/DROMMartin3.

McFadden, Leslie. "8 Major Benefits of New Credit Card Law." *Bankrate*, August 20, 2009. http://tinyurl.com/DROMMcFadden.

National Highway Traffic Safety Administration. "Traffic Safety Facts: 2010 Data." *U.S. Department of Transportation*, June 2012. http://tinyurl.com/DROMNHTSA.

Peter G. Peterson Foundation. "Despite Recent Declines, U.S. Household Debt Is Still Very High Relative to Disposable Income." February 1, 2013. http://tinyurl.com/DROMPGPF.

Prater, Connie. "What the Credit Card Reform Law Means to You." *Creditcards.com*, June 13, 2012. http://tinyurl.com/DROMPrater.

RT. "700k Windfall: Russian Man Outwits Bank with Handwritten Credit Contract." August 8, 2013. http://tinyurl.com/DROMRT.

Silver-Greenberg, Jessica. "Problems Riddle Moves to Collect Credit Card Debt." *New York Times*, August 12, 2012. http://tinyurl.com/DROMSilver5.

Stark, Lisa. "Your Debt May Raise Your Credit Card Rates." *ABCNews.com*, June 2, 2009. http://tinyurl.com/DROMStark.

Unger, Nadine, Tami C. Bond, James S. Wang, Dorothy M. Koch, Surabi Menon, Drew T. Shindell, and Susanne Bauer. "Attribution of Climate Forcing to Economic Sectors." *Proceedings of the National Academy of Sciences of the United States of America* 107, no. 8 (2010): 3382–3387. http://tinyurl.com/DROMUnger.

U.S. Congress. "H.R. 627—111th Congress: Credit Card Accountability Responsibility and Disclosure Act of 2009." *111th Congress*, 2009. http://tinyurl.com/DROMCARD.

U.S. Government Accountability Office. *Credit Cards: Increased Complexity in Rates and Fees Heightens Need for More Effective Disclosures to Consumers*. Washington, DC: GPO, 2006. http://tinyurl.com/DROMGAO.

Weyler, Rex. "Oil Wars." *Greenpeace International*, October 19, 2012. http://tinyurl.com/DROMWeyler.

THREE
MEDICAL DEBT

AMERICA'S SICK CREATION

WHAT IS MEDICAL DEBT?

If you're having trouble paying medical bills, you are certainly not alone. About 62% of all personal bankruptcies in the United States are linked to medical bills, and three-quarters of those bankrupted had health insurance when they got sick.[1] That's about one medical bankruptcy every ninety seconds. This is not surprising when we consider that seventy-two million people in the United States have trouble paying medical bills.[2]

Individuals accrue medical debt when they are charged, but don't or can't yet pay for, out-of-pocket health-care-related expenses charged by the hospital, clinic, or doctor (provider). As soon as you pull out the plastic and put it on your credit card—something strongly advised against when trying to manage medical bills—it becomes personal or consumer debt.

There are many ways you can incur medical debt. According to the *American Journal of Medicine*, "among medical debtors, hospital bills were the largest medical expense for 48%, drug costs for 19%, doctors' bills for 15%, and insurance premiums for 4%."[3] A grim reality in the United States is that when it comes to health care, you are often faced with taking on debt or losing your life. Every year, forty-five thousand people die preventable deaths because of lack of health insurance.[4]

---

[1] David U. Himmelstein, et al., "Medical Bankruptcy in the United States, 2007: Results of a National Study," *American Journal of Medicine* 122, no. 8, 2009. http://tinyurl.com/DROMHimmelstein, 3.

[2] Sara R. Collins et al., "Losing Ground: How the Loss of Adequate Health Insurance Is Burdening Working Families," *Commonwealth Fund*, August 2008. http://tinyurl.com/DROMCollins, 1–3.

[3] Himmelstein, "Medical Bankruptcy in the United States," 4.

[4] Andrew P. Wilper, et al., "Health Insurance and Mortality in U.S. Adults," *American Journal of Public Health* 99, no. 12, 2009. http://tinyurl.com/DROMWilper, 2292.

Dr. David Himmelstein, MD, founder of Physicians for a National Health Program, has stated, "private health insurance is akin to an umbrella that melts in the rain. It simply isn't there for you when you most need it."[5]

WE'RE ALL AT RISK

Almost everyone is affected by medical debt. The for-profit healthcare industry is designed to benefit a few at the expense of the rest. Debtors and non-debtors alike are forced to pay out-of-pocket for everything from basic care to life-saving operations. As patients, most of us understand instinctually that someone is making out like a bandit when we get sick. This becomes clear the minute you walk into a doctor's office or a hospital where you open your wallet to make an upfront payment, sometimes called a copay, before even seeing a doctor. The costs can start piling up from there, even if you have insurance.

If you have a serious illness or accident, it's unlikely that your insurance will cover all—or even most of—the care you need. What insurance doesn't pay, you're responsible for. Predictably, medical debt discriminates along familiar lines. Low-income people, who are disproportionately people of color, are the most likely to incur medical debt. Astonishingly, more than half of working-age Blacks (52%) report problems paying medical bills, in contrast with 34% of Latino/as and 28% of Whites.[6]

"We are a typical middle class family. We have 3 sons. My husband has worked blue collar his entire adult life which means he has paid taxes and Social Security. I am now in school to become an RN to help better our lives. Our debt comes from medical bills. We have insurance so the doctors and hospitals get some sort of payment immediately. They then hound us for the rest for what seems like forever. I try to make some kind of payment, but when it comes down to it: food on the table, mortgage, and electricity win out."[7]

"Sickness can destroy you in America. When my partner got sick, we began living on credit cards. I think people

---

[5] Mark Almberg, "Illness, Medical Bills Linked to Nearly Two-Thirds of Bankruptcies," *EurekAlert!*, June 4, 2009. http://tinyurl.com/DROMAlmberg.

[6] Michelle M. Doty, Jennifer N. Edwards, and Alyssa L. Holmgren, "Seeing Red: Americans Driven into Debt by Medical Bills," *Commonwealth Fund*, August 2005. http://tinyurl.com/DROMDoty, 2.

[7] "We Are a Typical Middle Class Family," *Why Strike Debt*, December 16, 2012. http://tinyurl.com/DROMWSD02.

have a lot of assumptions about how people get into credit card debt. For us, it was how we survived during the most difficult time in our lives. The fact is that insurance doesn't cover everything, and you can't work if you're sick. Even people with health care are affected by medical costs. We'll be paying off our credit card debt into retirement. People who have insurance and a little money in the bank think nothing bad is going to happen to them. But what happened to us can happen to them too. It can happen to anyone."[8]

PAY MORE, GET LESS

People in other wealthy countries have no concept of medical debt. That's because they have a system of universal health care that spreads risk across the population. U.S. health care does exactly the opposite; the financial burden is placed on the most vulnerable individuals, while the cost of care increases and coverage becomes skimpier. Health insurance is supposed to guarantee that you get the care you need without going bankrupt, but in the United States, it may very well do neither.

The World Health Organization places the United States healthcare system first in spending (per capita) and thirty-seventh in quality of care.[9] Spending was estimated at over $8,500 per person (or 17.9% of the GDP) last year.[10] At the same time, the United States ranked last among high-income countries on amenable mortality—that is, deaths that could have been prevented with access to effective health care.[11] The reason is that private, for-profit insurance companies dominate the U.S. healthcare system. One out of every three healthcare dollars is spent on advertising, underwriting costs and lavish payouts to executives and shareholders, but not care.[12] To give you an indication of the profit-seeking mentality at the root of this problem, the "loss" in the common insurance industry term "medical loss ratio" refers to the money that is spent on care instead of profits. In the eyes of insurers, providing care becomes an unfortunate cost of doing business.

---

[8] Personal interview with Strike Debt.

[9] *The World Health Report 2000: Health Systems: Improving Performance* (Geneva: World Health Organization, 2000). http://tinyurl.com/DROMWHO, 155.

[10] *National Health Expenditure Accounts: Methodology Paper, 2010: Definitions, Sources, and Methods* (Baltimore: Centers for Medicare and Medicaid Services, 2010). http://tinyurl.com/DROMCMS, 5.

[11] Ellen Nolte and Martin McKee, "Variations in Amenable Mortality: Trends in 16 High-Income Nations," *Health Policy* 103, no. 1, 2011. http://tinyurl.com/DROMNolte, 47.

[12] Mark Smith, et al., *Best Care at Lower Cost: The Path to Continuously Learning Health Care in America* (Washington, DC: The National Academies Press, 2012). http://tinyurl.com/DROMSmith4.

The Affordable Care Act:
Written by and for the Health Insurance Companies

Unfortunately, Obama's signature health care policy, the Affordable Care Act, is inadequate when it comes to eliminating medical debt. The Affordable Care Act (ACA) is a huge expansion in the role of private health insurance and for-profit care. It will rapidly transfer public money to private hands leaving patients in the dust. The law was largely written by Liz Fowler, vice president of policy at the nation's largest and most profitable health insurance company, WellPoint.

The ACA will deliver over twenty million new customers and $447 billion in taxpayer subsidies directly to the private health insurance companies, but leave at least twenty-three million uninsured, and millions more underinsured with inadequate health insurance coverage.

The cornerstone of the ACA is the individual mandate. This regressive policy requires that if you are not eligible for a public program—Medicare, Medicaid, Veteran Benefits (VA)—you will then be forced to buy private health insurance, or remain uninsured and pay a fine. Lower-income people will have to pay a much higher percentage of their income than the affluent for their coverage, and older people under the age of sixty-five will have to pay more than younger people.

As noted above, having insurance is no guarantee that you won't go bankrupt should you have a serious illness or accident. In Massachusetts, which implemented the individual mandate model in 2006, two-thirds of all bankruptcies are linked to medical debt. Most people had insurance at the time of illness.[13]

HOW TO BETTER UNDERSTAND MEDICAL BILLS[14]
Hospital bills

> **"A few months ago, I was in the hospital for a week. I'm still getting bills. There are so many bills, and they are from different departments in the same hospital! How can I tell them apart?"**

When you receive a medical bill:

- Keep every bill.

---

[13] David U. Himmelstein, Deborah Thorne, and Steffie Woolhandler, "Medical Bankruptcy in Massachusetts: Has Health Reform Made a Difference?" *American Journal of Medicine* 124, no. 3, 2011. http://tinyurl.com/DROMHimmelstein4, 224.

[14] The content in this section is primarily modified from *How to Prevent and Fix Medical Debt: A Handbook for Community Advocates Assisting New Yorkers with Medical Debt* (New York: Legal Aid Society, 2010). http://tinyurl.com/DROMLAS.

- Separate doctors' bills from the hospital's bills. Not every service provided during your hospital stay will be included in the hospital's bill.
- The origin of the bill is a significant factor in determining whether you're entitled to a discount.
- Different account numbers on the bills may help indicate the different providers.
- Ask the hospital's billing office for an itemized bill. This bill will separately list all hospital charges. You have a right to know what you're being charged for.
- If you have trouble understanding which services you're being charged for and by whom, call the telephone number listed on the bill to help clarify.
- If you're insured, review your insurance policy to better understand the expenses for which you are responsible versus those covered by the plan.
- In addition to making sure you receive coverage that you're eligible for, avoid putting medical bills on your credit card.[15] Doing so converts your medical expenses to consumer debt, which puts you in an even worse place. Having credit card debt instead of medical debt likely means greater fees and penalties, and greater difficulty securing a job or mortgage.

You can challenge your hospital bills for many reasons:

- If you believe the bill was not calculated correctly.
- If you believe you're being charged twice for a single service.
- If you believe your insurance—either public or private—should have covered some or all of the charges for which you are being billed.

Private insurance bills

If you get insurance through your employer, or buy it on the individual market, be careful about referrals! Sometimes patients admitted to an in-network hospital by their in-network provider incur huge bills as a result of out-of-network referrals during their hospital stay. This is because commercial insurance plans do not require their in-network doctors to refer patients to other in-network doctors.

If you have a plan with limited out-of-network coverage, or with none at all, tell your doctor not to refer you to out-of-network doctors. Ask each specialist who treats you in the hospital whether they accept your health plan. Anesthesia bills can be very costly; request an in-network anesthesiologist who accepts your plan and ask to have this request written in your chart.

---

[15] Stephanie Barton, "How to Avoid Medical Debt," *Investopedia*, May 4, 2011. http://tinyurl.com/DROMBarton.

Doctors' bills

- Call your doctor right away if you think your bill is wrong.
- Find out what the bill is for. You may be responsible for copays or deductibles, depending on your plan.
- Make sure that the doctor has *all* of your insurance information. If you have coverage from multiple sources—private insurance, Medicare, or Medicaid—make sure that the doctor knows about all insurance plans and has sent claims to all. Some insurance sources require payment to be made in a certain order, so if the doctor fails to submit a claim to all sources, your claim may be denied. For example, Medicaid pays last. As a result, Medicaid will deny payment if the claim was not first submitted to your other insurers such as Medicare or commercial plans for payment.
- If you receive care from an out-of-network doctor, you may have to pay up front and submit the claim yourself. Clarify this with your doctor. For help submitting a claim, call the insurer.
- Most insurance plans have time limits for submitting claims. Make sure not to miss these deadlines.

Persuading doctors to reduce their bills

- Tell your doctors if you're having a hard time paying a bill. You can ask for a discount and offer to send recent financial information such as proof of income, recent bank statements, and proof of major expenses.
- If you received financial aid for your hospital bill, ask the private doctor if they would be willing to reduce the bill on that basis.
- Ask your doctor for an installment plan instead of sending the bill to a collection agency. If the doctor agrees to an installment plan, ask for it in writing. However, if you can no longer afford the payment plan the account may be sent to a collection agency.

Challenging medical bills in collections

The best way to challenge a medical bill in collections is to request that the collector provide you with a fee breakdown—which is almost impossible to provide without violating the patient-information privacy rights set out in HIPAA (Health Insurance Portability and Accountability Act of 1996). If the collector does provide you with prohibited details of the care you received, you now have legal grounds to dispute the debt. (*See Appendix C for a sample letter for this purpose.*)

WHAT DO YOU DO IF YOU NEED CARE NOW?
Going to the emergency room

If you have to go to the hospital, you cannot be turned away from the emergency room. All you can do is get the care you need and figure out how to pay for it later. If you receive a bill that you cannot afford, go as soon as you can to the hospital's financial aid or billing center. Some hospitals can lower your payments based on your level of income. Be persistent.

Stories of lying about identity to avoid emergency room bills have been reported to us confidentially. You could consider changing your identifying information so they cannot track you down to bill you, but use *extreme* caution to avoid getting caught.

Free care

See "Health and Care" in Chapter Eleven for resources on how to find free/low-cost care.

How to choose a hospital

There are different types of hospitals with different types of programs in all fifty states. Many states offer "urgent care" or "free clinics," which provide very basic services, but you may still need insurance to access even these services. Private and public hospitals also have different programs. Public hospitals receive more state and federal funding and should be able to help you find ways to lower your medical bills. If you know this information in advance, you can request which hospital to be taken to if you end up in an ambulance. The National Association of Free and Charitable Clinics (nafcclinics. org) allows you to find free clinics near you.

Denied treatment?

Protest to get the care you need. We've heard reports from people who received favorable responses from health insurance companies after complaining on Twitter and Facebook. If you are denied health care, you can organize public demonstrations to demand that you're given the care you need. Once controversy is created, corporations may reverse their decision to withhold care. In 2007, seventeen-year-old Nataline Sarkisyan was approved for a liver transplant that had a 65% chance of saving her life. At first, Cigna denied coverage for this expensive operation, resulting in valuable time lost. The community and family rallied together at the hospital and protested Cigna until the transplant was approved. It was too late for Nataline. She passed away shortly after the Cigna reversed their decision. The tragic loss of Nataline highlights the cruelty of the system but also the power we have when we organize collectively to challenge corporations.[16] The important thing to remember is that corporations want to avoid bad press and you should not be shy about making a lot of noise in public and online if you are denied care or receive a bill that you can't pay.

END MEDICAL DEBT BY FIGHTING FOR UNIVERSAL HEALTH CARE

The only real solution is to change the system from its current for-profit model to a nonprofit model that is publicly controlled, which has proved sustainable elsewhere in the world. Of the thirty-three wealthiest countries, the United States is the only one without universal health care. Half of the other thirty-two nations have single-payer health care—that is, the state provides insurance and pays for all expenses except copays and coinsurance.[17] This could be achieved in the United States by extending Medicare to all.

Some states are experimenting with single-payer systems. Vermont is working on implementing a publicly funded universal health-care system. This could prove to be a model for the nation in reversing the trend toward greed and profit that dominates our health care.

Join the fight for single-payer universal health care and help build the movement to end medical debt!

- Activists and advocates can contact Healthcare-NOW! at healthcare-now.org.
- Health professionals can contact Physicians for a National Health Program at pnhp.org.
- If you're in a union, contact National Nurses United at nationalnursesunited.org.
- Organize with Occupy Wall Street. Contact Healthcare for the 99% or Doctors for the 99% at owshealthcare.wordpress.com.

The above are all important ways to achieve the goal of ending for-profit health care and medical debt. But even single payer is not the ultimate solution. State-financed care is a stop on the road to what we really need. It would give us, above all, a chance to take a step back from the relentless bills and the anxiety that come from not knowing if we'll be able to afford to care for ourselves and our loved ones. It would give us a chance to ask if there are really only two choices: private or public, corporate or federal. It would give us, at long last, the freedom to ask larger questions about the meaning of health and how we can work together to re-embed care in our communities.

---

[16] Pauline W. Chen, "When Insurers Put Profits Between Doctor and Patient," *New York Times*, January 6, 2011. http://tinyurl.com/DROMChen.

[17] Praveen Ghanta, "List of Countries with Universal Healthcare," *True Cost*, August 9, 2009. http://tinyurl.com/DROMGhanta.

We have a difficult road ahead. But there is no doubt that the private insurance industry is wholly inadequate to the task. Our lives are in jeopardy because medical care in the United States is a profit-making enterprise that enriches the few at the expense of the rest of us. Reform won't do in the long run. Politicians do not have the will to take the necessary steps. As Dr. Steffie Woolhandler, of PNHP, makes clear:

> It's not your fault if you're in debt and it's particularly not your fault if you're in debt because of a medical problem. This is unfair. No other developed nation forces people to go into debt because they get sick.[18]

The situation we face is not our fault, but it's our job to take a stand together. The only real solution is a bottom-up, grassroots movement that puts people before profits.

RESOURCES

Websites

- Doctors for the 99% (doctorsforthe99.org)
- Healthcare-NOW! (healthcare-now.org)
- Healthcare for the 99% (owshealthcare.wordpress.com)
- National Association of Free and Charitable Clinics (nafcclinics.org)
- National Nurses United (nationalnursesunited.org)
- Physicians for a National Health Program (pnhp.org)
- Vermont Workers' Center (workerscenter.org/healthcare)

Articles

- Brian Grow and Robert Berner with Jessica Silver-Greenberg, "Fresh Pain for the Uninsured." *Bloomberg Businessweek*, December 2, 2007, http://tinyurl.com/DROMGrow.
- Galen Moore, "Mixed Response for Companies That Buy Hospital Debt." *Boston Business Journal*, November 30, 2009, http://tinyurl.com/DROMMoore.
- Jessica Silver-Greenberg, "Medical Debt Collector to Settle Suit for $2.5 Million." *New York Times*, July 30, 2012, http://tinyurl.com/DROMSilver2.

REFERENCES

Almberg, Mark. "Illness, Medical Bills Linked to Nearly Two-Thirds of Bankruptcies." *EurekAlert!*, June 4, 2009. http://tinyurl.com/DROMAlmberg.

Barton, Stephanie. "How to Avoid Medical Debt." *Investopedia*, May 4, 2011. http://tinyurl.com/DROMBarton.

Centers for Medicare and Medicaid Services. *National Health Expenditure Accounts:*

---

[18] Steffie Woolhandler and Margaret Flowers, "Time to End Medical Debt, Medical Bankruptcy," *Physicians for a National Health Program*, March 16, 2013. http://tinyurl.com/DROMWoolhandler.

Methodology Paper, 2010: Definitions, Sources, and Methods. Baltimore: Centers for Medicare and Medicaid Services, 2010. http://tinyurl.com/DROMCMS.

Chen, Pauline W. "When Insurers Put Profits Between Doctor and Patient." *New York Times,* January 6, 2011. http://tinyurl.com/DROMChen.

Collins, Sara R., Jennifer L. Kriss, Michelle M. Doty, and Shiela D. Rustgi. "Losing Ground: How the Loss of Adequate Health Insurance Is Burdening Working Families." *Commonwealth Fund,* August 2008. http://tinyurl.com/DROMCollins.

Doty, Michelle M., Jennifer N. Edwards, and Alyssa L. Holmgren. "Seeing Red: Americans Driven into Debt by Medical Bills." *Commonwealth Fund,* August 2005. http://tinyurl.com/DROMDoty.

Ghanta, Praveen. "List of Countries with Universal Healthcare." *True Cost,* August 9, 2009. http://tinyurl.com/DROMGhanta.

Himmelstein, David U., Deborah Thorne, Elizabeth Warren, and Steffie Wool- handler. "Medical Bankruptcy in the United States, 2007: Results of a National Study." *American Journal of Medicine* 122, no. 8 (2009): 741–746. http://tinyurl. com/DROMHimmelstein.

Himmelstein, David U., Deborah Thorne, and Steffie Woolhandler. "Medi- cal Bankruptcy in Massachusetts: Has Health Reform Made a Difference?" *American Journal of Medicine* 124, no. 3 (2011): 224–228. http://tinyurl.com/ DROMHimmelstein4.

Legal Aid Society. *How to Prevent and Fix Medical Debt: A Handbook for Community Advo- cates Assisting New Yorkers with Medical Debt.* New York: Legal Aid Society, 2010. http://tinyurl.com/DROMLAS.

Nolte, Ellen, and Martin McKee. "Variations in Amenable Mortality: Trends in 16 High-Income Nations." *Health Policy* 103, no. 1 (2011): 47–52. http://tinyurl. com/DROMNolte.

Smith, Mark, Robert Saunders, Leigh Stuckhardt, and J. Michael McGinnis. *Best Care at Lower Cost: The Path to Continuously Learning Health Care in America.* Washington, DC: The National Academies Press, 2012. http://tinyurl.com/DROMSmith4.

"We Are a Typical Middle Class Family." *Why Strike Debt,* December 16, 2012. http://tinyurl.com/DROMWSD02.

Wilper, Andrew P., Steffie Woolhandler, Karen E. Lasser, Danny McCormick, David H. Bor, and David U. Himmelstein. "Health Insurance and Mortality in U.S. Adults." *American Journal of Public Health* 99, no. 12 (2009): 2289–2295. http://tinyurl.com/DROMWilper.

Woolhandler, Steffie, and Margaret Flowers. "Time to End Medical Debt, Medi- cal Bankruptcy." *Physicians for a National Health Program,* March 16, 2013. http:// tinyurl.com/DROMWoolhandler.

World Health Organization. *The World Health Report 2000: Health Systems: Improv- ing Performance.* Geneva: World Health Organization, 2000. http://tinyurl.com/ DROMWHO.

FOUR

STUDENT DEBT

FORECLOSING ON THE FUTURE

In the not-too-distant past, high school graduates in the United States seeking a meaningful college education could likely have received one from an in-state or city university at little to no cost. And it would have been reasonable for them to assume that the degree they earned would significantly increase life opportunities. Though that era was relatively short-lived here, many other countries have made access to free or low-cost higher education an enduring priority, insisting on it being a basic right and a good that benefits society as a whole.

These days though, back here in the United States, higher education has sadly become one of the biggest debt traps of all—turning many of us into lifelong debtors. Even in the midst of the Great Recession, college costs have continued to skyrocket. Funding for our once robust and affordable state university system—a symbol of a collective commitment to broadening opportunity and shared prosperity—has been whittled away over time, with the burden of education costs shifted onto students and their families in the form of severe tuition and fee hikes. The story at private schools is equally grim, with already out-of-reach average tuition nearly tripling in cost since 1980.[1] And though it's become common knowledge that a college degree is a prerequisite for obtaining a decent job, we are increasingly being told that we need an expensive master's degree too, with few grants available to those scrambling to enroll.

In the absence of free or low-cost options, students are taking on life-altering debts to cover astronomically high tuition, fees, and living costs, coerced through fears of an uncertain financial future and false promises of stable careers. Lenders, loan servicers, Wall Street investors, school administrators, predatory for-profit colleges, and even the government are raking in profits at students' expense. As a result, in 2012, the total amount of student debt owed in the United States

---

[1] Sandy Baum and Jennifer Ma, "Trends in College Pricing, 2012," *College Board*, 2012. http://tinyurl.com/DROMBaum2, 14.

surpassed the $1 trillion mark—higher than credit card debt or any other kind of consumer debt with the exception of mortgage debt.

Two-thirds of U.S. students are leaving college with an average of $27,000 in debt, with the burden falling disproportionately on Native Americans, Blacks, and Latino/as. And with too few jobs on the horizon, it's no surprise that defaults are now occurring at the astonishing rate of one million per year. Almost one in six borrowers is in default, with many others on the brink. Of the class of 2005, 41% are already delinquent or in default.[2] Experienced on a personal level, this combination of chronic underemployment and massive indebtedness has given many the sense that their futures have been foreclosed upon, leading them into depression and some even to suicide.

Given the enormous sticker price for college, students often don't even qualify for enough crushing loans to pay the full cost. As such, parents are increasingly taking out or cosigning loans on their children's behalf and facing the same repayment problems as their offspring. It's no wonder then that seniors are now the fastest growing population of student debtors. At the same time, unemployment for people under twenty-five is almost twice the national average, meaning that young people are being forced to depend on their parents for longer periods of time after graduating. As a result, many parents are putting off retirement in order to continue to provide for their families while struggling to cover the added expense of student loan repayment.

The Federal Reserve Bank of New York reported that, in 2012, seniors owed around $36 billion in student loans, or about 4.2% of total U.S. student loan debt. For the sizeable number of those who are in default, their Social Security benefits are subject to seizure. This growing predicament piles layers of guilt on top of the fear and depression experienced by younger debtors when they realize that not only are they unable to assist their parents through their retirement years, they are also a direct cause of their parents' added economic burden.

Given this grim picture, some analysts argue that there is a student debt "bubble" about to burst. Unlike the housing bubble, a mass devaluation of outstanding student loans might not be a bad thing for debtors. After all, the creditors can't repossess your degree or your brain—or at least not yet! But there are harsh penalties for defaulting, making any bet that your debt-burden will someday be reduced a risky one at best.

---

[2] Alisa F. Cunningham and Gregory S. Kienzl, "Delinquency: The Untold Story of Student Loan Borrowing," *Institute for Higher Education Policy*, March 2011. http://tinyurl.com/DROM-Cunningham, 5.

This chapter explains how student debt was created, who profits from it and how you can survive as a debtor. Above all, you should know that you are not alone if you are facing default. There are ways of resisting, especially by acting together.

HOW IT GOT SO BAD

Going to public college used to be pretty affordable, especially for those on the GI Bill, or those who went to public colleges like the City University of New York or the University of California. Alarmed at the rise of student activism and guided by simplistic free-market ideals of "personal responsibility," conservatives took advantage of the fiscal crises in the mid-1970s to clamp down on free tuition and open admissions policies. A temporary season of austerity measures turned into an enduring epoch as cuts by state lawmakers continued throughout the 1980s and down to this day. Neoliberal policy-making, aimed at privatizing public responsibilities, has increasingly transferred the financial burden from the state onto individual students. As an example of the results, in 1976, a student at the University of California paid only $647 in annual fees; by 2012, the bill had reached $13,181.[3] When these are the most "affordable" options, students from low-income homes regularly end up owing a third, half or even more of their family's annual earnings for a year of tuition.[4]

Overall, the costs of a college education have risen by more than 1,100% in the last three decades. With grants and scholarships lagging far behind tuition increases, student loans are the only option for most who want a college education. And in a knowledge economy, where a college degree is considered a passport to a decent livelihood, there's really not much of a choice but to take on loans, committing large chunks of your future earnings to pay back the debts you got stuck with simply trying to prepare yourself for employability in the first place. This kind of contract is the essence of indenture.

To make matters considerably worse, in 1998 Congress took the extraordinary step of making federally backed loans all but impossible to discharge through bankruptcy. After prolonged pressure from Wall Street creditors, private loans became ineligible in 2005, making student debt virtually the only kind of loan that doesn't allow debtors the option of bankruptcy. As if that's not enough, the government also granted enormous collection powers to lenders. Lending agencies can now garnish wages and seize tax returns without even

---

[3] "Budget and Capital Resources," *University of California*, December 2011. http://tinyurl.com/DROMUC, 2.

[4] Renee Schoof, "Public Colleges Are Often No Bargain for the Poor," *McClatchy*, May 29, 2013. http://tinyurl.com/DROMSchoof.

requesting a legal hearing first. Even Social Security and disability wages are subject to garnishment.[5]

The knowledge that students have little choice but to debt-finance their education however high the cost has created some perverse incentives for college and university administrators, warping educational priorities and putting further upward pressure on tuition. In order to make up for financial shortfalls, colleges have increasingly turned to issuing bonds, using tuition as collateral to secure loans from Wall Street. For example, in 2012, the University of California sold almost $1 billion in bonds set to mature over the next hundred years. That means UC students' tuition dollars will be used to line the pockets of big investors over the next ten decades. To ensure a steady flow of riches, financiers hold colleges hostage by threatening to ruin their credit ratings if tuition does not go up.[6]

Given the cultural shift from a model based more on public funding to one where education is seen largely as a commodity for individual purchase, many administrators have quite logically responded by marketing their schools as luxury goods. They fill their ever-expanding campuses with extravagant dorms and "state-of-the-art" facilities designed by big-name architects, and invest in non-academic "lifestyle" services and perks. They certainly don't skimp when it comes to their own salaries. Average pay for administrators increased dramatically in recent years, with many private and public school presidents, provosts, and chancellors falling well within the top 1% of income "earners." And when endowments fail to cover the tab, faculty who do the apparently less important work of actual teaching can always be replaced by adjunct professors who get paid far less and receive little in the way of benefits.

A luxury education might be fun for some, but upon graduation, debtors must quickly learn to walk a treacherously thin tightrope. Student debt can endure for decades, employment prospects are more and more precarious, and wages have been stagnating. But a credit report damaged by even one or two delayed payments can generate additional obstacles to finding work, as employers are now increasingly demanding that potential hires agree to undergo intrusive and unreliable credit checks as part of the application process. Thus debtors tend to put their preferred career paths on hold (and therefore risk abandoning them) until they have finally paid off their loans through employment options that are much less desirable. Ironically, one of

---

[5] Tyler Kingkade, "Private Student Loan Bankruptcy Rule Traps Graduates with Debt amid Calls for Reform," *Huffington Post*, August 16, 2012. http://tinyurl.com/DROMKingkade.

[6] Chris Mondics, "Rutgers' Credit Rating Falls," *Philadelphia Inquirer*, June 2, 2013. http://tinyurl.com/DROMMondics.

the quickest paths to paying off debts for some students is to find work in the finance industry, issuing loans or speculating on derivatives.

Wall Street lenders have made a killing on the debt-financing of education, especially in the decades before federal loans were re-organized in 2010. Sallie Mae, sometimes referred to as the "queen" of student lending, was created in 1972 as a government-sponsored enterprise. But in 1977, as the business of student loans became more and more lucrative, the push to privatize began. By 2004, Sallie Mae was fully publicly traded. The company now has a hand in both federal and private student loans and draws its profits from every aspect of the student loan industry: originating, servicing, and collecting.[7]

Between 1972 and 2010, under the FFELP (Federal Family Education Loan Program) lending system, federal loans originated by financial institutions (including Wall Street banks) were fully guaranteed and subsidized by the government. In 2010, the Obama administration cut out the middlemen, which means that any federal loan taken out now is originated directly by the federal government. However, these government loans are still serviced by a group of select private institutions, including Sallie Mae. That means that the government pays these servicers millions of dollars a year in order to handle the billing and other maintenance of the loan.

Even more recently, under the thin guise of easing the burden of debtors, Congress and the president did away with the unjustifiably high 6.8% interest rate on federal loans, replacing it with a *temporarily* lower adjustable rate tied to returns on ten-year treasury notes—creating a time bomb that will explode in students' faces once treasury rates go up again, as they surely will. But don't worry! The rate for loans is capped at 8.25%. Now don't you feel better?

As if all that weren't bad enough, Federal loans rarely meet the full cost of education, leaving many students with no choice but to take out private loans to make up the difference. Even though only 20% of all current student loans are private, at the current rate of issuance their overall volume will have surpassed that of federal loans in ten to fifteen years. These private student loans are subject to different terms and have much higher interest rates.

Many college financial aid officials are in cahoots with private lenders. A 2006 investigation by the New York State Attorney General's Office concluded that the business relationship between lenders and university officials amounted to an "unholy alliance." Lenders paid kickbacks to universities based on the loan volume that financial aid offices steered their way; they also gave all-expenses-paid Car-

---

[7] U.S. Department of the Treasury, *Lessons Learned from the Privatization of Sallie Mae* (Washington, DC: GPO 2006). http://tinyurl.com/DROMTreasury.

ibbean vacations to financial aid administrators and even put them on their payroll. In addition, lenders set up funds and credit lines for schools in exchange for being placed on preferred-lender lists.[8] In spite of these scandals, and despite the NYS Attorney General's recommendation that bankruptcy protections be restored to student lenders, nothing really changed. The student loan racket was just too profitable to be reined in by a few grandstanding regulators.

The lack of protection for consumers has made default quite profitable for lenders. On average, 120% of the principal on a defaulted loan is ultimately collected. In fact, in 2003 Sallie Mae disclosed that its record-breaking profits were due in significant part to collections on defaulted loans. Two years earlier, the company was caught declaring loans to be in default before even trying to collect the debt. This rapacious conduct is the norm in some quarters of the student lending industry.[9]

As in the subprime mortgage market, many private loans are securitized—packaged and sold to the highest bidder as Student Loan Asset-Backed Securities (SLABs). These SLABs account for almost a quarter—$234.2 billion—of the aggregate $1 trillion debt. Since SLABS are often bundled with other kinds of loans and traded on secondary debt markets, investors are not only speculating on the risk status of student loans but also profiting from resale of the loans though collateralized derivatives.[10]

The uneven social impact

The human toll of all this is becoming increasingly visible. For a host of disturbing accounts of student debt, it's well worth reading Alan Collinge's book *Student Loan Scam: The Most Oppressive Debt in U.S. History—and How We Can Fight Back*. And it's certainly not hard to find student debt horror stories all over the internet, especially in the wake of Occupy Wall Street, which inspired many debtors to "come out" online. A military veteran reports that he has paid $18,000 on a $2,500 loan and Sallie Mae claims the man still owes $5,000; the bankrupt husband of a social worker, bedridden after a botched surgery, tells of a $13,000 college loan balance from the 1980s that ballooned to $70,000; a grandmother subsisting on Social Security has her payments garnished to pay off a $20,000 loan balance from a ten-year-old $3,500 student loan she took out before undergoing

---

[8] Doug Lederman, "'Deceptive Practices' in Loan Industry," *Inside Higher Ed*, March 16, 2007. http://tinyurl.com/DROMLederman.

[9] Alan Collinge, *Student Loan Scam: The Most Oppressive Debt in U.S. History—and How We Can Fight Back* (Boston: Beacon Press, 2009).

[10] Malcolm Harris, "Bad Education," *n + 1*, April 25, 2011. http://tinyurl.com/DROMHarris.

brain surgery. Loans like these grow rapidly due to a combination of compounding interest and forbearance programs. In fact, only 37% of student loans are in repayment at any given time. The other 63% are accruing interest, adding fees and becoming more and more likely to add to the six million student loans already in default.[11]

While the single largest debt loads are racked up by students from middle-income families seeking a private university degree, the overall impact of debt is magnified among low-income families. Of those who have earned bachelor's degrees, about 81% of Black students and 67% of Latino/a students leave school with debt, compared to 64% of White students.[12] As a result of the home equity losses suffered since 2008, Black people lost a huge portion of the economic gains they had made in the post–civil rights era. Reflecting those losses, Black students have had to borrow more for education than Whites, and the racial inequity of the employment landscape means they are twice as likely to be unemployed on graduation. Also, students of color are much more likely to enroll in for-profit schools, which have high non-completion rates and account for nearly half of student loan defaults. These proprietary colleges (we should call them "Wall Street's colleges") engage in reverse redlining, explicitly targeting students of color for recruitment, loading them with debt in return for a dubious educational experience. It's no surprise then that the default rate for Black people is four times that of Whites.[13]

One of the worst examples of debt-financing in the for-profit sector stems from the introduction of the new GI Bill, introduced by Congress in 2008 to help veterans of the wars in Iraq and Afghanistan enter the higher education system. Almost a third of the GI Bill monies have ended up in the coffers of for-profit colleges.[14] These colleges have exploited a legislative loophole that allows them to count GI Bill money as part of the 10% of revenue they are required to raise from non-public sources in order to be eligible to receive federal student loans, which account for the other 90% of their revenue. The result has been an aggressive recruitment of ex-soldiers—some were so brain-damaged from their injuries they had no idea what they were signing[15]—with an inevitable impact upon veterans of color, who

[11] Anne Johnson, Tobin Van Ostern, and Abraham White, "The Student Debt Crisis," *Center for American Progress*, October 25, 2012. http://tinyurl.com/DROMJohnson, 10.

[12] Sandy Baum and Patricia Steele, "Who Borrows Most? Bachelor's Degree Recipients with High Levels of Student Debt," *College Board*, 2010. http://tinyurl.com/DROMBaum, 6.

[13] Julianne Hing, "Study: Only 37 Percent of Students Can Repay Loans on Time," *Colorlines*, March 17, 2011. http://tinyurl.com/DROMHing.

[14] Adam Weinstein, "How Pricey For-Profit Colleges Target Vets' GI Bill Money," *Mother Jones*, September 2011. http://tinyurl.com/DROMWeinstein.

[15] Tamar Lewin, "Obama Signs Order to Limit Aggressive College Recruiting of Veterans," *New*

serve disproportionately in the armed services. Excluded from most of the homeownership and education benefits of the original GI Bill, Native Americans, Blacks, and Latino/as are being preyed upon and debt-burdened by the latest bill.

AVOIDING DEFAULT

Your loan becomes *delinquent* the first day after you miss a payment. The delinquency will continue until all back payments are made. Loan servicers report delinquencies of at least 90 days (and in some cases as early as 30 days) to the three major credit bureaus. As we've seen in Chapter One, a negative credit report may make it difficult for you to meet your basic needs.

Student loans are generally considered to be in *default* when you fail to make a payment for 270 days for a federal loan or 120 days for a private loan, though the industry standard for private loans is 180 days. Though the consequences of delinquency can be hard to bear, the penalties for default are of a much greater magnitude. If you can't avoid delinquency but want to avoid default, try to make at least one payment every 120 (private) or 270 (federal) days.

If you haven't defaulted but are alarmed about not being able to pay your student loans, do not panic. If you just graduated, many loans provide an automatic six-month deferment period. And if you have federal loans, you can extend this period on an annual basis either through deferment or forbearance programs. Deferment on certain loans halts interest during periods of unemployment, economic hardship or temporary disability, or while the debtor is in school. Forbearance—granted by a loan servicer to borrowers who don't qualify for deferment—does not stop interest from accruing, but it does allow for some breathing room. But keep in mind that forbearance will cause the amount that you owe to increase. Typically, the interest is compounding annually, which means that at the end of a year it will be added to the principal and you will have to pay interest on that too. This can cause loans to mushroom, so check to see if you qualify for deferment before entering into forbearance.

It may also be helpful to consolidate all of your loans into one. To learn about requirements for loan consolidation, you can visit studentaid.ed.gov/repay-loans/consolidation. The application for Direct Loan Consolidation is available at loanconsolidation.ed.gov.

There are a couple of newer programs that may also be helpful to those with federal loans: the Income-Based Repayment Plan (IBR) and Public Service Loan Forgiveness (PSLF). Income-based repayment allows you to adjust payment to meet your income by capping payment at 15% of income based on family size. A single individual with no children making under $20,000 would pay 2.4% of income toward student debt whereas a family of four making under $100,000 would pay 9.9% of their income toward student debt. After twenty-five years, any remaining student loan debt would be forgiven. But there is a major caveat with this type of loan forgiveness. The government taxes loans that are written off, including IBR student loans, as *earned income*. This means that, after twenty-five years, the remainder of that loan is written off, but you will now owe what may be a significant amount in taxes, whether or not you can pay it.

Public Service Loan Forgiveness (PSLF) provides forgiveness of federal student loan debt after ten years of continuous employment by any nonprofit, tax-exempt 501(c)(3) organization, a federal, state, local, or tribal government agency including the military, public schools, and colleges, or while serving in AmeriCorps or the Peace Corps. You may also be eligible if your employer is not a religious, union, or partisan political organization and provides public services.[16] Loans forgiven through PSLF, unlike IBR, do not get taxed as earned income.

Being in default

If you are about to default on a student loan, remember that you are not alone. There are approximately six million other Americans that have already done so. While default can be a political act (especially when done collectively), any such decision should be made with full knowledge of the following possible consequences:

- Your loans may be turned over to a collection agency.
- You will be liable for the costs associated with collecting your loan, including court costs and attorney fees.
- You can be sued for the entire amount of your loan.
- Your wages may be garnished. Federal law limits the amount that may be garnished to 15% of the borrower's take-home or "disposable" pay—the amount of income left after deducting any amounts required by law to be deducted. The wage garnishment amount is also subject to a ceiling that requires the borrower to be left with weekly earnings after the garnishment of at least thirty times the federal minimum wage.
- Your federal and state income tax refunds may be intercepted.
- The federal government may withhold part of your Social Security benefit payments. The U.S. Supreme Court upheld the government's ability to col-

---

[16] "What Are These Programs? IBR and PSLF," *IBRInfo*. http://tinyurl.com/DROMIBR.

lect defaulted student loans in this manner without a statute of limitations in *Lockhart v. United States* (December 2005).

- Your defaulted loans will appear on your credit history for up to seven years after the default claim is paid, making it difficult for you to obtain an auto loan, mortgage, or even credit cards. A bad credit record can also harm your ability to find a job. The U.S. Department of Education reports defaulted loans to TransUnion, Equifax, and Experian (*see Chapter One*).
- You won't receive any more federal financial aid until you repay the loan in full or make arrangements to repay the overdue amount and make at least six consecutive, on-time monthly payments. You will also be ineligible for assistance under most federal benefit programs.
- You will be ineligible for deferments.
- Subsidized interest benefits will be denied.
- You may not be able to renew a professional license you hold.[17]
- If you had a cosigner on your loan (this is usually a parent or grandparent), they will be held legally responsible to pay back your loans. The penalties that apply to the person who took out the loan are also applied to cosigners who default.

These measures are harsh, but you can continue to fight as an individual. Unfortunately, bankruptcy is not an option for student debtors, except occasionally in cases of permanent disability or "undue hardship." Although it is difficult to get credit reporting agencies (CRAs) to remove defaulted student debt from reports, it is not impossible. You can use the strategies and resources outlined in Chapter Nine to demand that CRAs and debt collectors prove that the amount of your debt is fully verifiable. This will require a concerted letter-writing campaign, but you may be pleasantly surprised by the results. Often, recordkeeping is poor and the collector will not have access to any records that actually tie you to a debt, especially if your student loan was securitized into a SLAB. Although a court judgment is not required before your paycheck, bank account, or tax return is garnished, you are entitled to an administrative hearing if you request one.

If you want to get out of default, you can often rehabilitate your loan by entering into an agreement to make twelve consecutive on-time payments to the original lender or the guarantee agency in exchange for the removal of the prior delinquency history from your credit report. Be sure to get this agreement in writing and to be clear about how this will be entered on your credit report, since amnesty agreements like this are technically noncompliant with the Fair Credit Reporting Act.

---

[17] Mark Kantrowitz, "Defaulting on Student Loans," *FinAid*, 2012. http://tinyurl.com/DROMKantrowitz2.

Know your loans

As the number of middle-people standing between you and your original loan continues to increase, it can be hard to ascertain exactly who guarantees, originates, services, and collects your loans. To find out this information about your federal loans, visit the national student loan database at *nslds.ed.gov/nslds_SA*. The Neighborhood Economic Development Advocacy Project also offers a step-by-step guide at *nedap.org/resources/studentloanguide.php*. Things are a little more complicated when dealing with private loans. FinAid is a great first resource for understanding the variety of institutions involved: *finaid. org/loans/studentloans.phtml*. It's important to fully understand your own situation, since the laws apply unevenly to different kinds of financial institutions. For example, state guarantee agencies are exempt from the Fair Debt Collections Practices Act, but any private collection agency hunting you down must comply with this law. Be aware of their illegal practices and know your rights. This FinAid page about defaulting on student loans is a good place to start: *finaid.org/loans/ default.phtml*. Abusive debt collection behavior is also highlighted in Chapter Nine of this book. We recommend you read it carefully.

COLLECTIVE ACTION TOWARD CHANGE

If we fight this system alone, the best we can hope for is to keep our heads above water. Collective action is the only true solution. There's plenty of inspiration to be found outside of the United States, where powerful movements fighting to reclaim education as a basic right seem to be popping up everywhere. A wave of governments under the sway of neoliberal ideologues have been doing their best to undermine once well-funded university systems in hopes of imposing U.S.-style debt-financing on their students. But the immense suffering that system has created is no secret, and students across the globe have begun to draw lines in the sand, staging massive protests, strikes, and direct actions to resist.

In 2010, when the British government announced plans to cut funding and drastically raise tuition fees, students across the United Kingdom erupted in a series of massive protests. In London alone, fifty thousand students took to the streets on one day, many of them surrounding and occupying the Conservative Party headquarters. Starting in 2011 in Chile, where access to higher education has long been pitifully unequal, hundreds of thousands of students have filled the streets over and over again, paralyzing the education system and weakening government resolve to implement debt-financing and privatization. And in 2012, over three hundred thousand students went on strike in Québec, mobilizing mass popular support and virtually shutting down the university system in their struggle to resist tuition hikes. And the struggles continue.

But here in the United States, we're at a crossroads. After two generations of students and families suffering under punishing burdens of student debt, it seems to have finally become clear to most everyone that we are in a crisis. An insurgency of student debtors is on the rise. But the question remains as to where that momentum will lead us. Politicians—heavily beholden to the finance industry—campaign on promises of reform, offering market-based "solutions" that would further commit students to a debt-driven system where education is first and foremost a profit engine for financiers, asset speculators, and real estate developers.

And some well-meaning groups organizing around student debt seem to be similarly stuck on solutions that continue to treat education as a commodity primarily benefitting individuals who purchase it. A recent grassroots effort put Oregon on the path to a system where the state pays tuition costs at public colleges upfront and students pay it back as a percentage of income for years into the future. However much such a program may increase access to education in the short term, requiring individual students to fund universities out of their paychecks normalizes the idea that education is a personal responsibility and in the long run could accelerate the replacement of publicly funded schools with lifetimes of indebtedness.

Other moderate, pro-capitalist reform proposals—including efforts to restore bankruptcy protection or to receive partial debt "forgiveness"—have produced little in the way of legislative change. While we are of course deeply in favor of building a movement around the debt crisis, any such movement must target the root of the problem, rather than pruning the foliage. In a truly democratic society, nobody would have to go into debt to earn a diploma. The pathway to this outcome does not lie in futile pleas for economic reform, but through a political movement driven by self-empowerment and direct action on the part of debtors.

If you're a current student, learning about your school's governance and demanding fiscal transparency and accountability from your administrators and board is a powerful way to fight back. In April of 2013 in New York City, the president and board of directors of one of the very few tuition-free colleges left in the United States—the Cooper Union—announced that they would forsake the school's 150-year-old mandate to provide free education and begin charging students up to $20,000 a year. Students who had been organizing in coordination with school faculty and staff in anticipation of such a move quickly occupied the office of the president, demanding not just a return to free tuition, but that decisions regarding the management of Cooper be opened up to the entire school community going forward. After sixty-five days, the board agreed to convene a working group composed of students, faculty, alumni, and administrators with the intention of restoring founder Peter Cooper's vision of education that's "as free as air and water." Students also won a seat on the board and a permanent space to continue organizing.

At the time of writing, the fall semester is about to begin and students from colleges and universities across New York City have organized disorientation campaigns, staging events and direct actions and distributing thoroughly researched guides to arm incoming students with the tools they'll need to continue the struggle against the neoliberalization of our schools. Campaigns like these are spreading to schools across the country. Find out what's going on in your area. Or start your own disorientation campaign!

The demand for a student debt jubilee was heard often during Occupy Wall Street, and the Occupy Student Debt Campaign (OSDC) that grew out of it did much important work toward articulating a vision of the what true change would look like. Others across the country—including Strike Debt, a direct descendent of OSDC—have begun to converge around a set of interlocking principles that should be central to any movement seeking to restore education as a social good and a right. To begin with, the federal government must make all two- and four-year public colleges tuition-free for all students. Any future student loans from the government should be offered at zero interest. All current student debt should be cancelled as part of a one-time corrective jubilee. And all university institutions must open their books; transparency and accountability to students and their families, as well as to their employees, is essential.

If you think providing free public education sounds like pie in the sky, it would probably cost way less than you think. By our estimates, the total amount of new money necessary is less than $13 billion a year.[18] That's a lot of money, to be sure, but within the scope of the federal budget it is less than 0.1% of yearly spending—merely a rounding error. For the sake of comparison, U.S. taxpayers are currently subsidizing too-big-to-fail banks at the rate of $83 billion every year.[19] To offer another comparison, tax subsidies to just twelve corporations totaled about $20 billion per year from 2008 to 2010.[20]

---

[18] Strike Debt, "How Far to Free?" August 15, 2013. http://tinyurl.com/DROMSD2.

[19] "Why Should Taxpayers Give Big Banks $83 Billion a Year?" *Bloomberg*, February 20, 2013. http://tinyurl.com/DROMBloomberg.

[20] Rick Ungar, "How Our Largest Corporations Made $170 Billion During Great Recession and Paid No Taxes," *Forbes*, June 1, 2011. http://tinyurl.com/DROMUngar.

Until the conventional debate is opened up to include alternatives that genuinely reflect the needs of students and debtors, Strike Debt believes that the only sensible thing to do is to resist student debt. It is immoral, illegitimate, odious, and a drain on both those who must bear it and the society in which they live. We believe that a true grassroots movement of student debtors—the movement we want to be a part of—will organize a collective refusal to pay. When student debtors realize their collective power in this way, then we may suddenly find ourselves in a world where politicians are forced to treat education as a public good. Momentum is growing. Join the resistance!

RESOURCES
Websites
- All Education Matters (alleducationmatters.blogspot.com)
- Dēmos (Dēmos.org/category/tags/student-loans)
- FinAid (finaid.org)
- Free Cooper Union (cusos.org)
- Income-Based Repayment Info (ibrinfo.org)
- Occupy Student Debt Campaign (occupystudentdebtcampaign.org)
- Project on Student Debt (projectonstudentdebt.org)
- Student Bloc NYC (studentblocnyc.org)
- Student Debt Crisis (studentdebtcrisis.org)
- Student Loan Justice (studentloanjustice.org)

Articles and Books
- Jerry Ashton, "America's Financial Institutions and Student Lenders—Attention: OWS 'Occupy Student Debt' Committee Has Something to Say," *Huffington Post*, November 21, 2011, http://tinyurl.com/DROMAshton.
- Pamela Brown, "Education Debt in the Ownership Society," *AlterNet*, June 27, 2012, http://tinyurl.com/DROMBrown.
- George Caffentzis, "Plato's *Republic* and Student Loan Debt Refusal," *Interactivist*, December 31, 2011, http://tinyurl.com/DROMCaffentzis3.
- Alan Collinge, *The Student Loan Scam: The Most Oppressive Debt in U.S. History—and How We Can Fight Back* (Boston: Beacon, 2009).
- Herman De Jesus, "Resolving Defaulted Federal Student Loans: A Step-by-Step Guide for Advocates," *Neighborhood Economic Development Advocacy Project*, July 2012, http://tinyurl.com/DROMDeJesus.
- Tamara Draut, *Strapped: Why America's 20- and 30-Somethings Can't Get Ahead* (New York: Anchor, 2007).
- Brian Holmes, "Silence=Debt," *Occupy Student Debt Campaign*, 2012, http://tinyurl.com/DROMHolmes3.
- Sarah Jaffe, "Meet 5 Big Lenders Profiting from the $1 Trillion Student Debt Bub-

ble," *AlterNet*, November 28, 2011, http://tinyurl.com/DROMJaffe.

• Anya Kamenetz, *Generation Debt* (New York: Riverhead Books, 2006.

"Private [Student] Loans: Facts and Trends," *The Project on Student Debt*, July 2011, http://tinyurl.com/DROMPSD.

• Mike Konczal, "Stop Calling Student Loans 'Financial Aid'," *Salon*, September 15, 2012 http://tinyurl.com/DROMKonczal.

• Andrew Ross, "Mortgaging the Future: Student Debt in the Age of Austerity," *New Labor Forum* 22, no. 1 (2013), http://tinyurl.com/DROMRoss1.

• Andrew Ross, "NYU Professor: Are Student Loans Immoral?" *The Daily Beast*, September 27, 2012, http://tinyurl.com/DROMRoss2.

• "Some Options," *EDU Debtors Union*, 2011, http://tinyurl.com/DROMEDU.

• Jeffrey Williams, "Student Debt and the Spirit of Indenture," *Dissent*, Fall 2008, http://tinyurl.com/DROMWilliams3.

REFERENCES

Baum, Sandy, and Jennifer Ma. "Trends in College Pricing, 2012." *College Board*, 2012. http://tinyurl.com/DROMBaum2.

Baum, Sandy, and Patricia Steele. "Who Borrows Most? Bachelor's Degree Recipients with High Levels of Student Debt." *College Board*, 2010. http://tinyurl.com/DROMBaum.

Bloomberg View Editorial Board. "Why Should Taxpayers Give Big Banks $83 Billion a Year?" *Bloomberg*, February 20, 2013. http://tinyurl.com/DROMBloomberg.

Collinge, Alan. *Student Loan Scam: The Most Oppressive Debt in U.S. History—and How We Can Fight Back*. Boston: Beacon Press, 2009.

Cunningham, Alisa F., and Gregory S. Kienzl. "Delinquency: The Untold Story of Student Loan Borrowing." *Institute for Higher Education Policy*, March 2011. http://tinyurl.com/DROMCunningham.

Harris, Malcolm. "Bad Education." *n + 1*, April 25, 2011. http://tinyurl.com/DROMHarris.

Hing, Julianne. "Study: Only 37 Percent of Students Can Repay Loans on Time." *Colorlines*, March 17, 2011. http://tinyurl.com/DROMHing.

IBRInfo. "What Are These Programs? IBR and PSLF." Accessed March 26, 2013. http://tinyurl.com/DROMIBR.

Johnson, Anne, Tobin Van Ostern, and Abraham White. "The Student Debt Crisis." *Center for American Progress*, October 25, 2012. http://tinyurl.com/DROMJohnson.

Kantrowitz, Mark. "Defaulting on Student Loans." *FinAid*, 2012. http://tinyurl.com/DROMKantrowitz2.

Kingkade, Tyler. "Private Student Loan Bankruptcy Rule Traps Graduates with Debt Amid Calls for Reform." *Huffington Post*, August 16, 2012. http://tinyurl.com/DROMKingkade.

Lederman, Doug. "'Deceptive Practices' in Loan Industry." *Inside Higher Ed*, March 16, 2007. http://tinyurl.com/DROMLederman.

Lewin, Tamar. "Obama Signs Order to Limit Aggressive College Recruiting of

Veterans." *New York Times*, April 27, 2012. http://tinyurl.com/DROMLewin.

Mondics, Chris. "Rutgers' Credit Rating Falls." *Philadelphia Inquirer*, June 2, 2013. http://tinyurl.com/DROMMondics.

Schoof, Renee. "Public Colleges Are Often No Bargain for the Poor." *McClatchy*, May 29, 2013. http://tinyurl.com/DROMSchoof.

Strike Debt. "How Far to Free?" August 15, 2013. http://tinyurl.com/DROMSD2.

Ungar, Rick. "How Our Largest Corporations Made $170 Billion During Great Recession and Paid No Taxes." *Forbes*, June 1, 2011. http://tinyurl.com/DROMUngar.

University of California. "Budget and Capital Resources," December 2011. http://tinyurl.com/DROMUC.

U.S. Department of the Treasury. *Lessons Learned from the Privatization of Sallie Mae.* Washington, DC: GPO, 2006. http://tinyurl.com/DROMTreasury.

Weinstein, Adam. "How Pricey For-Profit Colleges Target Vets' GI Bill Money." *Mother Jones*, September 2011. http://tinyurl.com/DROMWeinstein.

FIVE

HOUSING DEBT

HOW THE AMERICAN DREAM BECAME A BAIT-AND-SWITCH NIGHTMARE

Many people struggle to find sympathy for those who have borrowed beyond their means to pay for something we all must provide for ourselves: housing. From the perspective of those who rent, have resisted taking on debt, or were fortunate enough to purchase and hold onto a home, it can be difficult to empathize with what appear to be bad choices. But when morality and debt intersect, appearances are often extremely misleading. The reality is that a great deal of what lenders, investors, and government agencies told the public about the housing market was never true. Decades of false promises, irresponsible practices, and collusion between banks and the government created a system in which lenders exploited the hopes and ambitions of people in the name of endless profit.

This chapter will explain how this culture emerged, how it exploits the most vulnerable among us, and what we can do about it.

THE STORY OF THE AMERICAN HOMEOWNER

You can't escape the need for shelter. But in the United States, this basic need is entangled with a pervasive and often fervent belief in the American Dream—that anyone who works hard enough can achieve some version of comfortable "middle-class" status. For many of us, this status is most visibly realized by the purchase of a home. Given the prevalence of this sentiment, it can be easy to imagine that the relationship between homeownership and the "American Dream" existed from the beginning of time. But this central feature of our collective American identity was largely created in the 1930s when, in response to the Great Depression, the U.S. government began a partnership with private lenders. In order to stabilize the existing housing market, they began to construct an idea of homeownership as a fail-proof investment.

A new deal and the mortgage industry we know today

Before the 1930s, the majority of people in the United States did not own their homes.[1] At that time, the ability to buy a house required that you either pay cash, or that you knew someone who would lend you the money. The lender could be a bank, but only if you had a good relationship with your local banker. Even then, they would only allow you to borrow 50% of the property value, and you had to pay it off in three to five years.

In spite of the relatively low ownership rates and direct limits on mortgage access, a housing debt crisis similar to the one in 2008 emerged. Property values plummeted and mortgages destabilized. Lenders refused to renegotiate and borrowers defaulted. At the lowest point of the crisis, one in every ten homes was in foreclosure. In the 1930s, most banks had no government support or backing to sustain them during a crisis. Without money coming in, they were unable to lend, which resulted in freezing credit and dragged the country further into depression. In order to stabilize the market and open the flow of credit, the federal government intervened and established the entities we have today: the Home Owners' Loan Corporation (1933), the Federal Housing Administration (1934), and the Federal National Mortgage Association (1938), later known as Fannie Mae. These institutions were created to underwrite the lending system, create new terms for borrowers, and unlock credit for the banks to continue lending. Essentially, these institutions functioned so that the private banks could continue making loans and profit from the higher interest, while shifting the increased risk to the public. This partnership between the banks and government agencies continues today with almost all mortgages on the books of FHA, Fannie Mae, Freddie Mac, and Ginnie Mae—in other words, they are guaranteed by taxpayers. In 2011, the federal government guaranteed more than 95% of all mortgages, making the U.S. taxpaying population the largest backer of home loans and shielding the profiting industry from resistance or further collapse.

The ownership society as a tool
Against the workers

Expanding homeownership was a response by government and banks to the debt crisis of the Depression—a means of maintaining credit in the system and restoring faith in a failing economic order. It is quite apparent how the banks benefit in this relationship, outsourcing the risk of their own practices to the public via government intervention. But what is in it for the government? Why go through

---

[1] "Historical Census of Housing Tables: Homeownership," *U.S. Census Bureau*, October 31, 2011. http://tinyurl.com/DROMUSCB.

such lengths to expand an ownership society that was clearly struggling to maintain itself?

During the Depression, union membership hit record highs, growing from 7% in 1930 to 25% in 1940. This development threatened the power of industry and employers, and seemingly had the potential for continued growth. Public dollars were used to create a state-supported market where workers would individually receive support for financing their homes. This had the effect of propping up the competitive housing market without further strengthening the working class as a whole through direct aid. Far from an American dream, the resulting system of homeownership has created a mass of disenfranchised debtors, beholden to the debt system. As homeownership (and mortgage debt) climbed, union membership began its steady decline in 1945.[2]

Against veterans

During the same period of union growth, World War I veterans mobilized against the government. In payment for their war service (1914–1918), veterans were offered bonus certificates in 1924 that would not be redeemable until 1945, a full twenty-seven years after the war. As the country moved into the Great Depression, veterans were particularly vulnerable to joblessness. With few alternatives, forty-three thousand marchers took to the U.S. Capitol building in 1932 demanding that they receive their payment. Even after their camp was cleared, belongings burned and several veterans killed by police, resistance continued. To pacify the movement, jobs were offered to the veterans within the New Deal. Most of them took the jobs before Congress agreed in 1936 to pay the bonuses early.

This powerful movement and others like it illustrated the threat that organized veterans could pose at the end of each subsequent war. In response, complex packages were developed to compensate service members for their duty. Just as before, however, the choice was made to provide forms of compensation that encouraged entrance into competitive markets and the taking on of individual debt to avoid further empowering group strength. Mortgage options became a feature of individual veteran compensation. Under the GI Bill, the Veterans Administration Mortgage Insurance Program was developed as part of the deferred compensation package for service in the armed forces. Returning veterans of World War II were given very low mortgage rates to encourage entrance to the market as individuals, and the practice of the thirty-year loan with 95% financing became a new norm. With the "success" of these new long-term loans, banks began

---

[2] Michael Wachter, "The Rise and Decline of Unions," *CATO Institute*, 2007. http://tinyurl.com/DROMWachter, 27.

to offer them to the general population with government backing. The market expanded enormously, and by the 1970s homeownership had grown to 63% of the American public—and mortgage debt became an all-too-essential part of the American experience.

Communities of color and links to the poor

The link between racial disparities and homeownership began early on. In the early 1900s, the homeownership rate for Blacks was at 21% while that of Whites was 49.4%—a nearly 30-point ownership gap that continues to this day.[3] Regulations such as the Jim Crow laws purposefully kept Blacks from expanding into the housing market and joining the ranks of those accumulating wealth for their subsequent generations. The New Deal packages referenced earlier were largely reserved for working-class Whites, placing them at odds with workers of color and further fracturing the working class along racial lines. During the Civil Rights era, peaking in 1960, a new kind of consolidated power emerged. As communities of color organized and created powerful movements, the familiar tool of individual debt was used again.

The competitive market was again expanded to contain a surge in power. In the 1970s, growing anger about the longstanding practice of redlining (lending discrimination that divides communities along racial lines) moved the government to pass the Community Reinvestment Act (CRA), which required banks to conduct business in the entire geographic area in which they operated—the idea being that one area could not be more favored (or ignored) than another in terms of approved mortgages and lending. Rating systems were established to penalize those banks showing evidence of bias. Still, as late as 1992, a study by the Federal Reserve Bank of Boston claimed that people of color were denied mortgages at higher rates than Whites.[4] In response, the industry, backed by the federal government, was called on to broaden access to mortgage credit and homeownership by reducing its qualifying standards.

The stated goal of President Clinton's "National Homeownership Strategy: Partners in the American Dream" program was to extend homeownership to eight million low-income buyers. But the government's perverse response to racial economic inequality increased availability of credit and the *expansion* of crushing mortgage debt, rather than the provision of direct assistance through extended public or subsidized

---

[3] Barry Bluestone, "Is Homeownership Now Just a Dream? Implications of Potential New Federal Housing Policies on the Distribution of Homeownership," *Northeastern University School of Public Policy and Urban Affairs*, March 2012. http://tinyurl.com/DROMBluestone, 27.

[4] Alicia H. Munnell et al., "Mortgage Lending in Boston: Interpreting HMDA Data," *Federal Reserve Bank of Boston Working Paper Series* 92, no. 7, 1992. http://tinyurl.com/DROMMunnell.

housing—further enlarging the market and incorporating a significant new segment of the population into the ownership/debtor relationship.

Through these direct government mandates and the promise of trillions of dollars in revenue, the door was open for the lending industry to develop complex new products, specifically targeted at low-income households and communities of color—all of which were intentionally confusing, overwhelming, and generally designed to fail the borrower. While the burden of public housing was lifted off of the government's shoulders, mortgage debt was coming down like a ton of bricks on unsuspecting families. "Get-rich-quick" schemes used new financial products to exploit the hopes of millions. A litany of how-to books reinforced the blind faith of the market: *How to Make Millions in Real Estate in Three Years Starting with No Cash* (2005); *Frank McKinney's Maverick Approach to Real Estate Success: How You Can Go from a $50,000 Fixer-Upper to a $100 Million Mansion* (2005); *Wise Women Invest in Real Estate: Achieve Financial Independence and Live the Lifestyle of Your Dreams* (2006); *Why the Real Estate Boom Will Not Bust—And How You Can Profit From It: How to Build Wealth in Today's Expanding Real Estate Market* (2006).

Let's say you were dubious about the promises being offered. Like anyone ready to make a major decision, you did your research. You took a trip to Fannie Mae's mortgage calculator and tried to assess the risks. You imagine your worst-case scenario—your property value goes down. What would that look like? You would have received an error— literally. The mortgage calculator was incapable of forecasting a future of zero or negative growth because they assumed that property values *always* rise. The message became, "The time to invest is *now*." Unfortunately, that is exactly what many people did, entangling themselves in unforeseen obligations, a lifetime of debt, and a bubble about to burst.

Some of the worst lending practices include adjustable rate mortgages (ARM) where after several years the initial interest rate adjusts (often substantially higher), placing a lender in a situation where the original math that made the loan affordable no longer applies, only the interest is paid and the principle debt grows endlessly. "Piggyback mortgages" made the down payment for a first mortgage possible with the taking out of a second "piggyback" mortgage. Stated income loans (a.k.a. "liar" loans) allowed borrowers to simply state their income with no verification and enter into mortgages beyond their means. Interest-only payments, negative amortization, and hybrids of all of the above empowered the banks to entangle anyone with a desire for a home, stability, and wealth in a debt scheme they previously would have never qualified for.

In order to back these high-risk loans, banks divided the debt into pools with mixtures of risk, making it impossible to separate the reliable from the dangerous and selling units of these pools in secondary markets with completely unwarranted guarantees of security. It turned out to be a huge success—for the banks.

And yet, despite lenders' consistently reckless and predatory behavior, the dominant narrative is so often warped by the "morality" of the debt system. Again and again, we are told the story of the irresponsible homeowners who borrowed beyond their means and must now live with their poor choices. But the risk of a loan is supposed to be assessed both by the borrower and the lender. After all, if you are asked to lend someone money, determining the likelihood that you'll actually get it back is part of your decision process. However, in the current financial system, the government has underwritten the majority of the banks' risks. The government has guaranteed that these lenders will always get their money back, plus interest. And even if you wanted to hold someone accountable, the actual originators of these toxic loans are often obscured by complex chains of repackaging, offloading, and reselling—leaving millions of borrowers with no direct lender to negotiate with, no access to federal aid, and all of the blame.

THE CURRENT NIGHTMARE

- Approximately 14% of all homes in the United States are vacant.[5]
- Pockets of extreme decline exist across the country. In Dayton, Ohio, for instance, the vacancy rate is 21.1% and median income has fallen 10.7% in two years.[6]
- The rate of homeownership in the United States has dropped to 1996 levels (65.3% from its 69% peak in 2004).[7]
- Over four million homes have been foreclosed on since September 2008.[8]
- Negative or near-negative equity accounted for 27% of all U.S. mortgages in 2012, affecting 10.8 million borrowers.[9]
- Approximately 25% of all Black and Latino/a mortgage-holders lost their home to foreclosure or are in threat of foreclosure, as opposed to just under 12% of White borrowers.[10]

---

[5] Robert R. Callis and Melissa Kresin, "Residential Vacancies and Homeownership in the Third Quarter 2012," U.S. Census Bureau News, October 30, 2012. http://tinyurl.com/DROMCallis, 4.

[6] Jack Riordan, "Disposing of Vacant Land and Abandoned Homes," Ohio Conference of Community Development, January 30, 2013. http://tinyurl.com/DROMRiordan.

[7] Steve Cook, "The Homeownership Rate Skips a Beat," Mortgage Professional America, January 30, 2013. http://tinyurl.com/DROMCook.

[8] "CoreLogic Reports 767,000 Completed Foreclosures in 2012," CoreLogic, February 1, 2013. http://tinyurl.com/DROMCL3.

[9] "CoreLogic Reports Number of Residential Properties in Negative Equity Decreases Again in Second Quarter of 2012," CoreLogic, September 12, 2012. http://tinyurl.com/DROMCL4.

[10] Debbie Gruenstein Bocian et al., "Lost Ground, 2011: Disparities in Mortgage Lending and Foreclosures," Center for Responsible Lending, November 2011. http://tinyurl.com/DROMBocian2, 4.

With figures as far-reaching as these, housing debt needs to be understood as a highly complex issue concerning us all both financially and ethically. The common "blame the victim" account of the sub-prime mortgage crisis ignores the fact that the industry developed complex financial instruments to expand the market through unsound and, in an overwhelming number of cases, fraudulent means, ultimately causing the system to collapse. Many of these "mortgage innovations" or "relaxed lending practices" were in fact trapdoor schemes to extract wealth from borrowers with false promises and exploited desires.

If you are currently struggling with a mortgage or foreclosure, you are not alone. Review the resources below to consider your options and where you can find aid. If you are not going through difficulties with your mortgage, support those you know who are by sharing this information and expressing your solidarity.

PREVENTING FORECLOSURE ON YOUR (AND YOUR NEIGHBOR'S) HOME

Let's say you're having trouble making your mortgage payments, or you've already gone into foreclosure but you want to stay in your home. What can you do? You have several options, ranging from individual to collective, low-risk to high-risk, legal to not-so-legal.

Individual strategies

1. *Explore federal mortgage modification programs.* You may qualify for government relief under a range of programs established in the wake of the housing market collapse, most of which are administered through the Treasury Department and the Department of Housing and Urban Development (HUD). These include the Making Home Affordable Program (MHA), the Home Affordable Modification Program (HAMP), and the Principal Reduction Alternative (PRA) (for significantly underwater mortgages). If your mortgage is insured by the Federal Housing Administration (FHA), there are additional loss mitigation programs available. Each program has complicated eligibility requirements, which you can learn about on the HUD website by going to http://tinyurl.com/DROMHUD. Then, ask your lenders and loan servicers about your options. If you run into difficulties, the HUD website has a list of organizations that can contact lenders and servicers on your behalf.

2. *Negotiate with your lenders, ideally with some help.* In seeking professional help, generally watch out for frauds and scams (for example, if you're asked for a lump-sum fee up front). Anyone looking to take your

mortgage payment and give it to the bank is untrustworthy; you'll want to pay the bank directly. Anyone who promises you a silver bullet is probably lying.

- *Consult a housing counselor.* Organizations like the Neighborhood Association Corporation of America (NACA) can point you to an accredited housing counselor experienced in negotiating with banks. Note that some housing counselors have a vested interest in building up their businesses and may be funded by banks; some are straight-up frauds.
- *Consult a lawyer.* If you cannot afford a lawyer, seek out local legal aid organizations, bar associations, or community-based organizations (e.g., housing justice organizations) for discounted or free legal services.
- *Consult community-based organizations specializing in housing issues.* Particularly in major metropolitan areas, there are organizations that can offer general advice and support with your housing issues. Some unions also do this. These organizations may also help you partake in collective action to win larger victories (see "Collective Action" below).

A Note on MERS

Mortgage Electronic Registration Systems (MERS) is a national electronic registration and tracking system for mortgage loans. MERS was conceived in the early 1990s by lenders and other entities including Bank of America, Countrywide, Fannie Mae, and Freddie Mac. Its stated purpose was to save mortgage purchasers money.

In the past, it was your lender that was on the deed as the beneficiary until you paid the loan in full. Your deed and loan note were recorded with the local County Recorder's office. The recording of the deed and the note created a public record for the transaction. Any ownership change had to be recorded to create a clear "chain of title"—a record of ownership that protects the owner from false claims to ownership.

When the banks decided they could make money by securitizing loans privately, they needed a way to manage the paperwork that involved selling of notes and deeds repeatedly. If they actually filed with the County Recorder each time, it would cost them time and money. So they figured out a way around it by cutting corners. Instead of your lender's name on the deed, you'll find MERS named instead. The problem with this is that MERS is really not the owner of your loan. How can MERS claim titles to loans they merely track, but do not own? If your foreclosure was "robo-signed" by MERS, you may be able to fight back on this basis. Discuss this with a lawyer.

3. *Walk away.* Walking away from—that is, strategically defaulting on—your mortgage is always an option. The personal finance world went ballistic when Suze Orman advised homeowners who are more than 20% underwater to walk away. But if you're that far in the hole, cutting your losses may be your best option. Entire communities are finding themselves in a vicious cycle of foreclosures driving down property values, which in turn reduces property taxes and therefore municipal income. Municipal indebtedness grows and public services suffer, further driving down property values. This death spiral is often impossible to escape. By strategically defaulting, you remove yourself from the poisonous cycle of individual and collective indebtedness and depreciation.

You can decide to walk away immediately, or after taking some intermediate steps to explore the full range of options. These steps include:

- Ask your lender to modify the loan by reducing the principal to the actual current value of the property.
- If they say no—which is likely—then ask for a short sale. A short sale is a sale for less than the amount owed for a property, and the bank takes the loss. Most often banks will say no to this, too.
- As a last step, ask for a deed in lieu of foreclosure. This will allow you to transfer the property deed to the bank without going through formal foreclosure proceedings. The advantage for you is that it allows you to walk away immediately and with no attachment to the property. The advantage to the bank is that they may save money and lower the risk of borrower vandalism of the property.

Of course, this exit doesn't come for free. Before you walk away, be aware of the consequences of foreclosure. Aside from the loss of your home, your credit report and credit score will take a big hit. You can expect your score to drop by 85 to 160 points. The foreclosure stays on your report for seven years and will impact your credit for that period, although it is impossible to know how much the impact will dissipate over time since credit reporting agencies do not disclose their algorithms. But without a doubt, it will be difficult to get another loan for quite some time. One thing you should certainly do is dispute the foreclosure with the credit reporting agency, forcing them to validate your credit report. CRA records are often inaccurate, so dispute them until they show you your signature on the loan documents (*see Chapter One*).

> *Important: Walking away only works if you are in a state where the law prevents the bank from suing for your other assets.* Many states prevent buyers from strategically defaulting through laws that entitle the bank to sue you for your other assets, including money in your bank account, stocks, and savings. *It is essential that you consult an attorney in your area to make sure that the bank cannot sue you and place a lien on your other assets.*

You might also consider walking away from your mortgage in strategic alliance with other homeowners facing foreclosure—in other words, participating in a mortgage strike. If done correctly, a mortgage strike could drastically increase your community's leverage against the banks. It is essential that you consult an attorney in this case because unlike tenants in a rent strike, homeowners in a mortgage strike have no support in the relevant laws.

4. *Rent instead of owning.* Although rent is not considered consumer debt, owing rent is certainly a form of indebtedness. This becomes obvious if you do not pay your rent. Your landlord will eventually evict you and you will owe "back rent." The similarity between owing a bank money for shelter and owing a landlord money for shelter becomes clear when the bank threatens to take away your home. Just as a bank keeps a down payment to cover a potential default, a landlord typically requires the tenant to provide a security deposit to be deposited in an interest-bearing escrow account to guarantee rent.

A recent Pew study showed that younger people in the United States have soured on buying and are less attached to the dream of homeownership.[11] The younger generation has seen its families suffer from underwater properties and fears the downside of ownership more than it desires the upside.

Be warned, however, that renting will not necessarily save you from the overall effects of housing debt. Since the foreclosure crisis, rents have overwhelmingly increased and in 2011, rental vacancies hit a ten-year low. Millions of foreclosed families have no choice but to rent, and since it takes seven years for a foreclosure to disappear from your credit report, many families are in it for the long haul. Of course, wages have not kept pace with rent increases and rent is eating up a growing portion of peoples' incomes. This outcome is also felt very unevenly. For example over 25% of Black and Latino/a families spend more than half their income on housing compared to 15% of White families.

---

[11] "Young Adults After the Recession: Fewer Homes, Fewer Cars, Less Debt," *Pew Research Center,* February 21, 2013. http://tinyurl.com/DROMPew2, 23.

Unfortunately, no one has been immune to the fraudulent practices that led to this mess. Unsustainable housing debt impacts us all.

Collective strategies: We are forty million strong

What does all this add up to? U.S. homeowners have been victims of a bank scheme to profit by creating a bubble that could only blow up in individual homeowners' faces. Since we are all affected by the housing crisis, the potential for collective action is enormous. For systemic change that benefits us all, we need to build power through acting together.

There are an estimated forty million residents of underwater homes today, greater than the entire population of California. There's $1.15 trillion in just the underwater portion of mortgages, and $4.8 trillion in total estimated property value of underwater homes.[12] Given these numbers, it's easy to see the potential for homeowners to unite under the threat of strategic default. In 2008, the federal government passed the $700 billion Troubled Asset Relief Program (TARP) to bail out banks. TARP specifically called for the government to encourage banks to modify loans to prevent foreclosures. However, very little money has actually been used to bail out homeowners and the banks have done little to change their lending practices to help people to avoid losing their homes. In fact, the review of loans in foreclosure by banks and their consultants was botched so badly that they reached a $3.6 billion settlement with regulators, providing cash relief to homeowners who entered foreclosure in 2009 or 2010. These homeowners suffered illegal foreclosures, including foreclosures despite never having missed a mortgage payment. More than half a million homeowners were deprived of a loan modification or other loss mitigation assistance.[13] Clearly, we can't rely on the government to clean up this huge mess that speculators caused.

Eviction/auction blockades

Activists have long used their bodies to blockade evictions of foreclosed homeowners and auctions of foreclosed homes. Blockades give you more leverage to negotiate a better deal with the bank because banks hate public pressure, especially around specific homeowners. Banks are softer targets than you might expect because so many cases are rife with legal irregularities and outright fraud; it's not uncommon

---

[12] Stan Humphries, "Negative Equity Declines Slightly on the Back of Modest Home Value Gains," *Zillow*, August 22, 2012. http://tinyurl.com/DROMHumphries.

[13] Jessica Silver-Greenberg, "First Checks to Be Issued in Mortgage Settlement," *New York Times*, April 9, 2013. http://tinyurl.com/DROMSilver11.

for customers to be mislead, crucial paperwork lost, and documents robo-signed. With a little help from your friends, you can use this against the banks.

Blockades raise the cost of foreclosing for the bank, which is helpful on both individual and collective levels. In Minneapolis, for example, thanks to the work of sixty activists from the grassroots group Occupy Homes MN, it took police four attempts and thirty-nine arrests to evict one family in the spring of 2012. The whole effort cost the city $40,000 (the city had to attack the front door with a battering ram), a fact that Occupy Homes MN publicized to shame elected officials for the misuse of public resources.[14]

Eviction and auction blockades can also serve as part of larger anti-eviction and anti-foreclosure campaigns that call on the legislature to put stronger legal protections in place for homeowners and moratoriums on evictions and foreclosures. Such reforms are a source of relief for many.

What are the economics that justify eviction and auction blockades? When a home is underwater, the lender has already lost its initial investment because it will have to resell the house at today's depressed fair market value. Who benefits from that resale to the market? Often they are "vulture fund" investors who have a lot of cash to shop for deals in distressed neighborhoods, only to gentrify those neighborhoods or quickly "flip" their investments in order to make a profit. They benefit from foreclosures at the expense of family, community and—if the mortgage is insured by Fannie Mae or Freddie Mac—taxpayers (who must repay the bank the amount of the original mortgage).

What demands should blockaders make? The most immediate demand is to halt or reverse foreclosure, or at least eviction in the wake of foreclosure. Our first goal is to stop a human being or family from becoming homeless. The next is a "principal reduction"—a new loan based on the house's current value. The benefits of principal reductions would ripple out far beyond any particular homeowner: Fannie and Freddie could save taxpayers billions by adopting principal reduction because odds are better the homeowner will be able to keep making payments and avoid default (or re-default).[15]

Those in charge argue that principal reductions—achieved by selling homes back to foreclosed homeowners—would create a "moral hazard," encouraging others to default on their mortgage. The

[14] Alexandra Bradbury, "Home Is Where the Fight Is," *Labor Notes*, March 5, 2013. http://tinyurl.com/DROMBradbury.

[15] "Review of Options Available for Underwater Borrowers and Principal Forgiveness," *Federal Housing Finance Agency*, July 31, 2012. http://tinyurl.com/DROMFHFA, 11.

term "moral hazard" is used to describe a situation where a person (or a corporation or other unit) takes undue risks because they know that someone else will bear the consequences of their risky action. The important thing to recognize is that corporations do this all the time—for example, corporations pollute with impunity because they do not bear the costs of such pollution themselves. In the housing market, banks extended risky, speculative mortgage loans to home-owners, knowing that if things were to go south, homeowners would suffer the consequences, not the banks. "Moral hazard" has nothing to do with morality and everything to do with particular distributions of power and risk. The question is, what types of "moral hazard" are we willing to tolerate?

Mortgage strikes

Rent strikes are a time-honored tactic for tenants to demand action from a delinquent landlord. Despite the lengthy history of rent strikes to gain repairs and other concessions, there is little history of mortgage strikes. There are many reasons property owners are unwilling to strike—attachment to homeownership, guilt about failing to pay debts, fear of bad credit, and hope that the market will improve. But as more and more victims of the housing market understand the complicated details of the game our government played with the banks at our expense, the potential for collective action grows.

Rent strikes work (although the risk of eviction is real) because under the lease and the landlord-tenant law regime, the landlord must perform its duties (such as keeping the premises habitable) for the tenant's duty to pay rent to kick in. How are mortgage strikes different from rent strikes? Unfortunately, the law does not protect homeowner-borrowers as much as it does tenants. This is a product of our society's pro-creditor bias, as well as the lack of a powerful mortgage debtors' movement. We mustn't forget that the legal protections for tenants making rent strikes possible did not always exist—they were obtained through collective action throughout the 1960s and '70s.[16]

People in the U.S. are beginning to come together to organize mortgage strikes. A community-based organization called Empowering and Strengthening Ohio's People (ESOP) has modeled its mortgage strike on rent strikes under Ohio law, which uses a court-

---

[16] The warrant of habitability in landlord-tenant law was first established by a DC Circuit case, *Javins v. First National Realty Corp.*, 428 F.2d 1071 (DC Cir. 1970). The court determined that if the premises become uninhabitable, the tenant is freed from their obligation to pay rent. The tenant's duty to pay rent was traditionally regarded as independent of whether the landlord fulfilled their duties.

supervised process. In a rent strike, tenants pay their monthly rent to the local court clerk, who holds the payments in escrow until the tenants' complaints are resolved. A mortgage strike would follow a similar structure, although it is not specifically authorized by Ohio law (making it highly risky). Participating homeowners would send money orders covering their regular principal and interest payments to a local attorney to hold in escrow until the homeowners explicitly release the payments. The attorney's role is to provide an escrow service so that the mortgage servicers and lenders are assured of payment after the strike. By collectively withholding mortgage payments through this escrow mechanism, underwater homeowners can increase their negotiating leverage vis-à-vis their shared lenders and servicers.

City Life/Vida Urbana (CLVU), a community-based organization in Boston has been actively organizing mortgage debtors' unions, or "Bank Tenant Associations"—a product of three decades of grassroots organizing. The model is being replicated across the country (and, for better or worse, is funded by national and international foundations). Bank Tenant Associations get the message out to the community, build solidarity, provide access to lawyers, organize creative actions that apply public pressure and attract media attention, and build leadership in the bank tenants themselves. CLVU has established Bank Tenant Associations with thousands of bank tenants who have stopped evictions, passed new laws, put pressure on the bank to sell back homes at half or less of the original loan value, and radically changed both lender and court culture. To give just one example, CLVU is initiating a pilot project in two organized neighborhoods to convert occupied foreclosed buildings into permanently affordable, resident-controlled homes. These grassroots movements can only lead to a broader, national demand for principal reduction and prioritizing affordable housing going forward.

CLVU has published a Bank Tenant Association Organizing Manual that details the myriad steps and dynamics of organizing a mortgage debtor's union.[17] Among other things, the manual includes creative ways to partner with community (not-for-profit) banks, which can buy underwater properties and sell them back to homeowners at their real value (a better result than in most loan modification efforts by for-profit banks), and much more.

---

[17] Sarena Neyman, *Bank Tenant Association Organizing Manual: Building Solidarity to Put People Before Profit* (Boston: City Life/Vida Urbana, June 2012). http://tinyurl.com/DROMCLVU2.

HOME IS WHERE OUR HEART IS:
CREATING A HOUSING COMMONS

Blockades and mortgage strikes are powerful tactics to prevent foreclosures right now, but let's not lose sight of our ultimate vision: a world where housing is a human right and an asset of the commons. To that end, we can continue historic commoning practices such as taking over and rehabilitating vacant homes and maintaining community land trusts (which allow the community to own land based on principles of democracy, affordability, and sustainability). We have seen how the irresponsible forces of the market have wrecked homes and lives. We must build our own resilient homes going forward, and that is most likely to succeed if we do it together.

RESOURCES
Websites
• Chicago Anti-Eviction Campaign (chicagoantieviction.org)
• City Life/Vida Urbana (clvu.org)
• Empowering and Strengthening Ohio's People (esop-cleveland.org)
• Housing Is a Human Right (housingisahumanright.org)
• Occupy Our Homes (occupyhomes.org)
• Right to the City Alliance (righttothecity.org)
• Take Back the Land (takebacktheland.org)

Articles
• John Atlas, "The Conservative Origins of the Sub-Prime Mortgage Crisis," *American Prospect*, December 17, 2007, http://tinyurl.com/DROMAtlas.
• Barbara Ehrenreich and Dedrick Muhammad, "The Recession's Racial Divide," *New York Times*, September 12, 2009, http://tinyurl.com/DROMEhrenreich.
• Ylan Q. Mui, "For Black Americans, Financial Damage from Subprime Implosion Is Likely to Last," *Washington Post*, July 8, 2012, http://tinyurl.com/DROMMui.
• Michael Powell and Gretchen Morgenson, "MERS? It May Have Swallowed Your Loan," *New York Times*, March 5, 2011, http://tinyurl.com/DROMPowell2.
• Maura Reynolds, "Refinancing Spurred Sub-Prime Crisis," *Los Angeles Times*, July 5, 2008, http://tinyurl.com/DROMReynolds.
• "The Rotten Heart of Finance," *The Economist*, July 7, 2012, http://tinyurl.com/DROMEconomist.

REFERENCES
Bluestone, Barry. "Is Homeownership Now Just a Dream? Implications of Potential New Federal Housing Policies on the Distribution of Homeownership." *Northeastern University School of Public Policy and Urban Affairs*, March 2012. http://tinyurl.

com/DROMBluestone.

Bocian, Debbie Gruenstein, Wei Li, Carolina Reid, and Roberto G. Quercia. "Lost Ground, 2011: Disparities in Mortgage Lending and Foreclosures." *Center for Responsible Lending*, November 2011. http://tinyurl.com/DROMBocian2.

Bradbury, Alexandra. "Home Is Where the Fight Is." *Labor Notes*, March 5, 2013. http://tinyurl.com/DROMBradbury.

Callis, Robert R., and Melissa Kresin. "Residential Vacancies and Homeownership in the Third Quarter 2012." *U.S. Census Bureau News*, October 30, 2012. http://tinyurl.com/DROMCallis.

Cook, Steve. "The Homeownership Rate Skips a Beat." *Mortgage Professional America*, January 30, 2013. http://tinyurl.com/DROMCook.

CoreLogic. "CoreLogic Reports Number of Residential Properties in Negative Equity Decreases Again in Second Quarter of 2012." September 12, 2012. http://tinyurl.com/DROMCL4.

CoreLogic. "CoreLogic Reports 767,000 Completed Foreclosures in 2012." February 1, 2013. http://tinyurl.com/DROMCL3.

Federal Housing Finance Agency. "Review of Options Available for Underwater Borrowers and Principal Forgiveness." July 31, 2012. http://tinyurl.com/DROMFHFA.

Humphries, Stan. "Negative Equity Declines Slightly on the Back of Modest Home Value Gains." *Zillow*, August 22, 2012. http://tinyurl.com/DROMHumphries.

Munnell, Alicia H., Lynn E. Browne, James McEneaney, and Geoffrey M.B. Tootell. "Mortgage Lending in Boston: Interpreting HMDA Data." *Federal Reserve Bank of Boston Working Paper Series* 92, no. 7 (1992). http://tinyurl.com/DROMMunnell.

Neyman, Sarena. *Bank Tenant Association Organizing Manual: Building Solidarity to Put People Before Profit*. Boston: City Life/Vida Urbana, June 2012. http://tinyurl.com/DROMCLVU2.

Pew Research Center. "Young Adults after the Recession: Fewer Homes, Fewer Cars, Less Debt." February 21, 2013. http://tinyurl.com/DROMPew2.

Riordan, Jack. "Disposing of Vacant Land and Abandoned Homes." *Ohio Conference of Community Development*, January 30, 2013. http://tinyurl.com/DROMRiordan.

Silver-Greenberg, Jessica. "First Checks to Be Issued in Mortgage Settlement." *New York Times*, April 9, 2013. http://tinyurl.com/DROMSilver11.

U.S. Census Bureau. "Historical Census of Housing Tables: Homeownership." October 31, 2011. http://tinyurl.com/DROMUSCB.

Wachter, Michael. "The Rise and Decline of Unions." *CATO Institute, 2007*. http://tinyurl.com/DROMWachter.

SIX

TAX DEBT

THE CERTAINTY
OF DEBT AND TAXES

The story we're usually told goes like this: The tax system is paying for things that make society function, and paying them is a good thing, since we all want those things to function. Taxes redistribute money to those in need, so paying them is practically a duty. When you don't pay taxes, you're not only a disloyal citizen, but also subject to the long arm of the law in the form of IRS harassment.

This narrative only tells part of the story. Tax money finances public spending, but what the government spends tax dollars on isn't necessarily what's needed for a healthy society. The most obvious example is the expansion of the military-industrial complex; the War Resisters League estimates that 47% of the total budget, or $1.355 trillion per year, goes to current military spending and debt service payments on past military spending.[1] Tax dollars also fund the state, local, and federal police forces and prison systems that oppress so many of us. Nationwide spending on prisons was $50 billion in 2011, contributing to the serious budget crises states have faced since the global recession of 2009.[2] Very often, our tax dollars go toward paying the government to enact violence on people in the United States or in other countries.

Less dramatic examples exist as well. The tax system isn't just about taking money from point X and moving it to point Y—it's also about regulating the economy more generally by allocating government support to certain industries over others. At the local level, city governments often give tax abatements for condo development, meaning that city residents collectively subsidize this kind of housing over more sustainable or affordable options. Implicit in these policies are decisions about what's best for the public. It sounds good on paper, but in reality, private interests often strongly influence government deci-

---

[1] "Where Your Income Tax Money Really Goes: U.S. Federal Budget 2013 Fiscal Year," *War Resisters League*, February 2012. http://tinyurl.com/DROMWRL3.

[2] Adam Skolnick, "Runaway Prison Costs Trash State Budgets," *Fiscal Times*, February 9, 2011. http://tinyurl.com/DROMSkolnick2.

sions, resulting in subsidies for private development projects that benefit a narrow part of the population while the rest foot the bill.

In this chapter, we'll look at taxes as a system of debt that often worsens problems in our society while claiming to fix them. We'll explore the history of tax resistance in United States, suggest practical means to pay less in taxes, and provide advice for defaulters.

WHO BENEFITS?
The wealthy

The U.S. tax system is regressive, meaning that poor people pay a higher proportion of their income in taxes than wealthy people. Taking into account all state, local, and sales taxes, the Institute on Taxation and Economic Policy 2013 report "Who Pays?" concludes:

> The main finding of this report is that virtually every state's tax sys-
> tem is fundamentally unfair, taking a much greater share of income
> from middle- and low-income families than from wealthy families. The
> absence of a graduated personal income tax and the over reliance on
> consumption taxes exacerbate this problem in many states. Combining
> all of the state and local income, property, sales and excise taxes state
> residents pay, the average overall effective tax rates by income group
> nationwide are 11.1 percent for the bottom 20 percent, 9.4 percent for
> the middle 20 percent and 5.6 percent for the top 1 percent.[3]

When everyone is required to pay taxes, having to pay *less* is certainly a benefit. Many tax rules systematically favor the wealthy; one obvious example is the fact that capital gains (taxes on the sale of investments) are often taxed less than wages. The 2013 "Fiscal Cliff" deal raised the capital gains tax rate from 15% to 20%, still leaving it below the wage tax rate applied disproportionately to low-income brackets.[4] This glaring unfairness in the tax system appears when a secretary pays a 33% tax rate compared to their boss, whose net worth might be $50 billion and pays a mere 17.4% of their income in taxes.[5]

Even if everyone followed these rules, the system would still be unfair. But not everyone follows the rules, and those doing the biggest cheating are wealthy individuals and large corporations, among whom tax avoidance is common and widespread.[6]

---

[3] "Who Pays? A Distributional Analysis of the Tax Systems in All 50 States" (4th ed.), *Institute on Taxation and Economic Policy*, January 2013. http://tinyurl.com/DROMITEP, 18.

[4] "Topic 409: Capital Gains and Losses," *Internal Revenue Service*, January 4, 2013. http://tinyurl.com/DROMIRS1.

[5] Warren E. Buffett, "A Minimum Tax for the Wealthy," *New York Times*, November 25, 2012. http://tinyurl.com/DROMBuffett.

[6] Lynnley Browning, "Critics Call Delaware a Tax Haven," *New York Times*, May 29, 2009. http://tinyurl.com/DROMBrowning.

Corporations

A look at who benefits from the tax debts that have been shifted onto the shoulders of individuals lends a more expansive view of how the government interacts with and regulates the economy. Over the last thirty years, the government has implemented neoliberal economic policies, which generally include the push for privatization of public services, lower wages for the majority of workers, and loosening restrictions on businesses.

"Corporate welfare" is the term used to describe these government policies that use tax revenues to support businesses in direct and indirect ways. Some examples include low-cost leases to energy companies that drill on public land, the bank bailout of 2008, and price support for large agribusiness in the Farm Bill. On the local and state level, corporate welfare can be seen in the numerous tax-breaks Walmart has received for new construction.[7] Additionally, corporations benefit from public spending on the services that make their business possible, such as transportation networks, and publicly funded research and development.

The tax preparation industry

The withholding of federal taxes from paychecks throughout the year can be difficult for many who live paycheck to paycheck. During tax season, when a sizeable portion of that money is often returned all at once, tax preparation companies take advantage of one of the few times during the year when working families have a chunk of extra income.

Until 2013, tax preparation companies offered refund anticipation loans (RALs) to those for whom they had prepared taxes. Upon receiving confirmation from the IRS that the taxpayer didn't have any back taxes or liens, they would loan the expected refund to the taxpayer in advance, after assessing a fee for this service in addition to a fee for tax preparation. These loans would average 150% APR, and sometimes as high as 400%, on par with the predatory payday loan industry.[8]

The tax preparation industry's promises of "Quick Cash" and "Instant Refunds" generally targeted poor communities and communities of color, like many other high-interest financial products offered by the fringe finance industry (*see Chapters Seven and Eight*). The

[7] Philip Mattera and Anna Purinton, "Shopping for Subsidies: How Wal-Mart Uses Taxpayer Money to Finance Its Never-Ending Growth," *Good Jobs First*, May 2004. http://tinyurl.com/DROMMattera, 15.

[8] Chi Chi Wu and Jean Ann Fox, "The Party's Over for Quickie Tax Loans: But Traps Remain for Unwary Taxpayers," *National Consumer Law Center* and *Consumer Federation of America*, February 2012. http://tinyurl.com/DROMWu2, 2.

consequences for many families are steep; in 2010, taxpayers paid an estimated $338 million in fees for these predatory loans.[9]

Now that changes to the IRS code have done away with refund anticipation loans, major tax preparation companies are offering new financial products called refund anticipation *checks* (RACs).[10] When a taxpayer can't afford the cost of tax preparation services, a temporary bank account is opened where the IRS deposits the tax refund. Once it is deposited, the preparer takes out preparation costs plus additional fees. RACs tend to be less expensive than RALs, but they can still cost individuals up to $55 in fees.[11]

WHO "PAYS"?

The highly regressive nature of the payroll tax means that those with incomes above $102,000 pay less than their fair share—the payroll tax doesn't apply beyond the first $102,000 of income paid. As a result, people who earn significantly more than $102,000 pay a payroll tax that is a lower percentage of their income than someone who makes less than $102,000.

Those who report their income with the 1099 form (freelancers and independent contractors) don't have taxes taken out of their checks by employers, but are required to file their taxes quarterly. Low-wage precarious workers who are forced to file this way forgo unemployment insurance, unions rights, and many workplace protections, as independent contractors are supposed to be "free" workers only bound by contracts, not by an employer-employee relationship.[12] Often people who are in effect regular employees of a business are misclassified as independent contractors so their employers don't have to pay things like Social Security and Medicare taxes. This form of employer tax evasion is widespread; studies estimate that anywhere from 10% to 30% of employers misclassify employees.[13] Efforts to challenge this practice have been undertaken by state and federal regulators. There have also been court cases and labor disputes, such

[9] Wu and Fox, "Party's Over," 7.

[10] Susan Tompor, "Your Money: Expect to Pay for Fast Tax Refund," *USA Today*, February 5, 2013. http://tinyurl.com/DROMTompor.

[11] Chi Chi Wu, Tom Feltner, and Jean Ann Fox, "Something Old, Something New in Tax-Time Financial Productions: Refund Anticipation Checks and the Next Wave of Quickie Tax Loans," *Consumer Federation of America* and *National Consumer Law Center*, February 2013. http://tinyurl.com/DROMWu5, 4.

[12] "1099'd: Misclassification of Employees as 'Independent Contractors,'" *National Employment Law Project*, April 2010. http://tinyurl.com/DROMNELP, 1.

[13] Sarah Leberstein, "Independent Contractor Misclassification Imposes Huge Costs on Workers and Federal and State Treasuries," *National Employment Law Project*, June 2010. http://tinyurl.com/DROMLeberstein, 1.

as when a group of FedEx drivers filed a class-action lawsuit against the company in 2010 for being categorized as independent contractors instead of company employees.[14]

BRIEF HISTORY AND LEGAL BACKGROUND

Resistance to taxes has a long and turbulent history. Throughout the ancient world, taxes were associated with foreign invasion, and a major cause of popular revolts against debt.[15] Jewish Zealots in Judea organized tax resistance to the Roman Empire in the first century CE.[16] Fourteenth-century London was invaded by tens of thousands of peasants revolting against Parliament's imposition of a poll tax.[17] Eighteenth-century Japan saw many tax revolts,[18] and heavy taxation was a major grievance in the French Revolution.[19] During the nineteenth century, tax resistance was a weapon of anti-colonial rebels resisting European colonial domination in African countries such as Ghana and Sierra Leone.[20] Tax resistance also had an important political impact during the twentieth century, helping India's campaign for independence from Britain,[21] supporting the first Palestinian Intifada,[22] and helping to oust Margaret Thatcher from power in the wake of Britain's anti–Poll Tax riots.[23]

Tax Resistance in North America predates the United States with the Algonquin refusal to pay taxes to Dutch Colonists to build a military base on Manhattan Island in 1637. Armed tax rebellion was a tactic of poor and indebted farmers before and after the American War of Independence. Henry David Thoreau famously called for those opposed to the Mexican-American War to refuse to pay

---

[14] Matt Wickenheiser, "Maine FedEx Drivers Sue Over Employment Status," *Bangor Daily News*, December 16, 2010. http://tinyurl.com/DROMWickenheiser.

[15] David Graeber, *Debt: The First 5,000 Years* (New York: Melville House, 2011). http://tinyurl.com/DROMGraeber, 13.

[16] James Stevenson Riggs, "The Zealots and Taxes in Judea," in *We Won't Pay! A Tax Resistance Reader*, ed. David M. Gross (CreateSpace, 2008), 1–3.

[17] "Tax Justice in History: The Peasant's Revolt," *Tax Justice Network*, July 12, 2009. http://tinyurl.com/DROMTJN.

[18] David F. Burg, *A World History of Tax Rebellions: An Encyclopedia of Tax Rebels, Revolts, and Riots from Antiquity to the Present* (New York: Routledge, 2004), 232.

[19] Burg, *World History*, 299.

[20] "The Story of Africa: Africa and Europe (1800–1914): Tax Wars," *BBC World Service*. http://tinyurl.com/DROMBBC.

[21] Mohandas Karamchand Gandhi, "Non-Payment of Taxes," in *We Won't Pay! A Tax Resistance Reader*, ed. David M. Gross (CreateSpace, 2008), 353.

[22] Karen Marysdaughter, "Palestinian Tax Resistance Update," *National War Tax Resistance Coordinating Committee*, April 1997. http://tinyurl.com/DROMMarysdaughter2.

[23] "1990: One in Five Yet to Pay Poll Tax," *BBC News*, August 14, 2008. http://tinyurl.com/DROMBBC2.

taxes—an anti-militarist form of tax resistance that has been echoed during many later U.S. wars. The War Resisters League, formed in 1923, continues to organize and advise people who refuse to pay for war with their taxes.[24] In the nineteenth and twentieth century, U.S., Chinese, Mexican, Greek, and Italian immigrants used tax resistance to protest the denial of social and economic rights.

Sadly, in recent decades, the political resistance to taxes has been taken up primarily as a right-wing effort to destroy social safety net programs and reverse the social gains of the 1960s and '70s. Beginning with California's "Taxpayers' Revolt" of 1978, and continuing with Ronald Reagan's campaign to lower taxes and "starve" federal social programs,[25] the right-wing version of tax-resistance may have found its clearest articulation yet in today's racist, anti-immigrant, and paranoid Tea Party movement. These contemporary "tax warriors" have made it hard to see the long and substantial history of left-wing, popular rebellions against unjust taxation.

WHAT HAPPENS WHEN YOU DEFAULT?

If you never pay your taxes and don't owe very much, the IRS will ignore you for a while, maybe years. But if your employers are filing tax forms (W-2s, 1099s) on their end, they'll likely catch up with you eventually. If you file a return but don't pay, they'll catch up with you much sooner. The IRS details the collection process on their website.[26]

What can and can't they do?

- You will receive a written notice stating how much you owe and are given the option to pay it in full and be done with it (until next year).
- If you don't have that money but are planning on paying, you can set up an installment agreement. It costs $105, although you can request a lower fee if you don't make very much money.[27] The IRS offers you different payment options—such as bank transfers, credit/debit cards, payroll deduction—and assesses different charges based on that.[28] IRS rules for repayment are confusing. If you're unable to hire an accountant, be sure to read their regulations multiple times and try to get them on the phone. Compare

[24] "History of War Tax Resistance," *War Resisters League*, 2008. http://tinyurl.com/DROMWRL2.

[25] Bruce Bartlett, "Tax Cuts and 'Starving the Beast,'" *Forbes*, May 7, 2010. http://tinyurl.com/DROMBartlett.

[26] "Topic 201: The Collection Process," *Internal Revenue Service*, December 27, 2012. http://tinyurl.com/DROMIRS3.

[27] "Form 13844: Application for Reduced User Fee for Installment Agreements," *Internal Revenue Service*, January 2013. http://tinyurl.com/DROMIRS4.

[28] "Payment Plans, Installment Agreements," *Internal Revenue Service*, March 12, 2013. http://tinyurl.com/DROMIRS5.

the different fees they charge for the different ways you can pay them, and see which is the most affordable and within your means.

- The IRS assesses fees for back taxes, and interest on the balance owed; the interest accumulates, and the fees don't. For older tax debts, retroactive fees and accumulated interest might mean that most of your monthly installments pay for fees and interest, not the principal of your debt.
- When paying off tax debts in installment plans, it's sometimes hard to find out exactly how much you owe, as the IRS assesses fees after payments. IRS letters with your balance on them do not show how they computed that figure, and talking to them on the phone often won't help in getting many more details. The IRS details the types of fees it assesses on its website.[29]
- The interest they charge you is relatively low, so for new tax debts (one to two years) it's most likely less than a credit card. If at all possible do *not* pay your taxes with a credit card.
- The statute of limitations for tax debt is ten years, meaning that once the IRS sends you a bill, they have ten years to get it from you. After that period of time, the remaining amount of debt can no longer be collected. This does not apply to years that you owe taxes but have not filed.

Collections
What they can do

If you continue to ignore the IRS, they will send you a "Final Notice" notifying you that you have thirty days to pay your taxes before they put a levy on your assets and begin to seize them, although it often does not begin right way. The IRS has the right to seize wages and bank accounts as well as property such as houses, land, cars and businesses. The IRS moves to seize bank accounts and wages first and will be less likely to seize properties for tax debts under $5,000, although this is not a hard and fast rule.

What they can't do

- The IRS states that it "can't seize your property if you have a current or pending installment agreement [see the section *Ways of getting out of tax debt*, page 104], offer in compromise [also see below], or if [they] agree that you're unable to pay due to economic hardship."[30]
- The IRS cannot seize more than 15% of federal payments such as a Social Security check.
- The IRS cannot seize the following payments: "unemployment benefits,

---

[29] "Failure to File or Pay Penalties: Eight Facts," *Internal Revenue Service*, April 17, 2012. http://tinyurl.com/DROMIRS6.

[30] "The IRS Collection Process: Publication 594," *Internal Revenue Service*, April 2012. http://tinyurl.com/DROMIRS7, 5.

certain annuity and pension benefits, certain service-connected disability payments, workers compensation, certain public assistance payments, minimum weekly exempt income, assistance under the Job Training Partnership Act, and income for court-ordered child support payments."[31]

- The IRS cannot seize personal and household property equal to or less than a total value of $6,250.
- The IRS cannot seize books or tools of the trade, business, or profession of the tax debtor equal to or less than a total value of $3,125.

If you haven't yet filed your taxes and are planning on filing

These tips can help reduce the expense and stress of paying taxes, and can reduce the total amount you owe.

- Get free tax help in person. For low- to middle-income taxpayers, many credit unions, community organizations, and government agencies will prepare your taxes for free, allowing you to receive your full refund and tax credits in seven to ten days. You can dial 1-800-829-1040 to find the government-funded free tax preparation site nearest you.
    - -Information: irs.gov/Individuals/IRS-Free-Tax-Return-Prepartion Programs
    - -Search tool: irs.treasury.gov/freetaxprep
- If you make $57,000 per year or less, you can have your taxes prepared and filed for free at freefile.irs.gov.
- Use free fillable forms: If you have some knowledge of how to file taxes but want an online account to save your information, do some of the math for you, and e-file for you, go to irs.gov/uac/Access-Free-File-Fillable-Forms-Here.
- 1099s / Independent Contractors: If you are receiving 1099s, you'll want to fill out a Schedule C form, which is for reporting profit or loss on a business. Since you're only taxed on your profit, you can reduce your tax bill by writing off business expenses such as tools, clothes, transportation, office equipment, cell phone bills, your car, and anything else used for your "business." Save your receipts in case you get audited in the future! If you keep the business profit below $400, you won't owe any self-employment tax either.

If you owe tax debt that you're planning on paying
Ways of getting out of tax debt

- Installment agreement: make a monthly payment plan for paying off the IRS.
- Offer in compromise: this is a way to settle your tax debts for less than what you owe, based on ability to pay, income, expenses, and asset

---

[31] "IRS Collection Process," 6.

equity. To see if you qualify, answer the questions at irs.treasury.gov/oic_pre_qualifier. If you qualify, you'll need to apply by going to irs.gov/Individuals/Offer-in-Compromise-1. A $150 non-refundable application fee is required, and you'll have to either make a lump sum payment or pay on a short-term payment plan.[32]

- "Currently not collectible": this is a program where the IRS voluntarily agrees not to collect on the tax debt for a year or so. There are specific eligibility conditions.[33]

- Tax debt can be discharged under Chapter 7 or Chapter 13 bankruptcy (*see Chapter Ten*) if it meets the following strict specifications:
  - The due date for filing a tax return is at least three years ago.
  - The tax return was filed at least two years ago.
  - The tax assessment is at least 240 days old.
  - The tax return was not fraudulent.
  - The taxpayer is not guilty of tax evasion.[34]

RESISTANCE STRATEGIES
If you plan on not filing your taxes and not paying your tax debt

The IRS isn't all-powerful and many people have avoided making payments on debt. However, failure to file tax returns *could* mean serving up to a year in prison and up to $25,000 in fines for each year not filed. If you are found guilty of deliberately evading taxes, you could serve up to five years and pay up to $100,000. This section borrows heavily from the National War Tax Resistance Coordinating Committee website (nwtrcc.org).

Wages

A big concern with being in tax debt is having your wages seized by the IRS. To avoid paying taxes, you'll need to make considerable lifestyle changes and probably adjust to having a lower, less regular income. The National War Tax Resistance Coordinating Committee recommends self-employment as the most reliable way to avoid collections. Working under the table or for small enterprises that don't report taxes is another way. Another option is to change jobs often, as it will take the IRS a while to catch up with you.

If you're not planning on filing and have a regular job, you can write "exempt" on your W-4 form so that no taxes will be withheld

---

[32] "Offer in Compromise," *Internal Revenue Service*, January 29, 2013. http://tinyurl.com/DROMIRS11.

[33] "Currently Not Collectible," *NFA Tax Help*. http://tinyurl.com/DROMNFA.

[34] William Perez, "Bankruptcy and Tax Debts: Five Rules for Discharging Tax Debts in Bankruptcy," *About.com: Tax Planning*. http://tinyurl.com/DROMPerez2.

from your paycheck. Or just increase the number of exemptions. If you don't have investments or itemized deductions, it would be simple to calculate how many exemptions you should claim in order to avoid a tax refund without getting a liability. Regardless of how many dependents you have, you can still claim, for example, five dependents for planning purposes. (When filing taxes, you would legally need to write the actual number of dependents.) Many websites, including the IRS website, feature a withholding calculator to help you make a more informed decision about this approach.

Bank accounts

The National War Tax Resistance Coordinating Committee writes, "It is possible to protect deposits from IRS seizure. The IRS learns the location of all interest bearing accounts because financial institutions are required to report interest payments of $10 or more to the IRS. Collection can be prevented by removing all deposits from interest bearing accounts as soon as you expect or receive a 'Final Notice' to pay from IRS. If you remove the deposits in cash and deposit them elsewhere, you can avoid leaving a paper trail from one institution to the next."[35]

Because banks are required to report transactions in excess of $10,000 to the IRS, the National War Tax Resistance Coordinating Committee recommends removing and depositing money in amounts less than $10,000. They also recommend using a bank in a different neighborhood or town from where you live as well as using a post office box as a banking address.[36]

Cars and houses

The best way to avoid seizure is to have cars and houses in the name of a trusted friend or relative. If you own a house that is your primary residence, another strategy is to avoid using it for mail and banking, and also having an unlisted phone number. The National War Tax Resistance Coordinating Committee writes, "This method isn't foolproof, but it certainly throws significant roadblocks in the way of IRS collection efforts. Experience shows that IRS collectors give up rather quickly when they run into several dead ends, because they can't waste too much time on any one case."[37]

---

[35] "Practical War Tax Resistance #3: How to Resist Collection, or Make the Most of Collection When It Occurs," *National War Tax Resistance Coordinating Committee*. http://tinyurl.com/DROMNWTRCC.

[36] "Practical War Tax Resistance #3."

[37] "Practical War Tax Resistance #3."

RESOURCES
Websites
• Citizens for Tax Justice (ctj.org)
• National War Tax Resistance Coordinating Committee (nwtrcc.org)
• War Resisters League (warresisters.org)

Articles and Books
• David F. Burg, *A World History of Tax Rebellions: An Encyclopedia of Tax Rebels, Revolts, and Riots From Antiquity to the Present* (New York: Routledge, 2004).
• David M. Gross, *We Won't Pay! A Tax Resistance Reader* (CreateSpace, 2008).
• "History of War Tax Resistance," *War Resistes League*, 2008, http://tinyurl.com/DROMWRL2.

REFERENCES
Bartlett, Bruce. "Tax Cuts and 'Starving the Beast.'" *Forbes*, May 7, 2010. http://tinyurl.com/DROMBartlett.

BBC News. "1990: One in Five Yet to Pay Poll Tax." August 14, 2008. http://tinyurl.com/DROMBBC2.

BBC World Service. "The Story of Africa: Africa and Europe (1800–1914): Tax Wars." http://tinyurl.com/DROMBBC.

Browning, Lynnley. "Critics Call Delaware a Tax Haven." *New York Times*, May 29, 2009. http://tinyurl.com/DROMBrowning.

Buffett, Warren E. "A Minimum Tax for the Wealthy." *New York Times*, November 25, 2012. http://tinyurl.com/DROMBuffett.

Burg, David F. *A World History of Tax Rebellions: An Encyclopedia of Tax Rebels, Revolts, and Riots From Antiquity to the Present.* New York: Routledge, 2004.

Gandhi, Mohandas Karamchand. "Non-Payment of Taxes." In *We Won't Pay! A Tax Resistance Reader*, edited by David M. Gross, 353. CreateSpace, 2008.

Graeber, David. *Debt: The First 5,000 Years.* New York: Melville House, 2011. http://tinyurl.com/DROMGraeber.

Institute on Taxation and Economic Policy. "Who Pays? A Distributional Analysis of the Tax Systems in All 50 States (Fourth Edition)." January 2013. http://tinyurl.com/DROMITEP.

Internal Revenue Service. "Collecting Process: Installment Agreements: Partial Payment Installment Agreements and the Collection Statute Expiration Date (CSED)." March 11, 2011. http://tinyurl.com/DROMIRS10.

Internal Revenue Service. "Failure to File or Pay Penalties: Eight Facts." April 17, 2012. http://tinyurl.com/DROMIRS6.

Internal Revenue Service. "Form 13844: Application for Reduced User Fee for Installment Agreements." January 2013. http://tinyurl.com/DROMIRS4.

Internal Revenue Service. "The IRS Collection Process: Publication 594." April 2012. http://tinyurl.com/DROMIRS7.

Internal Revenue Service. "Offer in Compromise." January 29, 2013. http://tinyurl.com/DROMIRS11.

Internal Revenue Service. "Payment Plans, Installment Agreements." March 12, 2013. http://tinyurl.com/DROMIRS5.

Internal Revenue Service. "Topic 201: The Collection Process." December 27, 2012. http://tinyurl.com/DROMIRS3.

Internal Revenue Service. "Topic 409: Capital Gains and Losses." January 4, 2013. http://tinyurl.com/DROMIRS1.

Leberstein, Sarah. "Independent Contractor Misclassification Imposes Huge Costs on Workers and Federal and State Treasuries." *National Employment Law Project*, June 2010. http://tinyurl.com/DROMLeberstein.

Marysdaughter, Karen. "Palestinian Tax Resistance Update." *National War Tax Resistance Coordinating Committee*, April 1997. http://tinyurl.com/DROMMarysdaughter2.

Mattera, Philip, and Anna Purinton. "Shopping for Subsidies: How Wal-Mart Uses Taxpayer Money to Finance Its Never-Ending Growth." *Good Jobs First*, May 2004. http://tinyurl.com/DROMMattera.

National Employment Law Project, "1099'd: Misclassification of Employees as 'Independent Contractors.'" April 2010. http://tinyurl.com/DROMNELP.

National War Tax Resistance Coordinating Committee. "Practical War Tax Resistance #3: How to Resist Collection, or Make the Most of Collection When It Occurs." Accessed March 26, 2013. http://tinyurl.com/DROMNWTRCC.

NFA Tax Help. "Currently Not Collectible." Accessed March 26, 2013. http://tinyurl.com/DROMNFA.

Perez, William. "Bankruptcy and Tax Debts: Five Rules for Discharging Tax Debts in Bankruptcy." *About.com: Tax Planning*. http://tinyurl.com/DROMPerez2.

Riggs, James Stevenson. "The Zealots and Taxes in Judea." In *We Won't Pay! A Tax Resistance Reader*, edited by David M. Gross, 1–3. CreateSpace, 2008.

Skolnick, Adam. "Runaway Prison Costs Trash State Budgets." *Fiscal Times*, February 9, 2011. http://tinyurl.com/DROMSkolnick2.

Tax Justice Network. "Tax Justice in History: The Peasant's Revolt." July 12, 2009. http://tinyurl.com/DROMTJN.

Tompor, Susan. "Your Money: Expect to Pay for Fast Tax Refund." *USA Today*, February 5, 2013. http://tinyurl.com/DROMTompor.

War Resisters League. "History of War Tax Resistance." Accessed March 26, 2013. http://tinyurl.com/DROMWRL2.

War Resisters League. "Where Your Income Tax Money Really Goes: U.S. Federal Budget 2013 Fiscal Year." February 2012. http://tinyurl.com/DROMWRL3.

Wu, Chi Chi, Tom Feltner, and Jean Ann Fox. "Something Old, Something New in Tax-Time Financial Productions: Refund Anticipation Checks and the Next Wave of Quickie Tax Loans." *Consumer Federation of America* and *National Consumer Law Center*, February 2013. http://tinyurl.com/DROMWu5.

Wu, Chi Chi, and Jean Ann Fox. "The Party's Over for Quickie Tax Loans: But Traps Remain for Unwary Taxpayers." *National Consumer Law Center* and *Consumer Federation of America*, February 2012. http://tinyurl.com/DROMWu2.

SEVEN
FRINGE FINANCE TRANSACTION PRODUCTS AND SERVICES

MAKING BANK ON THE UNBANKED

As James Baldwin once said, "Anyone who has ever struggled with poverty knows how extremely expensive it is to be poor." This is true now more than ever.

Some call it the "poverty tax"—the surcharge people pay for not having savings or access to "prime" credit and being consigned to "fringe finance." Fringe finance refers to the array of "alternative" financial services (AFS) offered by providers that operate outside of federally insured banks. Gary Rivlin, author of *Broke USA: From Pawnshops to Poverty, Inc*, does the math; adding up the profits from the AFS sector and dividing by the forty million households that survive on $30,000 a year or less, the industry receives an average of $2,500 per year from every low-income household. That's a "poverty tax" of around 10%, depleting the assets of low-income households.

This chapter and the next chapter break down the major perils of fringe finance into those related to transactions and those related to credit. This chapter deals with transaction products and services: check cashing and prepaid cards. Chapter Eight covers credit products and services: payday loans, auto-title and pawn loans, and rent-to-own financing. Among households without access to a bank account, 62% have used an AFS transaction product or service and 27% have used an AFS credit product or service. About 23% have used both.[1]

Both chapters offer analysis and information to help you identify the common tricks and traps of fringe finance so that you can avoid them. We consider alternatives to the most expensive products and

---

[1] Federal Deposit Insurance Corporation, *National Survey of Unbanked and Underbanked Households* (Washington, DC: GPO, 2009). http://tinyurl.com/DROMFDIC3, 28.

services, as well as how to save money if you're "locked in" or have no other options. There is no one-size-fits-all strategy for personal finance. We conclude Chapter Eight by outlining some individual and collective strategies that aim to minimize or eliminate our dependence on the current debt-finance system.

Investors, however, expect the stunning rates of financial extraction in the poverty industry to rise, and it has created funds to invest in startups and small firms with big growth potential in the fringe finance sector. The "market" that investors want to tap is the unbanked (people without checking or savings accounts) and the underbanked (people who rely on a combination of both "traditional" and "alternative" financial products). Why are investors so interested in this market? Not only is it a market that has previously been off their radar, it is a market that promises greater returns—even after adjusting for increased risk (otherwise, they wouldn't be interested). In a blog post titled "Not Unbanked: Untapped," a venture fund manager explains, "It is fair to say that most of these products are generally more expensive than what most of 'us' pay. APRs [annual percentage rates of interest] higher than 30% (if not 300%); transaction costs of $2+; money-transfer costs of $10+; access to payroll check for 2–4%."[2] The transaction services segment of AFS has seen some of the most spectacular growth in recent years, where prepaid cards are making inroads and recording profits that rival the always-profitable check-cashing outlets (CCOs).

This is the predicament of the poor in our debt-finance system: it costs poor people significantly more *to use money*—to spend it, to save it, to invest it, to borrow it, to send it "back home" (for immigrants whose families still live in their country of origin)—and they have less money to begin with. If you're poor, you are likely forced to engage with the debt-finance system, and the more wealth it takes from you, the more indebted you become. Meanwhile, AFS owners and investors, who enjoy lower financing costs than you and have more money to begin with, profit from your loss and acquire pieces of your debt. Thus, investors on Wall Street come to own pieces of your future. These are the workings of a two-tiered financial system, on the bottom of which are relatively high-cost services marketed to the growing and changing ranks of the unbanked and the underbanked.

The nearly ten million unbanked includes the working poor, the unemployed, the homeless, the undocumented, those who do not speak English fluently, those who are or have been incarcerated, those

[2] Arjan Schutte, "Not Underbanked: Untapped. Underserved Spend $45B on Financial Services," *Inside the Underbanked*, November 2, 2011. http://tinyurl.com/DROMSchutte.

with mental or physical health issues, older people, those working off the books, those hiding from creditors or the "authorities," those whose homes were stolen by robo-signing investment banks, youth who have been cut off from their parents, and anyone else who "traditional" financial institutions deem unworthy of service.

Demographically speaking, the unbanked population is broad and diverse, but it is disproportionately comprised of low-income households (71% of unbanked households earn below $30,000 a year), households of color, immigrant households, and individuals with negative banking histories.[3] (Of course, many of the unbanked fit into multiple categories.) In general, Latino/a and Black people are six and seven times more likely to be unbanked than Whites respectively. Households with an annual income under $30,000 are thirteen times more likely to be unbanked than those with an income between $50,000 and $75,000.[4] More than half of immigrants in New York City are unbanked, according to a recent survey. People of color and immigrants are more likely to have low, unreliable, or seasonal income, making it more difficult to save enough money to meet minimum opening-balance requirements at banks. Not having enough money is the number one reason that the unbanked do not have a bank account.[5] There's another significant commonality: many people of color, low-income individuals, and immigrants justifiably distrust banks.[6] Losing one's home or hard-earned property, or being denied credit for no reason but the color of one's skin—especially in a society focused on wealth accumulation—is traumatic. The effects can ripple across generations of a family, shaping how future generations interact with financial institutions. Banks have historically been places reserved for middle- or upper-class White men, and that explicitly exclusionary past makes its impact felt in today's world in various less overt ways. Because of the openly racist and classist history of U.S. credit practices, banks can feel like unfamiliar or even hostile territory to many poor people of color.[7]

---

[3] National League of Cities Institute for Youth, Education and Families, *Banking on Opportunity: A Scan of the Evolving Field of Bank on Initiatives*, U.S. Department of the Treasury (Washington, DC: GPO, 2011). http://tinyurl.com/DROMNLCI, 9–10.

[4] Preeti Vissa, "Debit Card Overdraft Fees: Reforms Welcomed but More Are Necessary," *The Greenlining Institute*, April 2010. http://tinyurl.com/DROMVissa, 3.

[5] FDIC, *National Survey*, 27.

[6] See Vikas Bajaj and Ford Fessenden, "What's Behind the Race Gap?" *New York Times*, November 4, 2007. http://tinyurl.com/DROMBajaj; "The Racial Gap in Debt, Credit and Financial Services," *Insight Center for Community Economic Development*, June 2009. http://tinyurl.com/DROMICCED, 1.

[7] See Bajaj and Fessenden, "What's Behind the Race Gap?"; Douglas Massey and Nancy Den-

Inconvenient locations, limited hours of operation, and language barriers often make access difficult for low-income households.[8] Undocumented immigrants generally lack the forms of ID required by many banks to open accounts, and furthermore fear that banks will share their immigration status with the authorities.

Some of the unbanked and underbanked rely on fringe finance because it helps them avoid unnecessary difficulties posed by mainstream financial products—difficulties which reflect their socially marginalized status. If you are a transgender person applying for a bank account, for example, you must use your legal name and gender, even if it is different from the name and gender that you identify as (though in Washington State, at least, transgender people have the right to be referred to by the name and gender of their choice when doing business at a bank). Preloaded debit cards, which do not have the owner's name printed on them, help trans people avoid harassment caused by a mismatch between the printed name and their gender presentation.[9]

It can become difficult for unbanked people to document and prove income when filing for benefits, workers' compensation, or filing cases against abusive employers. For many of the unbanked, the experience of second-tier status in the financial system mirrors their experience with the two-tiered justice system. Those who are socially marginalized in one way or another are more likely to occupy the bottom tier of the financial system, which makes it more likely they'll get caught up in the criminal justice system.

The criminalization of poverty, the criminalization of immigration, as well as racial and ethnic profiling are well-documented trends that push people to the fringes of finance. And being on the fringes of finance is itself increasingly criminalized. In at least a third of U.S. states, being in debt can now land you in jail.[10] In Washington State, for example, a Black man with mental health issues was incarcerated for two weeks for failing to pay $60 worth of "legal financial obligations" (LFOs). His jail stay, meanwhile, cost Spokane County over $1,500.[11]

In many cases, these barriers to the banking system can reinforce each other and create insurmountable walls between the banked and

---

ton, *American Apartheid: Segregation and the Making of the Underclass* (Cambridge, MA: Harvard University, 1993).

[8] National League of Cities Institute for Youth, Education and Families, 9.

[9] This information was obtained in a private email correspondence with the founder of a trans activist group. They relayed various members' experiences with banking and using fringe finance.

[10] Jessica Silver-Greenberg, "Welcome to Debtors' Prison, 2011 Edition," *Wall Street Journal*, March 16, 2011. http://tinyurl.com/DROMSilver3.

[11] "In for a Penny: The Rise of America's New Debtors' Prisons," *American Civil Liberties Union*, October 2010. http://tinyurl.com/DROMACLU, 73.

unbanked. The underbanked tend to share many of the same characteristics and face many of the same obstacles as the unbanked.[12]

CHECK-CASHING OUTLETS (CCOs)

For nine million households in the United States, cashing paychecks at a bank or credit union is not an option.[13] The unbanked generally do not have bank accounts for any number of the reasons discussed earlier. For many people, a CCO is the only option to transform their paycheck into cash.

According to the Federal Reserve, CCOs generally charge between 1.5% and 3.5% to cash a check.[14] For a $500 check, that comes out to between $7.50 and $17.50 in fees taken away. This is actually a conservative estimate. The Consumer Federation pegs average fees at 4.11%,[15] which means that CCOs get a cut closer to $20.55 of the original $500. With a checking account, by contrast, this service would be free. If you're unbanked and you make $500 every week, in one year you might spend $400 if you're relatively lucky, but possibly over $1,000, just so you can spend your own money. The average unbanked person with a full-time job can expect to spend more than $40,000 on such fees in their lifetime. That is, throughout the course of one's life, more than an entire year's worth of work goes exclusively toward turning one's salary into cash.[16]

Between 2000 and 2005, the number of CCOs in the country doubled, but the added competition did not lower fees. In fact, the price of cashing a check has gone up, with a 75.6% average growth rate between 1997 and 2006.[17] Companies like Walmart, Kmart, and Best Buy have also tapped into this market by offering check cashing at their stores. Although they charge less to cash a check than the regular outlets, they only keep lower prices so that people suddenly equipped with cash will spend it right where they are.[18]

As expensive as CCOs may be, and as much as they target people with lower incomes, if they all pulled up stakes and left, what would hap-

---

[12] FDIC, *National Survey*, 17.

[13] Christine Haughney, "City's Poor Still Distrust Banks," *New York Times*, August 17, 2009. http://tinyurl.com/DROMHaughney.

[14] Robin A. Prager, Federal Reserve Board, *Determinants of the Locations of Payday Lenders, Pawnshops and Check-Cashing Outlets* (Washington, DC: GPO, June 2009). http://tinyurl.com/DROMPrager, 6.

[15] Jean Ann Fox and Patrick Woodall, *Cashed Out: Consumers Pay Steep Premium to 'Bank' at Check Cashing Outlets* (Washington, DC: Consumer Federation of America, 2006). http://tinyurl.com/DROMFox, 2.

[16] William Clinton and Arnold Schwarzenegger, "Beyond Payday Loans," *Wall Street Journal*, January 24, 2008. http://tinyurl.com/DROMClinton.

[17] Fox and Woodall, 2.

[18] Brad Tuttle, "Big-Box Banking: Why the Unbanked Are Cashing Checks at Walmart," *Time*, February 1, 2011. http://tinyurl.com/DROMTuttle.

pen? Several alternatives may be available. You could make an arrangement with a trusted friend, family member, or even your employer—that is, someone with access to a checking account—in which you would write your check over to them and they would give you the full amount in cash. You could join with others in your community and approach a local community center or religious institution to ask if they would be willing to set up a free check-cashing service. You could talk to local credit unions about their free checking accounts and, to encourage the credit union to offer the services you need, organize others to join in your request. Your collective power and voice could open up new possibilities.

If you have exhausted other options and must resort to a CCO, it is important to know how to use it in a way that minimizes harm. For example, ask ahead of time for the fee *in dollar amounts* as opposed to the percentage. And be sure afterward to obtain and save an itemized receipt. Costs may vary not just from one CCO to the next, but by the time of day and other factors.[19] You can compare receipts to determine the optimal approach.

> Check cashers use a number of schemes to lure in the unbanked and the underbanked, and to keep them dependent. In an essay on the poverty tax, Gary Rivlin recalls, "A few years back, I attended the annual Check Cashers Convention, where I sat in on a 90-minute presentation dubbed, 'Effective Marketing Strategies to Dominate Your Market.' Speaking to a standing-room only crowd, a consultant named Jim Higgins shared his tips for turning the $1,000-a-year check cashing or payday customer into one worth '$2,000 to $4,000 a year.' Pens scribbled furiously as he tossed out ideas. Raffle off an iPod. Consider Scratch 'n Win contests. Institute the kind of customer reward programs that has worked so well for the airlines. And for those who are only semi-regulars offer a 'cash 3, get 1 free' deal. After all, Higgins told the crowd, 'These are people not used to getting anything free. These are people not used to getting anything, really.'"[20]

Remittances

In addition to exorbitant check-cashing fees, there are fees for money transfers. Nearly two-thirds of immigrants in New York City, according to a recent survey, reported using remittance services to send

---

[19] Tomorrow's Money for Young Adults: National Association of the State Treasurers Foundation, "Check-Cashing Stores," 2012. http://tinyurl.com/DROMTMYA.

[20] Gary Rivlin, "America's Poverty Tax," *Economic Hardship Reporting Project*, May 16, 2012. http://tinyurl.com/DROMRivlin.

money back to their families in their country of origin, 60% of whom send money every month. Most remittances go simply to pay for basic household needs, such as rent, utilities, and buying food. Immigrants hoping to send money outside of the United States may lose as much as 20% of the amount in the process.[21] While the Consumer Financial Protection Bureau recently introduced new disclosure rules aimed at stopping sudden and unexpected penalties, there's really nothing that limits the overall fee.[22] By contrast, banks and credit unions charge substantially less for this and other services. Some banks even offer special low-cost money transfers to certain countries. Services that could cost up to $500 annually at a CCO could cost between $30 and $60 annually at a traditional financial institution.[23] Many credit unions, and increasingly many banks, have flexible ID requirements, making it simpler for immigrants to open accounts. Be sure to find out if they require a minimum balance to maintain an account and if they require the recipient to have a bank account.

If you must use a money transfer service, be sure to ask what the exchange rate is and how much will actually be given to the recipient. Find out if the recipient will be charged any fees when picking up the money. Remember, you have the right to transfer money in U.S. dollars unless the receiving country has a law requiring money to be converted into the local currency. Be sure to use a licensed transmitter and to keep your receipts. The websites remesamex.gob.mx and remittanceprices.worldbank.org allow you to compare different options and costs when sending money to another country.

> Among the unbanked are many undocumented immigrants who believe that without a Social Security card they are unable to open up an account. The law does not require banks to ask you to provide a Social Security number to open an account, nor does it require them to inquire about your immigration status. The law simply requires that banks ask for your name, date of birth, street address, and one of several different kinds of identification numbers. While most banks have stricter policies, an increasing number of banks and credit unions who see opportunity in the growing immigrant population are more flexible.[24] Some banks will accept an Individual Tax Identity Number (ITIN) in the

---

[21] "The Remittances Game of Chance: Playing with Loaded Dice?" *Consumers International*, January 2012. http://tinyurl.com/DROMConsumer03, 4.

[22] Consumer Financial Protection Bureau, *Electronic Funds Transfer (Regulation E)* (Washington, DC: GPO, 2012). http://tinyurl.com/DROMCFPB2.

[23] Tomorrow's Money for Young Adults.

[24] "U.S. Banks Help Immigrants Send Money Home," *Work Permit*, January 30, 2006. http://tinyurl.com/DROMWP.

place of an SSN. Also, many consulates will provide their citizens with foreign ID cards that banks and credit unions are increasingly accepting. The most popular of these is the Mexican *matricula consular*. The Mexican consulate provides a list of banks and credit unions that accept this either as primary or secondary ID.

PREPAID CARDS

First there were credit cards. Then came debit cards. Now there are prepaid cards—and they're suddenly everywhere. Think about it this way: with credit cards you pay later, with debit cards you pay now, and with prepaid cards you pay early. Credit cards extend credit to consumers for free (with a grace period and assuming good credit). Debit cards give consumers free access to funds in their bank accounts. Prepaid cards charge consumers to access their own funds. So when you use a prepaid card you are essentially paying money to make an interest-free *loan* to the issuer, who then lends your money to other customers.

Charging us for the use of our own money is what banks do. They also provide useful services: the ability to store our money, to access cash, to pay for things without cash, and to turn checks into cash. Prepaid cards—now used by 13% of people in the United States[25]— do the same, although they're not attached to bank accounts. (Some banks have gotten into the prepaid card game—e.g., Chase Liquid, Bank of America CashPay, PNC *Smart*Access—but even their cards are not attached to accounts.) Branded with the logos of American Express, Discover, MasterCard, or Visa, they look like other plastic payment cards and provide ATM access and the ability to make purchases. There are a variety of prepaid cards, including gift cards, payroll cards, government benefits cards, and "general purpose reloadable" (GPR) cards, which let you add funds. Prepaid cards are usually more costly, less convenient, and less secure than comparable services from banks, and they tend to have poor disclosure policies and "gotcha" fees, replicating some of the most aggravating bank practices. Nonetheless, compared with a check-cashing outlet, getting cash from a prepaid card is usually cheaper. When it comes to making payments, prepaid cards are typically more expensive than credit or debit cards, but not necessarily. If you factor in overdraft charges, debit cards can cost more. If you factor in high ongoing balances, high interest rates, and late payment penalties, credit cards may cost considerably more than prepaid cards. Hence, there is no

---

[25] Catherine New, "Prepaid Cards Rise in Popularity as More Americans Are Shut Out from Traditional Banks," *Huffington Post*, April 11, 2013. http://tinyurl.com/DROMNew.

one-size-fits-all strategy for personal financial transactions. What's more, the rules governing the prepaid card industry are still in flux. In 2010 the Credit Card Accountability, Responsibility, and Disclosure Act of 2009 (CARD Act) took effect, tightening regulations for credit cards and traditional debit cards.[26] The new Consumer Financial Protection Bureau (CFPB) is presently considering how to bring the prepaid card market into the federal regulatory framework. In the meantime, barriers to cash continue to grow; transactions for an increasing range of basic services are impossible without plastic. Some employers only pay their employees via prepaid cards.[27] Soon many of us will have no choice but to use these cards when employers, government benefits administrators, and even colleges and universities begin to adopt them.

Purchasable, usable, and sometimes reloadable without identity verification, many prepaid cards offer the advantage of anonymity, which is why they've become the preferred means of laundering money and the de facto currency of the prison system.[28] There are also branded cards that are linked to celebrities, heroes, and social causes, and tend to be the most predatory corner of the market.

Many consumer advocates consider prepaid cards just the latest addition to the array of high-cost and inferior financial products for which the poor pay more. Not only do prepaid cards generally fail to serve their ostensible function of helping marginalized groups enter the financial mainstream, they also tend to intensify financial segregation. The predicament of Millennials, who appear to be the industry's latest target, is especially alarming. Not long after the CARD Act restricted credit card companies' access to college campuses and to customers under twenty-one, prepaid cards began moving in, looking to establish "partnerships." Now with prepaid cards increasingly serving as student IDs, enrolling in college also means enrolling in a bank.

General purpose reloadable (GPR) cards

GPR cards are the kind that you buy and set up yourself, like a gift card with fees. They range from competitively priced, no-frills cards to premium-priced celebrity cards, which are marketed as symbols of achievement or aspiration as often as they are advertised as financial tools. Beyond utility, the latter promise respect, empow-

---

[26] "Fact Sheet: Reforms to Protect American Credit Card Holders," *White House*, May 22, 2009. http://tinyurl.com/DROMWH.

[27] Jessica Silver-Greenberg and Stephanie Clifford, "Paid via Card, Workers Feel Sting of Fees," *New York Times*, June 30, 2013. http://tinyurl.com/DROMSilver12.

[28] See Ben Popken, "Why Money Launderers Love Prepaid Debit Cards," *The Consumerist*, May 25, 2011. http://tinyurl.com/DROMPopken; Adam Rust, "Prepaid Cards for Prisoners," *Bank Talk*, September 20, 2010. http://tinyurl.com/DROMRust.

erment and freedom. Of course, prepaid cards are not unique in this sense: everything we consume says something about who we are and what we believe. The problem with most celebrity cards is not simply that they don't deliver what's promised, but that they're designed to deliver exactly the opposite of what's promised, resulting in financial marginalization.

These cards can quickly extract money from their users. Consumers Union found many different types of fees for a range of prepaid cards. In addition to monthly fees, they found fees for activation, point-of-sale transaction, cash withdrawal, balance inquiry, transaction statements, customer service, bill payment, adding funds, dormancy, account closure, and overdraft.[29] Making matters worse, only a few of the fees charged by card issuers are disclosed prior to signing up for the card. Retail displays often contain only purchase prices and initial load amounts, and card company websites frequently require users to click on sign-up pages or registration forms in order to obtain fee information.

Consumer Action surveyed twenty-eight different prepaid cards and found that twenty of them carry a monthly maintenance fee, the highest being $14.95. Fees for out-of-network ATM withdrawals range from $1.95 to $3. A few cards charge users to reload money. Ten of the cards surveyed charge 50 cents to $2 to talk to a customer service agent and two of them charge 50 cents for automated help.

Like the worst practices in subprime mortgage lending, private student loans, and payday lending, the marketing and sales strategies of the celebrity prepaid card business are *predatory*; the best predators have a deep appreciation for the needs of their prey. "Well-banked" celebrities like Russell Simmons and Suze Orman are marketers of prepaid cards that target financially marginalized people. While their marketing suggests they are running charities, Simmons and Orman are managing private companies whose unequivocal objective is to profit from providing financial services to poor people. They deceptively present their enterprises as altruistic projects striving for collective emancipation (e.g., theapprovedcard.com). Yes, this is how capitalism works.

Electronic Benefit Transfer (EBT) cards and payroll cards

Over the past 15 years, the federal government and state governments have been gradually replacing paper benefits checks with Electronic Benefit Transfer (EBT) cards. For the unbanked, the shift to electronic payments means no check-cashing fees, less need

---

[29] Michael McCauley, "Consumers Union Report: Prepaid Cards Come with Long List of Fees and Weak Consumer Protections," *Consumers Union*, September 15, 2010. http://tinyurl.com/DROMMcCauley2.

to carry cash, faster payments, the ability to make purchases or pay bills electronically, and no ChexSystems screen (see *Chapter One* for information about ChexSystems). But overall, costs and benefits will vary depending on the fees and terms that apply to the particular prepaid card designated for your benefits program. These are administered by different federal and state government agencies, which contract with various prepaid card issuers. California and New Jersey are considered to have negotiated relatively good contracts for their unemployed workers, providing free and ample access to cash and transaction information with no penalty fees.[30] Tennessee workers, on the other hand, get slammed with the highest junk fees courtesy of JPMorgan Chase, the bank contracted to service that state's unemployment compensation (UC) prepaid card program.

For recipients of Social Security, Supplemental Security Income (SSI), or Veterans Affairs (VA) compensation, the Direct Express prepaid debit card has much lower fees than other prepaid cards and comes with strong consumer protections. Card accounts are insured by the Federal Deposit Insurance Company (FDIC) and are subject to federal consumer protection regulations (i.e., Regulation E).[31]

The prepaid card programs administered by the states to disburse UC, as well as Temporary Assistance to Needy Families (TANF) and food stamps (Supplemental Nutrition Assistance Program), are more problematic. They're generally less beneficial for recipients and more beneficial for banks and states. Forty states now use a prepaid card for paying some or all UC recipients. A survey by the National Consumer Law Center found significant shortcomings in fee structures, access to card information and payment options. Across the board, fees charged to benefit recipients are being used to cover the administrative costs of delivering UC benefits—in violation of federal law. Cards may charge ATM balance inquiry fees, denied transaction fees, $10 to $20 overdraft fees, and inactivity fees.[32] On top of this, card issuers such as Bank of America, Citibank, and JPMorgan Chase earn interchange fees—fees paid from one bank to another when accepting a transaction—as well as interest on the funds on deposit. Last year, card fees and ATM surcharges cost California welfare recipients over $17 million.[33]

---

[30] Lauren K. Saunders and Jillian McLaughlin, *Unemployment Compensation Prepaid Cards: States Can Deal Workers a Winning Hand by Discarding Junk Fees* (Washington, DC: National Consumer Law Center, 2011). http://tinyurl.com/DROMSaunders, 19.

[31] Consumer Financial Protection Bureau.

[32] Saunders and McLaughlin, 3.

[33] Monica Steinisch, "Governments Adopt Prepaid Cards for Benefits," *Consumer Action News*, April 2012. http://tinyurl.com/DROMSteinisch.

The bottom line: for those who have a bank account, prepaid cards offer little, if any, advantage over direct deposit. Benefit recipients with checking accounts will save money and time with direct deposit. Those who do not have that option—who lack access to a bank account or who live in one of the six states that have eliminated the direct deposit option—will be forced into the prepaid payroll card program(s) contracted to disburse your particular benefit(s). Since you have no choice about which card to use, familiarize yourself with the terms and fees that apply to the card designated for your program. This information should arrive in paper form with your EBT card. You can also look up the details of the particular prepaid payroll program online.

Survival strategies and resources

At a time when it's hard to use your own cash (if you're lucky enough to have any), prepaid cards can offer cash-like features such as anonymity, liquidity, and mobility. They'll also save you money compared with high-cost check cashing. Prepaid cards have also been sold as a way to reduce our reliance on the big banks. But Suze Orman probably came closer to the truth when she said her card is like having a bank in your pocket. Regardless of whose face is on the card, you can be sure somebody on Wall Street is getting their cut.

If you ultimately decide to get a prepaid card, you can visit nerdwallet.com to determine which is the least costly. Avoid cards with the most unnecessary fees and be aware of which fees are associated with the card you end up choosing. Be on the lookout for reloading fees, balance inquiry fees, and ATM cash withdrawal fees. When buying gas with a prepaid card, pay the attendant inside before you pump, otherwise the station may put up to a $75 hold on your balance for a few days. It is also important to read the card's privacy policy to make sure they aren't selling your personal information.[34]

For information on organizations that can help, go to the end of Chapter Eight.

RESOURCES
Articles and Books
General

- Candice Choi, "Reporter Spends Month Living Without a Bank, Finds Sky-High Fees," *Huffington Post*, December 11, 2010, http://tinyurl.com/DROMChoi.
- Sharon Hermanson and George Gaberlavage, *The Alternative Financial Services Industry*, AARP Public Policy Institute, August 2001, http://tinyurl.com/DROMHermanson.

---

[34] "Dos and Don'ts: Choosing and Using a Prepaid Card," *Consumer Action News*, Spring 2012. http://tinyurl.com/DROMCAN, 3.

- Dick Mendel, "Double Jeopardy: Why the Poor Pay More," in *Double Jeopardy: Advocasey Explores the High Cost of Being Poor*, 2005, http://tinyurl.com/DROMMendel2, 5–21.
- Gary Rivlin, *Broke USA: From Pawnshops to Poverty, Inc., How the Working Poor Became Big Business* (New York: HarperCollins, 2010).
- "The Truth about Immigrants' Banking Rights," *NEDAP*, http://tinyurl.com/DROMNEDAP03.
- John Ulzheimer, "Are Pawn Shops, Rent-to-Own and Other Loan Alternatives Worth It?" *Mint Life*, January 30, 2012, http://tinyurl.com/DROMUlzheimer.

Check–cashing outlets
- Jean Ann Fox and Patrick Woodall, "Cashed Out: Consumers Pay Steep Premium to 'Bank' at Check Cashing Outlets," *Consumer Federation of America*, November 2006, http://tinyurl.com/DROMFox.
- National Association of the State Treasurers Foundation: Tomorrow's Money for Young Adults, "Check-Cashing Stores," 2012, http://tinyurl.com/DROMTMYA.

Prepaid cards
- "Prepaid Cards: Loaded with Fees, Weak on Protections," *Consumer Reports*, March 2012, http://tinyurl.com/DROMConsumer02.
- Deyanira del Rio, "Perils of Prepaid Cards," *NEDAP*, December 22, 2010, http://tinyurl.com/DROMRio01.

REFERENCES

American Civil Liberties Union. "In for a Penny: The Rise of America's New Debtors' Prisons." October 2010. http://tinyurl.com/DROMACLU.

Bajaj, Vikas, and Ford Fessenden. "What's Behind the Race Gap?" *New York Times*, November 4, 2007. http://tinyurl.com/DROMBajaj.

Clinton, William, and Arnold Schwarzenegger. "Beyond Payday Loans." *Wall Street Journal*, January 24, 2008. http://tinyurl.com/DROMClinton.

Consumer Action News. "Dos and Don'ts: Choosing and Using a Prepaid Card." April 2012. http://tinyurl.com/DROMCAN2.

Consumer Financial Protection Bureau. *Electronic Funds Transfer (Regulation E)*. Washington, DC: GPO, 2012. http://tinyurl.com/DROMCFPB2.

Consumers International. "The Remittances Game of Chance: Playing with Loaded Dice?" January 2012. http://tinyurl.com/DROMConsumer03.

Credit Union National Association. "New Fin Lit Survey: 56% of U.S. Adults Don't Budget." April 4, 2012. http://tinyurl.com/DROMCUNA2.

Federal Deposit Insurance Corporation. *National Survey of Unbanked and Underbanked Households*. Washington, DC: GPO, 2009. http://tinyurl.com/DROMFDIC3.

Fox, Jean Ann, and Patrick Woodall. "Cashed Out: Consumers Pay Steep Premium to 'Bank' at Check Cashing Outlets." Washington, DC: Consumer Federation of America, 2006. http://tinyurl.com/DROMFox.

Haughney, Christine. "City's Poor Still Distrust Banks." *New York Times*, August 17, 2009.

http://tinyurl.com/DROMHaughney.

Insight Center for Community Economic Development. "The Racial Gap in Debt, Credit and Financial Services." June 2009. http://tinyurl.com/DROMICCED.

Massey, Douglas, and Nancy Denton. *American Apartheid: Segregation and the Making of the Underclass*. Cambridge, MA: Harvard University, 1993.

McCauley, Michael. "Consumers Union Report: Prepaid Cards Come With Long List of Fees and Weak Consumer Protections." *Consumers Union*, September 15, 2010. http://tinyurl.com/DROMMcCauley2.

National Association of the State Treasurers Foundation. "Check-Cashing Stores." Accessed March 26, 2013. http://tinyurl.com/DROMTMYA.

New, Catherine. "Prepaid Cards Rise in Popularity as More Americans Are Shut Out from Traditional Banks." *Huffington Post*, April 11, 2013. http://tinyurl.com/DROMNew.

Popken, Ben. "Why Money Launderers Love Prepaid Debit Cards." *The Consumerist*, May 25, 2011. http://tinyurl.com/DROMPopken.

Prager, Robin A. "Determinants of the Locations of Payday Lenders, Pawnshops and Check-Cashing Outlets." Washington, DC: Federal Reserve Board, 2009. http://tinyurl.com/DROMPrager.

Rivlin, Gary. "America's Poverty Tax." *Economic Hardship Reporting Project*, May 16, 2012. http://tinyurl.com/DROMRivlin.

Rust, Adam. "Prepaid Cards for Prisoners." *Bank Talk*, September 20, 2010. http://tinyurl.com/DROMRust.

Saunders, Lauren K., and Jillian McLaughlin. *Unemployment Compensation Prepaid Cards: States Can Deal Workers a Winning Hand by Discarding Junk Fees*. Washington, DC: National Consumer Law Center, 2011. http://tinyurl.com/DROMSaunders.

Schutte, Arjan. "Not Underbanked: Untapped. Underserved Spend $45B on Financial Services." *Inside the Underbanked*, November 2, 2011. http://tinyurl.com/DROMSchutte.

Silver-Greenberg, Jessica. "Welcome to Debtors' Prison, 2011 Edition." *Wall Street Journal*, March 16, 2011. http://tinyurl.com/DROMSilver3.

Silver-Greenberg, Jessica, and Stephanie Clifford. "Paid via Card, Workers Feel Sting of Fees." *New York Times*, June 30, 2013. http://tinyurl.com/DROM12.

Steinisch, Monica. "Governments Adopt Prepaid Cards for Benefits." *Consumer Action News*, April 2012. http://tinyurl.com/DROMSteinisch.

Tuttle, Brad. "Big-Box Banking: Why the Unbanked Are Cashing Checks at Walmart." *Time*, February 1, 2011. http://tinyurl.com/DROMTuttle.

U.S. Department of the Treasury. *Banking on Opportunity: A Scan of the Evolving Field of Bank on Initiatives*. Washington, DC: GPO, 2011. http://tinyurl.com/DROMNLCI.

Vissa, Preeti. "Debit Card Overdraft Fees: Reforms Welcomed but More Are Necessary." *The Greenlining Institute*, April 2010. http://tinyurl.com/DROMVissa.

White House Office of the Press Secretary. "Fact Sheet: Reforms to Protect American Credit Card Holders." May 22, 2009. http://tinyurl.com/DROMWH.

Work Permit. "U.S. Banks Help Immigrants Send Money Home." January 30, 2006. http://tinyurl.com/DROMWP.

EIGHT

FRINGE FINANCE CREDIT PRODUCTS AND SERVICES

CREDIT FOR THE PRECARIAT

"Respectable" banks and financiers have always tried to distance themselves from the taint of loan-sharking and other fringe financial services. For many people, non-bank lending has traditionally conjured up images of dilapidated storefronts on the edge of town, surrounded by vice and petty criminality. But if you're one of the twelve million Americans who took out a payday loan in the past year, it's more likely that you did it in a suburban strip mall or cyberspace. It's even possible that you got it from a bank—five large banks, including Wells Fargo, have begun to offer payday loans.[1] Although they seem to be worlds apart, in reality these banks and fringe finance are interconnected and overlapping; the biggest players in all segments of fringe finance are publicly traded, national corporations. Around 20% of all users of "alternative" financial services (AFS) also use traditional banks. And even fringe financial services earn profits for wealthy investors—via the very "asset-backed securities" that brought down the financial system not too long ago. Whether sourced in prime credit or subprime, student loans or pawn loans, the profits of our indebtedness flow to the wheelers and dealers on Wall Street.

But people are waking up to the bait-and-switch.

This chapter covers the debt traps encountered outside of the federally insured financial institutions: AFS credit products and services such as payday loans, pawnshop loans, auto-title loans, and "rent-to-own" agreements. Like traditional banks, these businesses provide ready access to cash and credit. However, their services are

---

[1] "Bank Payday Lending: Which Banks and Where?" *Center for Responsible Lending*, 2011. http://tinyurl.com/DROMCRL2. They call them "direct deposit loans," but don't be fooled; they're just as bad.

substantially more costly than those typically offered by major banks, and they frequently involve even more unfair, abusive, and deceptive practices. Unlike the transaction products from the previous chapter, these credit products involve lending money rather than charging people to access money they've already earned.

Enabled by friendly regulations at the local, state, and national levels, the poverty industry preys on the poor. For a long time the working poor have been its main target, but the Great Recession has supplied millions of new potential victims: people with busted credit, people who are desperate for cash, and people who have fallen from the ranks of the disappearing U.S. middle class. At a time of unprecedented inequality, poverty, and precarity, unprincipled money lenders are poised to make a killing; indebting people, possibly for life.

During the 1990s, deregulation tore through every segment of the U.S. financial system. Lending standards were loosened, increasing the availability of credit on Main Street as well as Malcolm X Boulevard. The resulting proliferation of high-cost subprime loans was celebrated as the "democratization of credit."[2] The rolling back of core financial consumer protections created an unprecedented opportunity for financial extraction—the prospect of making money off of people who have no money. On the fringes of finance, money comes easy, but debts are built to last.

Given that median net worth fell 38.8% from 2007 to 2010, rising demand for "Quick Cash, Few Questions Asked!" should come as no surprise.[3] When people have maxed out their credit cards and bank credit lines, they increasingly rely on AFS providers. Most AFS borrowers have tended to be the unbanked, which includes about 20% of Blacks and 20% of Latino/as. But today twenty-one million borrowers fall in the "underbanked" category, meaning they use AFS in combination with traditional banking services.[4]

About half of AFS users have incomes below the poverty line, but it's quite possible that many of the underbanked not too long ago qualified for *prime* mortgages and boasted incomes considerably higher than the national median. These are sure signs of precarity: insecure and unpredictable living conditions, which threaten both material and psychological welfare.

---

[2] Regina Austin, "Of Predatory Lending and the Democratization of Credit: Preserving the Social Safety Net of Informality in Small-Loan Transactions," *American University Law Review* 53, no. 1217, 2004. http://tinyurl.com/DROMAustin.

[3] Jesse Bricker et al., "Changes in U.S. Family Finances from 2007 to 2010: Evidence from the Survey of Consumer Finances," *Federal Reserve Bulletin* 98, no. 2, 2012. http://tinyurl.com/DROMBricker, 17.

[4] Federal Deposit Insurance Corporation, *National Survey of Unbanked and Underbanked Households* (Washington, DC: GPO, 2009). http://tinyurl.com/DROMFDIC3, 10.

Compared to traditional bank loans, fringe lending has a unique and peculiar set of tricks and traps. But like any extension of credit, it involves a set of expectations about the future. Lenders exploit borrowers' dreams. In fringe finance, the aspirations tend to be more immediate, like having a way to get to work, buying groceries for your kids, bailing your cousin out of jail, or treating your mother to lunch on her birthday.

PAYDAY LOANS:
HOW SHORT-TERM LOANS BECOME LONG-TERM DEBTS

Three-quarters of workers in the United States report living "paycheck-to-paycheck," defined as not having enough money saved up to cover six months' worth of expenses.[5] After years of insufficient income, we've drained our savings just to cover necessary expenses. Those of us who've never been able to accumulate savings already depend on short-term credit to get by. We've gone into debt in order to live.

In the early 1990s, there were fewer than two hundred payday lending stores in the United States. Today there are twenty-three thousand—more than there are McDonald's locations—making payday lending a $50 billion industry. The deregulation of interest rates at the end of the 1970s, which removed all caps and limits on interest, set the stage for the "rise of payday."[6] Today, fifteen large corporations, which together operate roughly half of all loan stores, dominate the industry. Of these fifteen, six are publicly traded companies: Advance America, Cash America, Dollar Financial, EZ Corp, First Cash Financial, and QC Holdings. Many of these companies also operate payday loan sites on the internet.

Having witnessed the rapid and socially destructive effects of these loans, fifteen states have renewed consumer protections and rolled back authorizations of payday loans, eliminating payday loan storefronts. Another eight states have limited the number of high-cost loans or renewals that lenders may offer. The reforms' effectiveness, however, has been limited by the advent of unlicensed online payday lending, which now comprises 35% of the market and allows for even more egregious practices.[7]

The appeal of payday loans is the flip side of the barriers to traditional banking: convenience, ease of transaction and few ques-

---

[5] "June 2013 Financial Security Index Charts," *Bankrate.com*, June 24, 2013. http://tinyurl.com/DROMBR2.

[6] "A Short History of Payday Lending Law," *Pew Charitable Trusts*, July 18, 2012. http://tinyurl.com/DROMPew3.

[7] Jessica Silver-Greenberg, "Major Banks Aid in Payday Loans Banned by States," *New York Times*, February 23, 2013. http://tinyurl.com/DROMSilver13.

tions asked. Payday loans are small-credit loans marketed as a quick and easy way to tide borrowers over until the next payday. However, the typical storefront payday loan leaves borrowers indebted for more than half of the year with an average of nine payday loan transactions at annual interest rates over 400%. And if you think that's bad, try 800–1,000% APR in the case of online payday loans.[8]

Make no mistake: payday lending is legal loan-sharking. The aim is to prolong the duration of debt in order to extract as many fees as possible; this is known as "churning," and doing this every two weeks makes up 75% of all payday loan volume. Typically, payday loan debt lasts for 212 days. Repeated payday loans result in $3.5 billion in fees each year.[9]

Payday loans are carefully structured to bring about this result. When you take out a payday loan (normally $100 to $500), you put down collateral (e.g., a postdated check or electronic access to your bank account) equal to the loan amount plus a fee ($15 to $35 per $100 borrowed). At the end of the typical two-week loan period, you either repay the total owed or renew the loan for another two weeks. Few borrowers (only 2%) are able to afford the entire payment, so instead they pay only the fee and renew the loan, which grows in size due to compound interest.[10] With every renewal, the amount owed grows bigger, making repayment ever more difficult. In the meantime, the lender goes on extracting fees every two weeks, and pretty soon, you've repaid the amount of the original loan (the principal), yet you are forced to continually renew the loan until you can repay the hugely inflated balance in one lump sum. According to the Federal Trade Commission, a number of online lenders obtain borrowers' bank account information in order to deposit funds and later withdraw the repayment, with a supposed one-time fee.[11] In actuality, withdrawals occur on multiple occasions, with fees each time. The FTC cites a typical example where someone borrowed $300 and, after the lender withdrew many times, the borrower was ultimately charged $975. With payday loans, the term "debt trap" takes on a whole new meaning.

The payday industry lobby group, which misleadingly calls itself the Community Financial Services Association (CFSA), tries to get some cover for its predatory behavior by warning, "Payday

---

[8] Nathalie Martin, "Online Payday Lenders Seek More Respect and Less Oversight: Call Them What You Like, They Are Still 1,000% Long-Term Loans," *Credit Slips*, July 26, 2012. http://tinyurl.com/DROMMartin.

[9] "Fast Facts: Payday Loans," *Center for Responsible Lending*. http://tinyurl.com/DROMCRL3.

[10] "Fast Facts: Payday Loans."

[11] "Online Payday Loans," *Federal Trade Commission*, February 2013. http://tinyurl.com/DROMFTC02.

advances should be used for short-term financial needs only, not as a long-term financial solution." In actuality, the vast majority of borrowers (69%) use payday loans for everyday expenses, just to get by. A recent Pew survey shows that only 16% of borrowers actually used them in emergencies.[12]

Still, twelve million Americans have used payday loans over the past year. And who can blame them? If you have lousy credit and need cash fast, a short-term, no-credit check loan seems like a lifeline, a feeling reinforced by ubiquitous advertising. No doubt, the loans offer short-term relief, but in exchange for long-term financial harm. According to the CFSA, "payday advance customers represent the heart of America's middle class."[13] This particular industry talking point has truth to it. The core market for payday loans are people with regular incomes and bank accounts who are expected to "secure" their loans with pay stubs, benefit stubs, or personal checks—that is, the growing class of the underbanked.

A recent survey of payday loan users conducted by the Pew Center finds that most borrowers are White, female, and from twenty-five to forty-four years old. However, certain groups disproportionately use payday loans: those without a four-year college degree, home renters, Blacks, those earning below $40,000 annually, and those who are separated or divorced.[14]

People of color are targeted by payday lenders and by fringe finance more broadly. Like other forms of AFS, the immense expansion of payday lending has overwhelmingly taken place in communities of color. In California, for example, Black people are more than twice as likely as Whites to live within a mile of at least one payday lender.[15] The CFSA and leading payday lenders have for years cultivated relationships with Black leaders and organizations—lawmakers, celebrities, elders of the Civil Rights struggle—as part of their lobbying and marketing campaigns.[16] "Just like they target minority groups to sell their products, they target minority groups to make their products look legitimate," says critic Keith Corbett, executive vice president of the Center for Responsible Lending.[17]

---

[12] Nick Bourke, Alex Horowitz, and Tara Roche, "Payday Lending in America: Who Borrows, Where They Borrow, and Why," *Pew Charitable Trusts*, July 2012. http://tinyurl.com/DROMBourke, 5.

[13] Daniel Brook, "Usury Country: Welcome to the Birthplace of Payday Lending," *Harper's*, April 2009. http://tinyurl.com/DROMBrook.

[14] Bourke, Horowitz, and Rouche, "Payday Lending in America," 5.

[15] William C. Apgar Jr. and Christopher E. Herbert, U.S. Department of Housing and Urban Development, *Subprime Lending and Alternative Financial Service Providers: A Literature Review and Empirical Analysis* (Washington, DC: GPO, 2006). http://tinyurl.com/DROMApgar, I-41.

[16] Stephanie Mencimer, "Civil Rights Groups Defending Predatory Lenders: Priceless," *Mother Jones*, August 1, 2008. http://tinyurl.com/DROMMencimer2.

[17] Mencimer, "Civil Rights Groups."

Backers of payday loans argue that payday lending represents the "democratization" of credit, but this claim is misleading at best. The kinds of credit payday lenders are selling leads only to cycles of ever-growing debt. It may provide access to credit, but for the majority of payday borrowers, it is a form of credit that makes their financial situation worse rather than better. Furthermore, "democratization" of finance, under any reasonable interpretation of the word, would mean enhanced ability to have a voice in one's financial situation. Extracting the little wealth that poor and middle-class people have with non-negotiable, misleading, barely legal, and intentionally unexplained contract terms does anything but.

Ways out

Alternative lending is an industry that profits from interest rates that used to be illegal, have always been illegal in just about every other country, and have been condemned in many faith traditions as usurious. Although limited, there are other options. Some community organizations and many credit unions offer small, short-term loans at much more favorable rates. While it is best to avoid payday lenders entirely, if you have outstanding debt with a payday lender, remember:[18]

- Payday loans are *unsecured* debt. This is any type of debt or general obligation that isn't collateralized by a lien on specific assets, like a house or car. In the event of default, the lender has no legal claim on your assets, no matter what the debt collectors say.
- Many people default, and expectations of that outcome are built into the business model. The typical "risk premium" (the cost increase required to compensate for credit risk) is so high that even with 15–20% default rates, payday lenders are *highly* profitable.
- In the event of default, lenders' only means of retaliation is to report the event to a credit reporting agency (CRAW). They commonly try to persuade borrowers that repayment of payday loans strengthens credit—the industry even funds research to peddle this myth—but it's not true. Most payday lenders don't report their loans at all to CRAs.

> **The following information comes from an anonymous former payday loan employee. It's perhaps a bit fanciful, but fun to imagine! And it points to the vulnerabilities of some of these seemingly powerful institutions.**

---

[18] The content in this section is adapted from: Anonymous payday loan insider, e-mail to author, July 29, 2012.

HOW TO DESTROY THE PAYDAY LOAN INDUSTRY

1. Identify a group of people planning to move between any of the four countries: United States, Canada, England, and Australia. Have each person take out a number of payday loans.

2. Once you get about $10,000 in loans, move the money to different bank accounts so the companies don't have access to it.

3. When you move to another country, your credit score will be a blank slate and you'll have free money to fight the system.

4. With about a thousand people willing to travel between the four countries, you can take out a few major international pay loan providers, like Wonga and Enova Financial.

PAWNSHOP AND AUTO-TITLE LOANS

A pawnshop loan is when a borrower gives property to a pawn-broker to secure a small loan. The loan is generally for half the item's value. If the borrower is able to repay the loan with interest by the due date—typically between one and three months—then the item can be retrieved.[19] The average pawnshop loan is for $70, and approximately one out of every five pawned items are not redeemed.[20] According to a survey by Think Finance, approximately one-quarter of eighteen- to thirty-four-year-olds who are un- or underbanked use pawnshops.[21] Because U.S. citizenship and regular income are not required for pawn loans, they are particularly appealing to undocumented immigrants and others who might have difficulty obtaining loans through traditional financial services. Ten states do not require any cap on monthly interest rates and forty states do not require the return of pawned items.[22]

An auto-title loan is a similar product to a pawnshop loan, but even more egregious—so much so that it is prohibited in thirty-one states.[23] A borrower in this case exchanges the title to their automo-

[19] "Give Me a Little Credit: Short-Term Alternatives to Payday Loans," *Cash Net USA*, March 2012. http://tinyurl.com/DROMCashNet2, 2.

[20] Sharon Hermanson and George Gaberlavage, *The Alternative Financial Services Industry* (Washington, DC: AARP Public Policy Institute, 2001). http://tinyurl.com/DROMHermanson, 2.

[21] "Millennials Use Alternative Financial Services Regardless of their Income Level," *Think Finance*, May 17, 2012. http://tinyurl.com/DROMThink.

[22] Signe-Mary McKernan, Caroline Ratcliffe, and Daniel Kuehn, *Prohibitions, Price Caps, and Disclosures: A Look at State Policies and Alternative Financial Product Use* (Washington, DC: The Urban Institute, 2010). http://tinyurl.com/DROMMcKernan, 6.

[23] "Title Loan: Don't Risk Losing Your Car," *Center for Responsible Lending*, 2011. http://tinyurl.

bile for cash. The vehicle can still be driven, however. Typically the loan is for about one-quarter of the vehicle's value. If it is not repaid with interest within thirty days, the lender could repossess the car or extend the loan for thirty more days and add further interest. When annualized, the rate of interest for title loans is in the triple digits, and often exceeds 900%.[24] LoanMax, an auto-title lender for which Reverend Al Sharpton, of all people, did a television commercial, says its average loan is $400.[25] Suppose you take out a $400 title loan from them at 360% APR—clearly a usurious interest rate yet far from the worst when it comes to these kinds of loans. Thirty days pass and you can't pay the $520 you now owe. Instead of repossessing your car, the merciful lender decides to renew the loan. And then again. And again. Title loans are renewed on average eight times per customer.[26] Therefore, within a typical timeframe, you may end up owing nearly three and a half times what you originally borrowed!

Having property repossessed and incurring further debt are the tragic yet unsurprising consequences of obtaining a loan through pawning. Despite state regulations such as APR caps, these alternative financial services are *inherently* predatory and cannot be modified to be substantially less harmful to borrowers. Pawnshop loans and auto-title loans should be avoided at all costs.

However, so long as viable alternatives remain inaccessible to those typically targeted by such institutions—traditionally low-income communities of color, but increasingly Millennials of all backgrounds[27]—the problem will remain and intensify. At the conclusion of this chapter, we contemplate a handful of suggestions for obtaining cash without having to be on the receiving end of predatory lending practices.

RENT-TO-OWN STORES

Rent-to-own (RTO) lenders offer appliances, electronics, and other items which, as the name suggests, people can eventually own. This is different from credit purchases where the customer immediately gains the title to the product. Aaron's and Rent-A-Center are two of the biggest such companies; their mascots are a self-proclaimed "lucky" dog and Hulk Hogan, respectively. On both company websites, product prices are not listed; you must provide some personal

---

com/DROMCRL.

[24] Hermanson and Gaberlavage, *The Alternative Financial Services Industry*, 7.

[25] Howard Karger, "Swimming with the Sharks," *AlterNet*, January 10, 2006. http://tinyurl.com/DROMKarger.

[26] "Title Loan: Don't Risk Losing Your Car."

[27] "Millennials Use Alternative Financial Services."

information, such as the last four digits of your Social Security number, in order to even receive a quote. Aaron's explicitly states that its stores are "strategically located in established working class neighborhoods and communities,"[28] which is a euphemism for *exploiting poor people and people of color*. This predation is also unabashedly reflected in RTO companies' own annual reports. Despite having fewer than half the number of customers as payday lenders, the RTO industry generates similar revenue.[29] What accounts for such high sales?

Unsurprisingly, there's a whole host of fees when using RTOs. Charges often include "security deposits, administrative fees, delivery charges, 'pick-up payment' charges, late fees, insurance charges, and liability damage waiver fees."[30] These costs are generally not revealed to customers until after the fact. Less than a third of U.S. states require disclosure of the total cost to own, and even then, many of these aforementioned charges are underestimated. With all of that on top of an average APR around 100%, consumers typically pay between two and five times more than if they had purchased the same item at a retail store. On average, RTO customers spend an extra $700 a year.[31] Failure to pay in full, or defaulting, results in the repossession of the product and loss of any money previously put toward the item.[32] Only eleven states require any cap whatsoever on the price of products or APR at RTO lenders.[33]

Items available at rent-to-own stores are readily available elsewhere, in some instances for one-fifth of the price; however, this may require saving up until one can afford the retail value rather than resorting to paid installments. If you need a computer, for example, consider borrowing one or using one at the library until you can pay for it at a not-so-predatory store. Avoiding RTO stores also might mean being willing to relinquish a bit of luxury and buy items secondhand. Either way, it ultimately beats the pitfalls of RTO lenders.

There are also many items that you can even obtain for free, although it may require waiting for just the right moment and taking time to do some research. Websites like the Freecycle Network (freecycle.org) and the free section on Craigslist (craigslist.org) have made this process much more convenient and accessible.

---

[28] Jim Hawkins, "Renting the Good Life," *William and Mary Law Review* 49, no. 6, 2008. http://tinyurl.com/DROMHawkins, 2059.

[29] Gary Rivlin, "America's Poverty Tax," *Economic Hardship Reporting Project*, May 16, 2012. http://tinyurl.com/DROMRivlin.

[30] Hermanson and Gaberlavage, *The Alternative Financial Services Industry*, 2.

[31] Rivlin, "America's Poverty Tax."

[32] John Ulzheimer, "Are Pawn Shops, Rent-to-Own and Other Loan Alternatives Worth It?" *Mint Life*, January 30, 2012. http://tinyurl.com/DROMUlzheimer.

[33] McKernan, Ratcliffe, and Kuehn, *Prohibitions, Price Caps, and Disclosures*, 6.

SURVIVAL STRATEGIES

Throughout the last two chapters, several strategies have been raised for avoiding or beating the various institutions that offer "alternative" financial services. These chapters have been written with the understanding that viable alternatives are hard to come by in many areas. In the course of doing this research, we have too often found that the recommended alternative to one segment of the fringe finance industry is often just to turn to a different segment.

The most important point is that we have to work together toward rendering all such institutions obsolete, toward a situation where people can have basic needs met without immense risk or sacrifice. *In the meantime, we need to be able to sustain ourselves.* Notably, at least one-quarter of unbanked households in the United States do not use any fringe finance products or services.[34] That is, over two million households are getting by without a checking account, without subprime loans, without cashing checks at CCOs, and without pawning their items. These households in particular have experiences worth sharing and learning from. In Chapter Eleven, we will discuss some strategies for decreasing our personal and collective dependency on these institutions.

The unbanked and underbanked can in certain instances avoid subprime loans. This may mean asking to borrow from friends or family, seeking emergency community assistance, and, if an option, asking your employer for advanced payment. Selling unwanted items on Craigslist or at thrift stores and consignment shops is a more reliable source of cash than pawning. Moreover, it's important to consider what you need the money for in the first place. Is there an alternative at a cheaper price, or perhaps a free alternative? Will buying something secondhand suffice? Is it worth obtaining something immediately if it means paying more?

While these questions are important for individuals to contemplate in order to avoid or at least minimize the harm done by AFS providers, we must go deeper. *The Debt Resisters' Operations Manual*, after all, is about *collective* action and radical transformation, not deepening personal sacrifice.

It is more difficult to point to an emerging movement around fringe finance than other aspects of financial capital outlined in this manual. Even so, some communities are beginning to take action in ways that might illuminate the contours of a possible social movement. In Dallas, communities have organized to enact local ordinances curbing payday lending. There has been a grassroots campaign in Sunset Park, Brooklyn, to pressure money transmitters to take

---

[34] Federal Deposit Insurance Company, *National Survey of Unbanked and Underbanked Households*, 29.

on more just practices. Community organizers in Jackson Heights, Queens, are working to establish a community development credit union in a largely immigrant neighborhood. While these campaigns are locally focused, and aim primarily for inclusion into mainstream banking and credit or to regulate the most egregious aspects of fringe finance, they indicate that communities affected by fringe finance are increasingly ready to take political action and that victories, albeit small for now, are possible. How would these local experiences translate into a national movement? What strategies would move beyond demands for inclusion and regulation, toward addressing the root causes of poverty and building sustainable alternatives?

While they may be designated as "fringe," the payday loan companies, the rent-to-own stores, the pawnshops, and the check-cashing outlets are all central to the debt landscape we are describing in this manual. We must come together to work toward the eradication of these venal institutions while creating better ways of obtaining what we need.

RESOURCES
Websites
Financial justice research and advocacy for low–income and underrepresented communities

• Center for Responsible Lending (responsiblelending.org)
• Consumer Action (consumer-action.org)
• The Consumerist (consumerist.com)
• Consumers Union—Defend Your Dollars (defendyourdollars.org)
• LawHelp.org
• National Consumer Law Center (nclc.org)
• Neighborhood Economic Development Advocacy Project (NYC) (nedap.org)

For filing complaints and reading complaints of other consumers

• Consumer Protection Financial Bureau (consumerfinance.gov/complaint)
• Ripoff Report (ripoffreport.com)

Articles and Books
General

• Candice Choi, "Reporter Spends Month Living Without a Bank, Finds Sky-High Fees," *Huffington Post*, December 11, 2010, http://tinyurl.com/DROMChoi.
• Dick Mendel, "Double Jeopardy: Why the Poor Pay More," in *Double Jeopardy: Advocasey Explores the High Cost of Being Poor*, 2005, http://tinyurl.com/DROM-Mendel2, 5–21.
• Gary Rivlin, *Broke USA: From Pawnshops to Poverty, Inc., How the Working Poor Became Big Business* (New York: HarperCollins, 2010).

- "The Truth about Immigrants' Banking Rights," *NEDAP*, http://tinyurl.com/DROMNEDAP03.

Payday loans

- Regina Austin, "Of Predatory Lending and the Democratization of Credit: Preserving the Social Safety Net of Informality in Small-Loan Transactions," *American University Law Review* 53, no. 1217, (2004) http://tinyurl.com/DROMAustin.
- Nick Bourke, Alex Horowitz, and Tara Roche, "Payday Lending in America: Who Borrows, Where They Borrow, and Why," *Pew Charitable Trusts*, July 2012, http://tinyurl.com/DROMBourke.
- Daniel Brook, "Usury Country: Welcome to the Birthplace of Payday Lending," *Harper's*, April 2009, http://tinyurl.com/DROMBrook.
- "Give Me a Little Credit: Short-Term Alternatives to Payday Loans," *Cash Net USA*, March 2012, http://tinyurl.com/DROMCashNet2.
- Stephanie Mencimer, "Civil Rights Groups Defending Predatory Lenders: Priceless," *Mother Jones*, August 1, 2008, http://tinyurl.com/DROMMencimer2.

Pawnshop and auto–title loans

- Christopher Neiger, "Why Car Title Loans Are a Bad Idea," *CNN*, October 8, 2008, http://tinyurl.com/DROMNeiger2.
- Valerie Williams, "Auto Title Loans: Are They the Best Alternative for Fast Cash?" *Suite 101*, September 2, 2010, http://tinyurl.com/DROMWilliams.

Rent–to–own stores

"Alternatives to Rent-to-Own Shopping," *Consumer Reports*, June 2011, http://tinyurl.com/DROMConsumer01.

REFERENCES

Apgar Jr., William C., and Christopher E. Herbert. *Subprime Lending and Alternative Financial Service Providers: A Literature Review and Empirical Analysis*. Washington, DC: U.S. Department of Housing and Urban Development, 2006, http://tinyurl.com/DROMApgar.

Austin, Regina. "Of Predatory Lending and the Democratization of Credit: Preserving the Social Safety Net of Informality in Small-Loan Transactions." *American University Law Review* 53, no. 6 (2004): 1217–1257. http://tinyurl.com/DROMAustin.

Bankrate. "June 2013 Financial Security Index Charts." June 24, 2013. http://tinyurl.com/DROMBR2.

Bourke, Nick, Alex Horowitz, and Tara Roche. "Payday Lending in America: Who Borrows, Where They Borrow, and Why." *Pew Charitable Trusts*, July 2012. http://tinyurl.com/DROMBourke.

Bricker, Jesse, Arthur B. Kennickell, Kevin B. Moore, and John Sabelhaus. "Changes in U.S. Family Finances from 2007 to 2010: Evidence from the Survey of

Consumer Finances." *Federal Reserve Bulletin* 98, no. 2 (2012). http://tinyurl.com/DROMBricker.

Brook, Daniel. "Usury Country: Welcome to the Birthplace of Payday Lending." *Harper's*, April 2009. http://tinyurl.com/DROMBrook.

Cash Net USA. "Give Me a Little Credit: Short-Term Alternatives to Payday Loans." March 2012. http://tinyurl.com/DROMCashNet2.

Center for Responsible Lending. "Bank Payday Lending: Which Banks and Where?" Accessed March 26, 2013. http://tinyurl.com/DROMCRL2.

Center for Responsible Lending. "Fast Facts: Payday Loans." Accessed March 26, 2013. http://tinyurl.com/DROMCRL3.

Center for Responsible Lending. "Title Loan: Don't Risk Losing Your Car." Accessed March 26, 2013. http://tinyurl.com/DROMCRL.

Federal Deposit Insurance Corporation. *National Survey of Unbanked and Underbanked Households.* Washington, DC: GPO, 2009. http://tinyurl.com/DROMFDIC3.

Federal Trade Commission. "Online Payday Loans." February 2013. http://tiny url.com/DROMFTC02.

Hawkins, Jim. "Renting the Good Life." *William and Mary Law Review* 49, no. 6 (2008): 2041–2117. http://tinyurl.com/DROMHawkins.

Hermanson, Sharon, and George Gaberlavage. *The Alternative Financial Services Industry.* Washington, DC: AARP Public Policy Institute, 2001. http://tinyurl.com/DROMHermanson.

Karger, Howard. "Swimming with the Sharks." *AlterNet*, January 10, 2006. http://tinyurl.com/DROMKarger.

Martin, Nathalie. "Online Payday Lenders Seek More Respect and Less Oversight: Call Them What You Like, They Are Still 1,000% Long-Term Loans." *Credit Slips*, July 26, 2012. http://tinyurl.com/DROMMartin.

McKernan, Signe-Mary, Caroline Ratcliffe, and Daniel Kuehn. "Prohibitions, Price Caps, and Disclosures: A Look at State Policies and Alternative Financial Product Use." *The Urban Institute*, October 21, 2010. http://tinyurl.com/DROMMcKernan.

Mencimer, Stephanie. "Civil Rights Groups Defending Predatory Lenders: Priceless." *Mother Jones*, August 1, 2008. http://tinyurl.com/DROMMencimer2.

Pew Charitable Trusts. "A Short History of Payday Lending Law." July 18, 2012. http://tinyurl.com/DROMPew3.

Rivlin, Gary. "America's Poverty Tax." *Economic Hardship Reporting Project*, May 16, 2012. http://tinyurl.com/DROMRivlin.

Silver-Greenberg, Jessica. "Major Banks Aid in Payday Loans Banned by States." *New York Times*, February 23, 2013. http://tinyurl.com/DROMSilver13.

Think Finance. "Millennials Use Alternative Financial Services Regardless of Their Income Level." May 17, 2012. http://tinyurl.com/DROMThink.

Ulzheimer, John. "Are Pawn Shops, Rent-to-Own and Other Loan Alternatives Worth It?" *Mint Life*, January 30, 2012. http://tinyurl.com/DROMUlzheimer.

NINE

DEBT COLLECTION

DON'T FEED THE VULTURES

Getting contacted by a debt collector can rank among one of the worst experiences of everyday life. And it happens over a billion times each year in the United States, according to industry estimates.[1] Debt collection has become a complex global industry, reliant on strong-arm tactics including harassing phone calls and threats that are often illegal. The coercion runs along a spectrum from moral persuasion to threats of violence, and increasingly involves institutions such as the courts and law enforcement. Given the complexity of debt collection laws and regulations that vary from state to state, there are hundreds of ways a debt collector can engage in illegal practices. It's important to know your rights and to record abusive and illegal practices. In many cases, your debt can be erased (due to collectors' misconduct) or reduced. In some cases, you might even have the right to sue for damages.

Debt collectors count on you to not do your homework. They count on you to be an easy mark and to be overwhelmed by bureaucracy, harassment, and shame. Our current economic downturn only amplifies the problem. Most people have less money and more debt. Debt collectors themselves are making less money per account (it's highly labor intensive with collectors making contact with only about fifteen out of two hundred or more targets),[2] causing more aggressive and increasingly illegal tactics. Even if collectors do not engage in activities and techniques that are technically illegal, they are likely to use intentionally deceptive practices.

In this chapter we briefly describe some of the laws around debt collection, the different ways debt is collected, who is hurt most by the debt collection industry, and what people can do to protect themselves,

---

[1] U.S. Government Accountability Office, *Credit Cards: Fair Debt Collection Practices Act Could Better Reflect the Evolving Debt Collection Marketplace and Use of Technology* (Washington, DC: GPO, 2009). http://tinyurl.com/DROMGAO1, 35.

[2] Patrick Sahr, "Debt and Its Discontents: The Depressing World of Collections, Part One," *Naked Capitalism*, August 27, 2012. http://tinyurl.com/DROMSahr.

their families, and their communities. While this chapter can't tell you everything you need to know to handle your specific situation, it provides a basic outline of how the debt collection industry works and points you to resources that can help you fight this system that wants you to fail.

WHAT IS A COLLECTION AGENCY AND WHY ARE THEY CALLING YOU?

A collection agency often works on behalf of an original creditor (OC). An OC can be a department store, a credit card company, or a hospital—basically wherever you open a line of credit. When bills go unpaid, the OC contracts with collection agencies or third-party debt collectors to collect the debt. Some collection agencies take a commission of every debt they collect on behalf of the OC, while other agencies lease or buy your debt outright from the OC after a period of non-payment. But the collection agency doesn't pay full price. In fact, it will almost certainly pay much less, usually 2–25% of the debt's face value. So if you owe $1,000, the collection agency might pay $150 for the right to collect that $1,000 from you. They then attempt to collect the full $1,000, and more if fees are attached, making a hefty profit in the end.

In short, the collection agency is essentially buying the right to take a gamble on your debt—debt that the OC may have already charged off. But they aren't just buying *your* debt. They are buying the debts of hundreds, even thousands, of people like you at a time. For their gamble to pay off, they need to convince only a small minority of consumers—through legal means or otherwise—to pay. The collection agency might also tack on additional late fees and interest all while harassing you by phone and by mail to collect.

The debt collection machine

The debt collection industry—also known as "accounts receivable management"—is financed by Wall Street and closely tied to credit card issuers and other lenders such as collection companies, offshore call centers, big law firms, and debt speculators. Each year, over three hundred thousand debt collectors amass more than $50 billion in debt, profiting over $10 billion total.[3] The collection industry has expanded significantly in recent years, shadowing the rise of consumer credit. From 2000 until the end of 2010, commercial banks *doubled* the total amount of consumer loans.[4] Should consumers

---

[3] Richard M. Alderman, "The Fair Debt Collection Practices Act Meets Arbitration: Non-Parties and Arbitration," *Loyola Consumer Law Review* 24, no. 4, 2012. http://tinyurl.com/DROM Alderman, 588.

[4] Board of Governors of the Federal Reserve System, "Consumer Loans, All Commercial

default, the debt collection industry is ready. The number of U.S. consumers subject to third-party debt collectors has doubled since 2000. Ten years ago, debt collectors pursued one in fourteen people in the United States; today, it's one in seven.[5] This includes many people who fell victim to illness, scams, divorce, or unemployment—even death. "Dead people are the newest frontier in debt collecting, and one of the healthiest parts of the industry," the *New York Times* reported in 2009.[6] Collection agencies like DCM Services are taking advantage of improved database technology to track down the kin of deceased debtors and pressure them to pay, even though they are not legally obligated to assume the debt of a spouse, sibling, or parent.[7]

Credit card debt and other small loans are bought and sold like other debt obligations, e.g., mortgages and student loans, as part of big portfolios. The biggest are managed by the largest debt buyers. The largest collection agency, NCO Group, is owned by the nation's biggest bank, JPMorgan Chase. JPMorgan Chase and other big banks supply enormous lines of credit to the leading debt buyers in order to "generate cash flow." Creditors profit at your expense on multiple levels, creating a dependent and exploitative relationship.

Today, debt collectors increasingly rely on the civil court system and local law enforcement to secure legal judgments to garnish wages, freeze bank accounts, and seize property. According to a report by the National Consumer Law Center, "Often, the grab extends to people who have already repaid or never owed the debts—parents, children, people with similar names, victims of identity theft. Harassment, threats, and even jail become tools of the collection trade."[8] Hundreds of district attorneys across the country have partnered with collectors in what amounts to a government-sponsored shakedown, lending out their official letterhead to give the impression that failure to pay up could lead to criminal charges. The collectors charge extra fees on top of the original payment, which typically go back to the DA's office.[9]

Banks," *Federal Reserve Bank of St. Louis*, 2013. http://tinyurl.com/DROMFed3.

[5] "Quarterly Report on Household Debt and Credit," *Federal Reserve Bank of New York*, November 2012. http://tinyurl.com/DROMFedNY, 15.

[6] David Streitfeld, "You're Dead? That Won't Stop the Debt Collector," *New York Times*, March 4, 2009. http://tinyurl.com/DROMStreitfeld.

[7] Jessica Silver-Greenberg, "For the Families of Some Debtors, Death Offers No Respite," *Wall Street Journal*, December 3, 2011. http://tinyurl.com/DROMSilver7.

[8] Rick Jurgens and Robert J. Hobbs, "The Debt Machine: How the Collection Industry Hounds Consumers and Overwhelms Courts," *National Consumer Law Center*, July 2010. http://tinyurl.com/DROMJurgens, 1.

[9] Jessica Silver-Greenberg, "In Prosecutors, Debt Collectors Find a Partner," *New York Times*, September 16, 2012. http://tinyurl.com/DROMSilver8.

How a collection agency thinks

It is key to understand how collection agencies think if you want to know how to best engage with them.[10] First, it is usually pointless to go back and contact the original creditor. The OC almost certainly has an agreement with the collection agency that prevents them from negotiating directly with you. Collectors often receive little training beyond, "Here's your desk, your phone, and your computer—now go make us some money." Many collection agency workers' pay is tied to a monthly quota of how many debts they collect, and it's common for collectors to employ more aggressive and illegal tactics toward the end of the month. Because they work on monthly commission, individual collectors are also most likely to pursue the people with the largest debts and the people who seem most likely to pay. Collectors usually start with a relatively low base pay and, at larger agencies, their bonus is usually 2% of the overall debt they collected, giving them an incentive to collect more debt by any means necessary.[11]

Remember that you are the most important variable to a collection agent. To quote one message board familiar with their tactics,

> It is *your* fears, *your* fantasies . . . *your* partial understanding of the truth that empowers the third-party debt collectors and each of these is a weapon to be used against you. . . . By carefully stating half-truths and letting your imagination run away the third-party debt collector can bend your mind so that it sees what truths the third-party debt collector wants it to see.[12]

There are two common types of collection agencies: letter writers—who write letters directing you back to the OC to make your payment—and just plain "collection agencies"—who require you to pay them directly so they can get their commission from the OC or make back the money they've already paid to buy your debt. Both must include a mini-Miranda (a required statement from the collectors stating they're collecting a debt and any information gathered will be used to collect that debt) in their letters or read aloud during their phone calls. If they do not, you may have grounds to sue.

If your first contact with a collection agency is over the phone, the mini-Miranda warning should sound something like this:

---

[10] "The Psychology of Collections," *Professional Recovery Personnel, Inc.*. http://tinyurl.com/DROMPRP.

[11] Sahr, "Debt and Its Discontents."

[12] "Understanding Collection Agencies," *Debtor Boards*, October 14, 2005. http://tinyurl.com/DROMDB.

> Hello, I am [name of collector]. I am [or "this office is"] a debt collec-
> tor representing [creditor]. Information obtained during the course of
> this call will be used for the purpose of collecting the debt.

If your first contact with the collection agency is via mail, the
mini-Miranda should look something like this:

> This correspondence is an attempt to collect a debt. Any information
> obtained will be used for that purpose. Unless within thirty days of
> your receipt of this notice, you notify us that you dispute the validity
> of this debt, it will be assumed to be correct. If you notify this office
> within thirty days that you dispute the validity of the debt, we will
> obtain verification of the debt or a copy of the judgment. If you
> request it within thirty days, we will provide you with the name and
> address of the original creditor (if different from the current creditor).

Do not ignore the call or letter. The biggest mistake people make when
they get letters or calls from debt collection agencies is to ignore them
and hope they will go away. Because you have thirty days to contest
the debt, you *must* act immediately. If you ignore the contact, you are
by default agreeing that the debt is legitimate. If it is legal in your
state, you can record your conversations and create a log of how often
they contact you. If you are uncertain about your state's laws, consult-
ing a lawyer would be wise.

Regardless of whether the debt is "legitimate" or not:

1. Write a letter to the office of the collection agency or attorney and state
   that you (a) dispute the bill, and that (b) you want a full accounting of the
   monies claimed to be owed (validation of debts). The Fair Debt Collections Practices Act of 1996 (FDCPA) requires they contact the original
   creditor to secure full account detail. Without a confirmed accounting of
   this debt, they cannot return to the collection process.[13]
2. In responding to a call, advise the collector that (a) you are disputing the
   debt and that you are doing so in writing to their offices, and that (b) you
   do not want to receive a call from this agency at your place of work and
   that they can only contact at your home (or on your cell phone if you
   don't have a home telephone) between the hours of X and Y.

There's a chance that you may not hear back. Remember, the
collection agency is most likely to pursue the people they think are
most likely to pay. You may have to continue to write to them, and
even threaten to sue. (*See Appendix D for sample letters.*)

---

[13] "Debt Settlement Letters and Sample Letters on Debt and Credit," *Debt Consolidation Care.*
http://tinyurl.com/DROMDCC.

SOME IMPORTANT THINGS TO KNOW
The Consumer Financial Protection Bureau

Over the past year, the newly established Consumer Financial Protection Bureau (CFPB) has set their sights on the debt collection industry. They will oversee three types of debt collectors: companies buying debt that other companies have given up on collecting, collectors going after debt on behalf of an original creditor, and companies litigating to collect debt.[14] The CFPB supervises 175 of the 4,500 companies officially classified as debt collectors. Although those companies take in about 63% of the industry's account receipts, they represent a small percentage of the industry itself. The bureau's rules only cover companies that have over $10 million in annual receipts, leaving smaller companies virtually free from these regulations. Because these larger companies tend to work with larger creditors (who have stricter requirements), they are often not the ones consumers have to worry about.[15] The CFPB is also looking to regulate collectors who use social media sites to track down and harass debtors.[16] There isn't much information on the CFPB because it is so new, but debtors of all stripes should be aware of the organization and keep up to date with its development.

Statute of limitations on debt

In every state there is a statute of limitations (SOL) for outstanding debts—a limit on the number of years in which a creditor may attempt to pursue payment. (It should be noted, however, that federal student loans, child support obligations, and income taxes in certain states like California do *not* have a statute of limitations.) Each state is different, so you should check.[17] Kentucky and Ohio have extremely long periods (fifteen years for written debt agreements) while Mississippi and North Carolina have much shorter periods (three years for written debt agreements). In most states, however, debt collectors can still attempt to collect debt after the SOL expires. Even after it expires, courts may award judgments against you if you fail to raise the SOL as a defense. Ordinarily it is up to the person being sued to point out that the SOL has expired. If there is a dispute about which state's laws apply, you can be sure that the collection agency will argue for the state with the longer period.

---

[14] Martha C. White, "CFPB Takes on Debt Collectors with New Oversight," *Time*, November 1, 2012. http://tinyurl.com/DROMWhite.

[15] Stephanie Eidelman, "Large Debt Collectors Now under Thumb of CFPB," *Forbes*, October 24, 2012. http://tinyurl.com/DROMEidelman.

[16] Carter Dougherty, "Debt Collectors Posing as Facebook Friends Spur Watchdogs," *Bloomberg*, January 24, 2013. http://tinyurl.com/DROMDougherty.

[17] LaToya Irby, "State-by-State List of Statute of Limitations on Debt," *About.com*. http://tinyurl.com/DROMIrby.

When does the SOL clock start?

The SOL clock starts running on the date of the last activity of your account. This is often the date of your last payment but—and this is key—it may also be the date when you entered into a payment agreement or simply acknowledged liability for the debt. This is why it is important to always contest liability. If your debt is beyond the SOL you can contest the debt on these grounds and, should you want to play offense, you can also attempt to set up the collection agency for an FDCPA violation and hit them with a lawsuit.

Know your FDCPA violations

Even if your debt falls within the SOL, there is a good chance the debt collector will engage in abusive or deceptive practices that are illegal under the FDCPA, but it is up to you to know your rights, be vigilant, and document any violations. Violations are grounds for dismissing debt and related lawsuits. Not all collectors are subject to the FDCPA's rules, however. Third party collectors, debt buyers, and law firms must comply with the FDCPA, but in-house collectors, or creditors who are trying to collect their *own* debts, do not have to follow the FDCPA.

Some common FDCPA violations

There are countless ways collectors violate the FDCPA and the longer you engage with a debt collector or agency (while continuing to dispute the debt), the greater the chance you will catch them in the act. Unfortunately (or fortunately if you're a debt collector) only a small fraction of violations go reported. You do not need a lawyer to contest debt obligations or report FDCPA violations; you can take action on your own and even win damages. If you decide to sue a collector, you must do so within one year from the date the law was violated. If you win, you could win up to $1,000 on top of any wages or reimbursements.[18]

Due to lax regulations and a lack of will to enforce them, debt collectors routinely break the law by verbally abusing and threatening debtors. Some debt collectors have "embedded" themselves in hospitals, pretending to be hospital employees and approaching people when they're at their most vulnerable. Jessica Silver-Greenberg writes, "To patients, the debt collectors may look indistinguishable from hospital employees, may demand they pay outstanding bills and may discourage them from seeking emergency care at all, even using scripts like those in collection boiler rooms."[19]

---

[18] "Debt Collection FAQs: A Guide for Consumers," *Federal Trade Commission*, February 2009. http://tinyurl.com/DROMFTC4, 4.

[19] Jessica Silver-Greenberg, "Debt Collector Is Faulted for Tough Tactics in Hospital," *New York Times*, April 24, 2012. http://tinyurl.com/DROMSilver6.

Debt collectors also call pretending to be police officers and claim that they have a warrant to arrest a debtor if they don't pay up. Collectors will often continually harass people for debts that they don't owe, have already paid, or have already been dismissed in court. Collectors frequently target the wrong person, mistaking one person for someone else with the same or similar name. Debt collectors will lie and say that they are calling on behalf of debt relief agencies, learn all about a debtor's situation and collect all of their personal information and then use it against them. Collectors have been known to illegally call employers and inform them of employees' debts. In the most extreme cases, debt collectors have made disturbing threats to seriously harm debtors and their families.[20] Although illegal, these tactics are widespread.

Even debt collectors who follow the law can legally mislead you or trick you in other ways. Credit card companies have started data-mining cardholder's purchases and using software to create psychological profiles of them. These profiles are then used by debt collectors to psychologically manipulate debtors to pay more than they have to, including artificial late fees that would otherwise have been waived. This tactic, although manipulative and immoral, is completely legal. After using a psychological profile to swindle one debtor out of an additional $2,000, debt collector Rudy Santana explained, "It's all about getting inside their heads and understanding what they need to hear."[21]

Debt buyers also contract with specialized collection law firms to collect on debts. In recent years, these firms have swamped small claims and other state courts, filing "mass-produced" lawsuits, mirroring reckless practices in the mortgage market, such as "robo-signing." Despite the fact that these suits typically lack proper documentation, most result in judgments, as the proceedings are skewed against debtors. If consumers are lucky enough to be properly "served," or notified of the lawsuits filed against them, many of them will not even have access to civil courts due to the forced arbitration clauses in millions of credit card and other consumer loan contracts. These lawsuits pay little regard to accuracy. Noach Dear, a civil court judge in Brooklyn who has presided over as many as one hundred credit card lawsuit cases in one day, estimates that "roughly 90 percent of the credit card lawsuits are flawed and can't prove the person owes the debt."[22]

---

[20] "As a Result of FTC Action, Two Defendants in Abusive Debt Collection Case Are Banned from the Industry, Will Surrender Assets," *Federal Trade Commission*, March 15, 2012. http://tinyurl.com/DROMFTC3.

[21] Charles Duhigg, "What Does Your Credit-Card Company Know about You?" *New York Times*, May 12, 2009. http://tinyurl.com/DROMDuhigg.

[22] Jessica Silver-Greenberg, "Problems Riddle Moves to Collect Credit Card Debt," *New York Times*, August 12, 2012. http://tinyurl.com/DROMSilver9.

Not all hope is lost, though. If you suspect you've fallen victim to "robo-signing," you can do a few things to fight back. First, you or an attorney should read the complaint and supporting documents carefully for any omissions, errors, or deceptions that could help you win. If your state requires debt buyers to be licensed, check whether the debt buyer is licensed. Suing without a license may constitute a violation of the FDCPA. You should also check to see if the plaintiff's name is the same party mentioned in the supporting documents and if they have proof of the underlying contract. Often a contract is not even attached to the complaint and, if it is, it's often photocopied and illegible. Carefully scrutinize the affidavit and make sure the affiant (the person who swears to the affidavit) has not been charged with malpractice before your case. If you look up the affiant's signature online and the signature in front of you does not match, you may have grounds for contestation. The burden of proof is with the affiant and the collectors, so make sure they can prove they know your case front to back. If they don't, you may be able to have the case dropped.[23]

KNOW YOUR RIGHTS

With all of this in mind, it's important to know what debt collectors legally can and can't do. Below is a basic list to help protect you:

- A debt collector can only call a third party once about you unless it believes the third party gave it false information the first time.
- Contacting you before 8:00 a.m. or after 9:00 p.m. is illegal.
- You must tell a collector not to contact you at work or by phone by sending them a cease and desist letter (*see Appendix D, sample letter #2*). You must send this certified mail and keep a copy for yourself so you have proof of receipt. If the collection agency contacts you again, other than to advise you of their intent to take action, then they are violating the FDCPA.
- It is your right not to speak with debt collectors; however, that doesn't cancel the debt.
- A debt collector cannot sell a debt to another collection agency knowing that it has expired (*see SOL*) or is in dispute.
- A debt collector may try to lead you to believe that you have no grounds for requesting a "validation of debt" (*see Appendix D, sample letter #1*).
- A debt collector may try to represent themselves as an attorney or law firm even if they are actually not an attorney or law firm. Regardless, collection attorneys have to follow the FDCPA just like collection agencies.
- If a debt collector sends an initial notice advising you of your right to a validation of debt, then they cannot demand payment within the next thirty days.

---

[23] Peter A. Holland, "Defending Junk-Debt-Buyer Lawsuits," *Clearinghouse Review Journal of Poverty Law and Policy* 46, no. 1–2, 2012. http://tinyurl.com/DROMHolland, 17.

- A collector cannot call your job and tell your HR department that they need your work information (wages, schedule) unless a valid suit was filed by them and tried in a court of law with a judgment in their favor. Until this happens (if it happens), they cannot contact your HR department or place of work, even if they claim to be looking for information to sue you. It is legal, however, for credit rating agencies to buy your personal data (employment and salary records) and sell it to debt collectors.[24]

- It is not unheard of for debt collectors to use fake case numbers and fake lawyers to scare an alleged debtor into paying. This is in clear violation of the FDCPA.

- The mini-Miranda (*see above*) should be on each and every communication you get from a debt collector.

- A collector is not allowed to reveal information about the envelope's contents on the outside of the envelope for others to see. Words such as "past due" or "collections" are in clear violation of the FDCPA.

- A debt collector cannot impersonate a law officer or claim they can throw you in jail for not paying your alleged debt.

THE SOCIAL IMPACT OF THE COLLECTION INDUSTRY

Hopefully you don't ever see a lawsuit, but if you do, you should know what you can expect and its implications on you and society at large. Plaintiffs file lawsuits because they assume: (1) the vast majority of consumers will not show up or contest lawsuits, and (2) a majority of judges will award a default judgment in the vast majority of cases, based often on inaccurate documents.[25] It is best that you do *not* ignore the lawsuit and educate yourself. Unfortunately, due to intimidation and illegal tactics, collectors and creditors often force debtors into the criminal justice system. These practices most directly affect working-class people and people of color, and they contribute to and sustain what is today known as the prison-industrial complex.

On debt row

In 1983, the U.S. Supreme Court made it illegal for indigent people to be imprisoned for failing to pay their debts. Yet to this day, people are locked up for being in debt. In 2009, for example, Minnesota courts issued 845 arrest warrants against debtors, half who owed less than $3,500 and one who owed only $85.[26] After serving time, they are burdened with legal financial obligations (LFOs). LFOs are fines, fees, and other costs associated with a criminal sentence, such as supervision fees if on proba-

---

[24] Bob Sullivan, "Your Employer May Share Your Salary, and Equifax Might Sell That Data," *NBCNews.com*, January 30, 2013. http://tinyurl.com/DROMSullivan.

[25] Holland, "Defending Junk-Debt-Buyer Lawsuits," 12.

[26] Chris Serres and Glenn Howatt, "In Jail for Being in Debt," *Minneapolis Star Tribune*, March 17, 2011. http://tinyurl.com/DROMSerres3.

tion, administrative fees, "pay to stay" fees, and prison fees.[27] LFOs pile up quickly, causing debtors to waive legal counsel because of those costs, which increases the likelihood of re-incarceration. This leads to a cycle of debt and imprisonment that many people are unable to escape.

Fees often begin even before one reaches the courthouse. The people sued—often low-income, elderly, or disabled people—frequently do not receive notice and are not aware of court proceedings. If they are notified, many people cannot defend themselves even though some of these lawsuits are filed without having proof of any debt owed. At least thirteen states, for example, authorize or mandate charging indigent individuals "defender fees"—sometimes thousands of dollars—for exercising their right to counsel.[28] Due to no money for adequate legal representation, language barriers, and sheer intimidation, debtors routinely lose court judgments. Between January 2006 and July 2008 alone, the top twenty-six debt buyers won more than $1 billion in judgments against New York City residents—mostly from low-income communities and communities of color—and only about 1% of those sued by creditors had legal counsel.[29] In some cases, courts seem to actively seek to punish members of marginalized groups. According to the American Civil Liberties Union, "in Washington [State], Hispanic defendants generally receive higher LFOs than white defendants convicted of similar offenses."[30] Anyone can be sued, but those with fewer resources—disproportionately, people of color—are most likely to be ensnared in a cycle of debt and prison.

WAGE GARNISHMENT AND WORK

Debts can also be collected through wage garnishment, which basically means that your employer withholds some of your wages if ordered to do so by a court or the government. The amount that can be seized depends on your "disposable income," or the amount left after legally required deductions are made (such as taxes and employee retirement systems). It is important that you check how much of your wages can be garnished based on your income so you don't end up in any more financial trouble. Although Title III of the Consumer Credit Protection Act (CCPA) forbids any employer from firing you because of any one debt, you *can* be fired if your wages need to be

---

[27] Alicia Bannon, Mitali Nagrecha, and Rebekah Diller, "Criminal Justice Debt: A Barrier to Reentry," *Brennan Center for Justice*, 2010. http://tinyurl.com/DROMBannon, 7.

[28] Bannon, Nagrecha, and Diller, "Criminal Justice Debt," 12.

[29] "Debt Deception: How Debt Buyers Abuse the Legal System to Prey on Lower-Income New Yorkers," *Legal Aid Society, Neighborhood Economic Development Advocacy Project, MFY Legal Services*, and *Urban Justice Center*, May 2010. http://tinyurl.com/DROMLAS2, 7.

[30] "In for a Penny: The Rise of America's New Debtors' Prisons," *American Civil Liberties Union*, October 2010. http://tinyurl.com/DROMACLU, 10.

garnished for two or more debts. If your employer commits any Title III violations, you may have grounds for reinstatement to your job, payment of back wages, and a restoration of the garnished amount.[31] Wage garnishment laws can differ from state to state, so it's best to look up what your state does and does not allow. If a state's garnishment law differs from Title III of the federal wage garnishment law, your employer must observe the law that requires the *smaller* garnishment amount. For specific information on how much your wages can be garnished, it's best to contact the Federal Trade Commission, the CFPB or your state's attorney general.

If you've had a judgment made against you, employers can choose not to hire you if they don't want to go through the trouble of having to dedicate their resources to fulfilling a court's order. Your bank may also freeze your account after they receive a garnishment order. If you've written checks or have your account tied to electronic payments, those payments may go unpaid. Depending on the bank, they may charge you with having insufficient funds. If your bank account has been frozen, you should seek an attorney right away. You should also tell the bank if your account has funds that are exempt from being frozen or garnished.

Debt collection is not merely a particular job of the collection industry. It is not just an aftershock of a credit transaction gone wrong. Rather, it is a powerful weapon—one that is used intentionally—that controls your time, your work, and your relationship with the people around you. Debt collection is a practice that extends to every level of society, from the courts and credit rating agencies to your workplace, your home, and your community. Debt collection isn't exclusively the domain of debt collection agencies, either. The federal government, municipalities, employers, and private companies all have the power to collect debt and view you as a means to make more money. Though the individual consequences are severe, debt collection—as a way of punishing and extracting profit from working people—preserves wider racial and economic inequalities, harming millions and undermining the struggle for a more egalitarian society.

IDEAS FOR COLLECTIVE ACTION

It remains to be seen how effective and "consumer friendly" the Consumer Financial Protection Bureau will be, but people should not always expect to rely on them or the Federal Trade Commission to solve their problems. There is no cure-all for resisting debt collection. Debt affects people differently and everyone has different experiences.

---

[31] U.S. Department of Labor, "Wages and Hours Worked: Wage Garnishment," *Employment Law Guide*, September 2009. http://tinyurl.com/DROMDOL.

A good first step is to try to educate yourself and your friends on how debt collection works, who the big players are, and what powers you potentially have to resist. Open up that conversation and talk to each other to find solutions together. Ask why you owe anything at all and how you got into the situation you're in. Are you "just irresponsible" (as debtors have often been told) or are there larger factors at play that have to do with employment, racism, and other forms of exploitation and oppression? Is it a matter of us spending beyond our means or is it about who controls our labor and wages, our value, and our worth?

In addition to sharing information, experiences, and strategies with others, there are two other main ways we can begin to fight back against debt collectors: letter-writing, and lawsuits for violating the FDCPA. Both could be made into mass actions that attempt to overwhelm debt collectors while also helping us reduce our debts. With the right organizational structure, debtors being chased by a common debt collector or debt collection agency can coordinate a well-timed letter-writing campaign to dispute their debts. If many debts with the same collector are disputed, it will disrupt and possibly halt their business. As far as we know, such a collective action has never been tried. But if a collector violates the FDCPA (which won't be hard to find out), a class-action lawsuit could be organized.

RESOURCES
Websites
- Carreon and Associates (carreonandassociates.com)
- The Consumerist (consumerist.com)
- Debtorboards (debtorboards.com)
- Fighting Collection Agency Debt (collectionagencydebt.blogspot.com)
- National Consumer Law Center (nclc.org)
- Written Off America (writtenoffamerica.com)

Reports and Articles
- Jude Chao, "How to Report Collection Agency Abuse," *eHow*, http://tinyurl.com/DROMChao.
- "Debt Collection FAQS: A Guide for Consumers," *National Association of Consumer Advocates*, http://tinyurl.com/DROMNACA01.
- "Debt Collection Info Packet," *NEDAP*, 2006, http://tinyurl.com/DROMNEDAP04.
- Alex Henderson, "'Am I Going to Have to Kill You?': The Horrific Ways Abusive Debt Collectors Threaten and Harass Their Victims," *AlterNet*, April 17, 2011, http://tinyurl.com/DROMHenderson.
- Lynnette Khalfani-Cox, "How to Handle Rude and Abusive Debt Collectors," *AARP*, January 16, 2012, http://tinyurl.com/DROMKhalfani.

- "Know Your Rights When You Owe a Debt," *National Association of Consumer Advocates*, http://tinyurl.com/DROMNACA02.
- Patrick Lunsford, "Debt Collectors Pursuing More than 14 Percent of Americans," *Inside ARM*, February 29, 2012, http://tinyurl.com/DROMLunsford.
- Chris Morran, "Debt Collectors Real & Fake: Top List of Most-Blocked Phone Numbers," *The Consumerist*, August 6, 2012, http://tinyurl.com/DROMMorran01.
- Chris Morran, "4 Things Debt Collectors Won't Tell You," *The Consumerist*, October 18, 2011, http://tinyurl.com/DROMMorran02.
- "Predatory Lending Practices," *National Association of Consumer Advocates*, http://tinyurl.com/DROMNACA03.
- Yves Smith, "How to Beat Vulture Debt Collectors," *Naked Capitalism*, August 16, 2012 http://tinyurl.com/DROMSmith3.

REFERENCES

Alderman, Richard M. "The Fair Debt Collection Practices Act Meets Arbitration: Non-Parties and Arbitration." *Loyola Consumer Law Review* 24, no. 4 (2012): 586–614. http://tinyurl.com/DROMAlderman.

American Civil Liberties Union. "In for a Penny: The Rise of America's New Debtors' Prisons." October 2010, http://tinyurl.com/DROMACLU.

Bannon, Alicia, Mitali Nagrecha, and Rebekah Diller. "Criminal Justice Debt: A Barrier to Reentry." *Brennan Center for Justice*, 2010, http://tinyurl.com/DROMBannon.

Board of Governors of the Federal Reserve System. "Consumer Loans, All Commercial Banks." *Federal Reserve Bank of St. Louis*, 2013, http://tinyurl.com/DROMFed3.

Debt Consolidation Care. "Debt Settlement Letters and Sample Letters on Debt and Credit." Accessed March 25, 2013, http://tinyurl.com/DROMDCC.

Dougherty, Carter. "Debt Collectors Posing as Facebook Friends Spur Watchdogs." *Bloomberg*, January 24, 2013, http://tinyurl.com/DROMDougherty.

Duhigg, Charles. "What Does Your Credit-Card Company Know about You?" *New York Times*, May 12, 2009. http://tinyurl.com/DROMDuhigg.

Eidelman, Stephanie. "Large Debt Collectors Now under Thumb of CFPB." *Forbes*, October 24, 2012. http://tinyurl.com/DROMEidelman.

Federal Reserve Bank of New York. "Quarterly Report on Household Debt and Credit." November 2012. http://tinyurl.com/DROMFedNY.

Federal Trade Commission. "As a Result of FTC Action, Two Defendants in Abusive Debt Collection Case Are Banned from the Industry, Will Surrender Assets." March 15, 2012. http://tinyurl.com/DROMFTC3.

Federal Trade Commission. "Debt Collection FAQs: A Guide for Consumers." February 2009. http://tinyurl.com/DROMFTC4.

Holland, Peter A. "Defending Junk-Debt-Buyer Lawsuits." *Clearinghouse Review Journal of Poverty Law and Policy* 46, no. 1–2 (2012): 12–24. http://tinyurl.com/DROMHolland.

Irby, LaToya. "State-by-State List of Statute of Limitations on Debt." *About.com*. Accessed March 25, 2013. http://tinyurl.com/DROMIrby.

Jurgens, Rick, and Robert J. Hobbs. "The Debt Machine: How the Collection Industry Hounds Consumers and Overwhelms Courts." *National Consumer Law Center*, July 2010. http://tinyurl.com/DROMJurgens.

Legal Aid Society, Neighborhood Economic Development Advocacy Project, MFY Legal Services, and Urban Justice Center. "Debt Deception: How Debt Buyers Abuse the Legal System to Prey on Lower-Income New Yorkers." May 2010. http://tinyurl.com/DROMLAS2.

Professional Recovery Personnel. "The Psychology of Collections." Accessed March 25, 2013. http://tinyurl.com/DROMPRP.

Sahr, Patrick. "Debt and Its Discontents: The Depressing World of Collections, Part One." *Naked Capitalism*, August 27, 2012. http://tinyurl.com/DROMSahr.

Serres, Chris, and Glenn Howatt. "In Jail for Being in Debt." *Minneapolis Star Tribune*, March 17, 2011. http://tinyurl.com/DROMSerres3.

Silver-Greenberg, Jessica. "Debt Collector Is Faulted for Tough Tactics in Hospital." *New York Times*, April 24, 2012. http://tinyurl.com/DROMSilver6.

Silver-Greenberg, Jessica. "For the Families of Some Debtors, Death Offers No Respite." *Wall Street Journal*, December 3, 2011. http://tinyurl.com/DROMSilver7.

Silver-Greenberg, Jessica. "In Prosecutors, Debt Collectors Find a Partner." *New York Times*, September 16, 2012. http://tinyurl.com/DROMSilver8.

Silver-Greenberg, Jessica. "Problems Riddle Moves to Collect Credit Card Debt." *New York Times*, August 12, 2012. http://tinyurl.com/DROMSilver9.

Streitfeld, David. "You're Dead? That Won't Stop the Debt Collector." *New York Times*, March 4, 2009. http://tinyurl.com/DROMStreitfeld.

Sullivan, Bob. "Your Employer May Share Your Salary, and Equifax Might Sell That Data." *NBCNews.com*, January 30, 2013. http://tinyurl.com/DROMSullivan.

"Understanding Collection Agencies." *Debtor Boards*, October 14, 2005. http://tinyurl.com/DROMDB.

U.S. Department of Labor. "Wages and Hours Worked: Wage Garnishment." *Employment Law Guide*, September 2009. http://tinyurl.com/DROMDOL.

U.S. Government Accountability Office. *Credit Cards: Fair Debt Collection Practices Act Could Better Reflect the Evolving Debt Collection Marketplace and Use of Technology*. Washington, DC: GPO, 2009. http://tinyurl.com/DROMGAO1.

White, Martha C. "CFPB Takes on Debt Collectors with New Oversight." *Time*, November 1, 2012. http://tinyurl.com/DROMWhite.

TEN

BANKRUPTCY

IT'S BETTER THAN NOTHING

If you happen to find yourself way out in the deep waters of debt, you should know tha Effects of Climate Change." Effects of Climate Change." t bankruptcy may be an option for rescuing yourself and getting a fresh start. Think of it as consumer protection for debtors, a lifeline in a financial contest that is generally rigged against you. As with many sets of legal codes, it reflects the society that created it and an economic system predicated on maximizing profit regardless of the human consequences. The protections offered by bankruptcy are anything but clear or straightforward. But bankruptcy can be more desirable than pursuing private negotiations with uncooperative creditors, going through sketchy debt management schemes, or refusing to pay and trying to go completely off-grid, especially if you can find a trustworthy legal representative to guide you through the process.

This chapter will recount some of the historical developments in this avenue of debt forgiveness, explain the two most common options for filing individual bankruptcy in the United States (Chapter 7 and Chapter 13), and clarify what possibilities bankruptcy may offer to you and where you can learn more about it. Bankruptcy as a form of debt relief is not just for big corporations like Enron, WorldCom, and Lehman Brothers; it's a legal and legitimate form of debt relief that all debt resisters should be aware of.

DISCLAIMER

The information contained in this chapter is an attempt to present general information about bankruptcy, its background in the United States, as well as a basic understanding of bankruptcy's current legal provisions. *We are not lawyers and cannot offer personal legal counsel* on how to make bankruptcy work in your case. While it is possible to file for bankruptcy without a lawyer, there is no substitute for a trusted financial advisor or legal counsel who will act in your interests, although such people are few and far between.

A SHORT HISTORY OF DEBT FORGIVENESS

Debt forgiveness has a long history. The Bible is full of passages about jubilees and other cancellations of debt. The Qur'an also advocates debt forgiveness for those who cannot pay: "If the debtor is in difficulty, grant him time till it is easy for him to repay. But if ye remit it by way of charity, that is best for you if ye only knew" (2:280).[1] Of course not every society has protected its citizen debtors—in ancient Greece, debtors unable to pay often lost their entire families to debt slavery.

On the whole, bankruptcy in the United States has been used by businesses more than individuals. Bankruptcy laws in favor of businesses were repeatedly passed and repealed throughout the nineteenth century. The first truly modern bankruptcy laws in the United States appeared during periods of "economic downturn" in the 1890s and 1930s. These laws were largely about saving companies and businesses deeply in debt. Businesses in the United States have consistently taken advantage of bankruptcy, especially in recent years, as companies have used it as a pretext to get out of pension obligations and to break union contracts.

But starting in 1978, the United States passed a law that made it significantly easier for individuals and families to get similar benefits and protections. In the 1980s, people increasingly took advantage of this potential liberation from debt. In the 1970s, just over one in a thousand Americans filed for bankruptcy every year. That number began to rise dramatically over the course of the next decade. By 1990, the rate had tripled to three in a thousand; by the late 1990s, it was up to five.[2]

A TALE OF TWO CHAPTERS

There are two chapters under which you can file for bankruptcy as an individual in the United States, named after relevant sections of the federal bankruptcy code.

Chapter 7 bankruptcy: Wipe out all of your debts

Chapter 7, often called "straight bankruptcy," is the simplest and quickest form of bankruptcy available. It discharges or wipes away all consumer and medical debt, as well as other unsecured debts such as payday loans. However, student loans and some tax debts *cannot* be discharged in bankruptcy.

---

[1] Quoted in Ajaz Ahmed Khan and Helen Mould, "Islam and Debt," *Islamic Relief*, April 2008. http://tinyurl.com/DROMKhan, 7.

[2] Thomas A. Garrett, "The Rise in Personal Bankruptcies: The Eighth Federal Reserve District and Beyond," *Federal Reserve Bank of St. Louis Review*, February 2007. http://tinyurl.com/DROM Garrett, 15.

Filing for Chapter 7 does not mean that you must give up your home or car, if you can continue paying the debts on them or claim them as exempt property when you file. Exempt property includes home, car, retirement accounts, and household furnishing, although the maximum value of any exemption depends on the exemption law of the state in which you file. Generally, you cannot claim an exemption for property that is security for a loan (unless you successfully remove the lien on the property). Consider the following details of the major federal exemptions:[3]

- Home: You can claim the federal homestead exemption for up to $22,975 of equity in your home per owner, after taking into account the cost of sale (generally 10%). You can also claim state exemptions, which are more favorable in some states than others (for example, in New York, you can protect up to $150,000 per owner, and in Florida, your home is exempt without limit).
- Car: You can claim a federal exemption of up to $3,675 of equity in your car.
- Retirement accounts: Retirement accounts (401ks, IRAs, and Roth IRAs) are, for all practical purposes, fully exempt.
- Household goods: You can claim a federal exemption of up to $12,250 per owner of household goods, furnishings and appliances, clothes, and other material possessions.
- Wild card: You can claim a federal exemption of $1,225 plus $11,500 of any unused portion of your homestead exemption for anything you own.

Any property that does not fit under these exemptions is sold off to pay the creditors. Filing for Chapter 7 gives you a way of becoming debt-free without becoming penniless.

Chapter 13 bankruptcy: Repay a portion of your debts

With a Chapter 13 bankruptcy, disparate debts are consolidated into a single sum owed to the bankruptcy court, and a rigorous payment plan is set up—usually lasting three to five years. This can be thought of as a "wage earner bankruptcy." It is intended for a situation where you have a home or a car and you have fallen behind on the payments—not where you couldn't afford the home or car in the first place prior to filing. In short, Chapter 13 strips away your unsecured debts in order to direct your income toward saving the home or car that you need in order to go on with life. It also requires that all creditor efforts to collect your debt (both secured and unsecured) must stop. Foreclosure actions are also suspended (though they can be resumed once the case is completed). Historically, many debtors

[3] Federal bankruptcy exemptions are adjusted every three years; the information above is accurate until March 31, 2016.

in Chapter 13 fail to comply with their payment plan during the payback period, which tragically leads to more debt. But in the best-case scenario, filing for Chapter 13 can offer some much needed breathing room from other debts while you catch up on payments for your necessary property.

The creditors fight back

The credit industry was alarmed by the boom in bankruptcies over the last thirty years, and it began a vast lobbying and propaganda campaign to tighten up the bankruptcy code. A "moral rot" was said to be spreading throughout the culture, and the old moral line about paying your debts was falling by the wayside along with other "traditional values."

Industry lobbying to cut back bankruptcies came up short at first. During the Clinton years, bankruptcy overhaul bills were introduced but never made it all the way through Congress. The efforts finally paid off in 2005, when George W. Bush signed the preposterously named Bankruptcy Abuse Prevention and Consumer Protection Act (BAPCPA), a heavily pro-creditor piece of legislation that made it harder and more expensive to file for bankruptcy.

The reform has been very good for creditors. Although there was a spike in bankruptcy filings in the year or two leading up to the passage of the bill—nearly seven out of every thousand Americans filed in 2005, an all-time record—filings then collapsed to just two per thousand in 2006. Filings soon began rising again, but even during the Great Recession of 2008, the filing rate never broke above five per thousand, essentially where it was in the late 1990s, when both the unemployment rate and debt levels were well below where they've been in recent years. A study by the Federal Reserve Bank of New York suggests that tightening up the bankruptcy code increased the number of foreclosures because many debtors were denied this avenue of relief.[4]

The battle over Chapter 13

Before BAPCPA, you had the option of choosing which chapter to file under. Under the guise of "abuse prevention," however, the new law requires that you pass a "means test" if your household is above your state's median income and you wish to file for Chapter 7. The means test is a formula based on your disposable income after certain expenses. (Means test calculators are available on the internet.) State medians run from about $37,000 in Mississippi to

---

[4] Donald P. Morgan, Benjamin Iverson, and Matthew Botsch, "Subprime Foreclosures and the 2005 Bankruptcy Reform," *Federal Reserve Bank of New York Economic Policy Review*, 2011. http://tinyurl.com/DROMMorgan.

$66,000 in Connecticut, with the national median around $50,000. Of course, you could have an above-median income in an expensive region like New York or San Francisco and not be living large at all. Despite the restrictions on Chapter 7 filings, they still account for about 70% of all bankruptcy cases, which isn't very different than the pre-reform share.

The 2005 reform also increased the amount of documentation required to file: tax returns, pay stubs, household budget information, and so on. Because of that, and the increased amount of time that lawyers now have to devote to a bankruptcy filing, fees have risen dramatically. The new law also requires you to complete a counseling course offered by a government-certified provider. All of this has contributed to lower filing rates than there would have been otherwise.

It is clear that in the name of "abuse prevention," the creditors and the government are forcing people to either not file for bankruptcy at all, or if they do, to file for Chapter 13. And it is not hard to see why. Unlike Chapter 7, creditors often recover up to 30% of the original loan with Chapter 13. Many of those who file for Chapter 13 end up completely failing: the rate of discharge (getting one's debts forgiven) is around one-third of cases according to many studies, and about one-half according to others. If your Chapter 13 filing fails, you are left in a worse situation than where you started.[5]

And from here it only gets worse. One detailed law study found that bankruptcy laws, specifically Chapter 13, implicitly favor a certain profile, an "ideal debtor," who is usually White and married. Most bankruptcy laws tend to favor wealth over income, ownership over renting, formal dependents over informal dependents, and straight married couples, all of which have significantly higher rates among Whites. Before 2005, Black people who filed for bankruptcy filed for Chapter 13 nearly 50% of the time, compared to less than 25% by Whites. A study found that when all other factors are equalized (identical financial cases), lawyers are twice as likely to steer Black clients toward Chapter 13 than they are White clients. The study could find no other cause besides racism in all forms: conscious, unconscious, structural, and institutional. This push toward Chapter 13—where one's race is far more often a determining factor as compared to Chapter 7—compounds the effect of the already racist terrain of bankruptcy law.

Black people are also 20% more likely to have their Chapter 13 cases dismissed by a judge. This discrimination has had a major impact on many Black debtors—they often avoid the option of bank-

---

[5] Wenli Li, "What Do We Know about Chapter 13 Personal Bankruptcy Filings?" *Federal Reserve Bank of Philadelphia Business Review*, 2007. http://tinyurl.com/DROMLi, 24.

ruptcy altogether and seek other solutions: hiding, adopting aliases, refusing to pay, or relying on highly predatory fringe financial services. It may appear at first glance that BAPCPA actually began to equalize the playing field across race and gender by introducing the fairly objective "means test," but it has, on the contrary, continued the trend of favoring wealth over income and made the whole process more intimidating and more expensive.[6]

WHO FILES FOR BANKRUPTCY? AND WHY?

The banks, government, and media would have you believe that people file for bankruptcy to scam the system, or because they are financially irresponsible. This is, of course, nonsense. Elizabeth Warren made her career by clarifying these myths around bankruptcy: most bankruptcies are simply not caused by financial carelessness but by life's misfortunes such as unexpected joblessness, illness, or divorce. The major social reason for the rise in bankruptcy over the decades has been the rise in consumer debt burdens, and the major reasons for the rise in these debts are wage stagnation, the elimination of caps on interest, and massive public sector service cuts. The line of argument advanced by the credit industry ignores the source of the debt to begin with: in a time of vulnerable work markets and mass cuts in basic social services, most people have no choice but to accrue debt to simply survive.

There has been a lot of talk about the role of medical debt in bankruptcies in the past few years—and for good reason. A whopping 62% of personal bankruptcies are traceable to medical debt. But it is not the only factor. Bankruptcy is not "caused" by any one type of debt. Most individuals and families filing for bankruptcy have auto debt, credit card debt, mortgage debt, student debt, and medical debt. The debt burden that households have been forced to take on is getting harder and harder to bear, such that mass bankruptcies and default in this system seem to be structurally inevitable, especially if bankers continue to force us to take loans that we cannot pay.

It would be a mistake to think that the U.S. bankruptcy laws and proceedings are fair across lines of gender, race, and class. In terms of gender, it's a complicated story. While the rates of bankruptcy filings are far higher for women, especially single and divorced mothers, they also benefit from the structure of bankruptcy laws. Individuals with child support obligations (usually men) who declare Chapter 7 are freed up to then satisfy these obligations, since consumer debt can be discharged but child support cannot. However, after the 2005 Act,

---

[6] A. Mechele Dickerson, "Race Matters in Bankruptcy," *Washington and Lee Law Review* 61, no. 4, 2004. http://tinyurl.com/DROMDickerson, 1726.

bankruptcy became more difficult for everyone, including both single mothers and those with child support obligations. All of this raises the question: why are so many single mothers (especially women of color) declaring bankruptcy? And instead of looking for policy solutions or resorting to moral chiding, how can we avoid these situations of indebtedness in the first place? We haven't seen these questions asked in any serious public forum.

In addition, there have been several reports in the last decade about the connection between race and bankruptcy. Anyone connecting the dots between race, predatory lending, and the 2008 financial crisis shouldn't be surprised by these results. Neil Ellington, executive vice president of a credit counseling agency in Raleigh, North Carolina, had this to say on the matter of race and bankruptcy: "The same underlying issues that created the problem in mortgage lending, with minorities paying higher interest rates than their white counterparts having the same loan qualifications, are present in all financial fields."[7]

So how bad is it? One study, focused on a neighborhood in Chicago, found that the rate of filings by Blacks is triple that of their White counterparts. The underlying cause isn't well documented, but it's not hard to guess: Black people have been systematically targeted by financial predators. Beyond predatory lending, people of color are targeted by fierce debt reduction schemes, rescue scams, and shady financial products promising to save them from their debt burdens.[8]

IN THIS SOCIETY, EVERYONE WANTS YOUR MONEY

Anyone contemplating bankruptcy or struggling with debt is likely to confront dubious operators. Worst of all are the characters who advertise on late-night TV or on the web offering debt-relief schemes. Google the term "debt relief" for examples. In the words of a Manhattan-based attorney who handles many bankruptcy cases, "I've never seen one that was legitimate." Avoid them at all costs.

But there are also more legitimate groups and financial advisors who will offer you still-dubious advice against filing for bankruptcy. The standard claim is that bankruptcy is an emotionally wrenching experience that will ruin your credit for years. According to these sources, you'll find it difficult or impossible to get a credit card or a mortgage after filing for bankruptcy. You might even find that it

---

[7] Tara Siegel Bernard, "Blacks Face Bias in Bankruptcy, Study Suggests," *New York Times*, January 20, 2012. http://tinyurl.com/DROMBernard.

[8] Geoff Smith and Sarah Duda, "Bridging the Gap II: Examining Trends and Patterns of Personal Bankruptcy in Cook County's Communities of Color," *Woodstock Institute*, May 2011. http://tinyurl.com/DROMSmith6.

"carries a stigma in your community," according to the National Foundation for Credit Counseling (NFCC), a trade association for the advice industry.[9] Better to tighten your belt and negotiate repayment plans with your creditors, they say. For example, one advocate, Dave Ramsey, who dispenses advice from the perspective of the religious right, suggests selling everything but the bare necessities to placate the creditors.

And they are right in one sense; bankruptcy is no picnic. But neither is private debt negotiation or settlement. Few people have the time and energy to fight with creditors for months, especially without a lawyer. Groups like the NFCC have been silent about releasing data showing success rates in private negotiations, debt settlement plans, and other alternatives to bankruptcy. It's hard to know whom to trust when everyone wants your money. Organizations like the NFCC will say terrible things about bankruptcy because they're funded by the financial industry and other private sector interests. While they divulge few exact details about their funders, the program for its most recent conference had sponsors such as Bank of America, Chase, Citi, MasterCard, and Experian (the credit rating agency). The conference also featured "breakout sessions" for creditors and a Creditors' Day (as if all the other days of the year weren't creditors' days, too).

NFCC's ideals are personified by the winners of their 2011 Client of the Year Award, Jerry and Sue Bailey of Jackson, Michigan. The Baileys "refused" the temptation of "walking away" from $92,000 in credit card debt, opting instead for a repayment program engineered by NFCC member firm GreenPath. They admit that paying off their debt was a struggle, but it was one "worth making." GreenPath (which, incidentally, paid its CEO about $600,000 in 2010) and other NFCC member firms are precisely the ones who run the counseling programs filers are required to attend.

So who *can* you trust? Bankruptcy lawyers? Let's not forget that they make money from debtors too. Every situation is different, and you should research the options that make the most sense for your situation.

So, should I file for bankruptcy or not?

Many of us are afflicted with a deep sense of guilt about not servicing our debt—it feels immoral. Worse still is the common myth that filing for bankruptcy means losing everything. In Chapter 7 you can avail yourself of exemptions for key assets, and Chapter 13 is designed so that you can save some non-exempt assets. We recom-

---

[9] "About Bankruptcy," *National Foundation for Credit Counseling*, 2013. http://tinyurl.com/DROMNFCC.

mend you research all of this carefully. In the end, filing for bankruptcy *can* be a tremendous relief.

There is no minimum amount of debt that must be owed before it is reasonable to file for bankruptcy; ultimately, it is based on the situation of the individual. Before filing, we highly recommend speaking to an attorney who specializes in bankruptcy. Many offer free initial consultations. For a referral, contact your state or local bar association and consider seeking free (pro bono) bankruptcy services in your area.

Contrary to claims by the credit industry (and the academics and counselors on their payroll), the rise in bankruptcy filings over the last couple of decades is *not* the result of spreading moral rot and a growing indifference to debt. Most people are close to their credit limit or behind on their payments—at a time when banks can raise the money they lend you for close to 0%—and getting rid of that rapidly compounding debt can be deliverance for many.

Compound interest can feel like endless sacrifice with no reward. If you have a $5,000 balance at 18% interest and make only the minimum payment, it will take you almost twenty-three years to pay off the debt and will cost you nearly $7,000 in interest (more than the original principal). Bankruptcy can reduce your credit card balance to zero in a matter of months—and put an end to calls from collection agents. There are consequences, of course, for your future ability to borrow, but being informed and doing it right makes it worth the risk.

The biggest relief bankruptcy offers is the "automatic stay," which means that creditors and collectors have to stop harassing you until the bankruptcy filing is completed and the court has ruled. In Chapter 13, your case is monitored so that you no longer have to deal with creditors as you pay back your debt for those three to five years (again, only if you are in the minority that successfully completes your plan).

It can cost as much as $3,000 to file for bankruptcy these days (Chapter 13 is more expensive), which, for people who are barely getting by, is a lot of money. You may be able to find a relatively cheap lawyer or get free legal representation by contacting your local bar association. It is possible to do it yourself using manuals and forms from online sources, but it can be a complicated process. The failure rate without a lawyer for Chapter 13 is at an astonishing 97%! So, we recommend getting a lawyer before filing; research carefully how to find a good one. And it can't hurt to know the law a bit before you go—the study mentioned above about lawyers' tendency to provide Black debtors with questionable advice shows the importance of this clearly.

What about my credit? And other risks?

The consensus in the credit counseling industry seems to be that, for many people, bankruptcy can actually be good for your credit score in the long run. How so? If you're considering bankruptcy, you've probably missed a few payments and are dealing with delinquency and default—which will wreck most people's scores. Also, before you file for bankruptcy, you have some income but a lot of debt; after filing, you will have the same income but no debt, which leads to a lower debt-to-income ratio. This ratio, in turn, is used as a factor in obtaining loans.[10] Counterintuitively, debt management programs or similar plans don't seem to do much for your credit, so at some point, you'll want to make a decision about bankruptcy.

It seems that Chapter 7 and Chapter 13 have an equivalent impact on credit scores. Either way, scores take a nosedive in the short term, and you may not have access to cheap or fair credit for a while. But it won't be long before you receive more credit card applications (sometimes as little as thirty days after filing). Why? Banks are not stupid: they know that you probably have income (or potential for it) and also that, due to your recently filed bankruptcy, you can't file another bankruptcy for eight years. To the bank, that means you'll have to pay back what you owe plus interest for the entire time.

Lenders will be more likely to lend to you after a Chapter 7. Few lenders will do any lending during the payback period of a Chapter 13, so it will take an extra three to five years to rebuild your credit. Notably, while a bankruptcy can stay on your credit score for seven to ten years, you can still qualify for a Federal Housing Administration-backed mortgage approximately two and a half years after filing a Chapter 7.

After bankruptcy, you will be an ideal target for the predatory loan sharks in the industry; they love people who are struggling. They will tempt you with low interest rates to start with, but then jack up rates and fees the minute that balances rise and payments fall behind. Be careful. The best strategy after bankruptcy is to accept a couple of cards. Study their terms and conditions and use them *very* carefully. Read up about how to build your credit (carrying a small balance, making regular payments, etc). Although a bankruptcy filing can stay on your credit report for a decade, even just six months after a filing, it's possible to get a credit score in the 700s.[11] That being said, it can be disastrous to declare bankruptcy a second time; few credit scores can recover from that (except patiently waiting seven to ten years).

---

[10] Erin Peterson, "Debt-to-Income Ratio Important as Credit Score," *Bankrate*, January 24, 2007. http://tinyurl.com/DROMPeterson.

[11] Lynnette Khalfani-Cox, "Life after Bankruptcy: 5 Steps to Rebuilding Your Credit, Finances and Emotions," *Daily Finance*, June 3, 2011. http://tinyurl.com/DROMKhalfani2.

Lastly, the biggest risk in filing for bankruptcy is that your case will be dismissed, in which case you've wasted time and money, accrued more debt (the interest accrues retroactively to the time of filing), and gained nothing. And, your bankruptcy would still be on your credit report. Though this is the worst-case scenario, remember that this happens for nearly 50% of those filing for Chapter 13.[12]

COLLECTIVE SOLUTIONS

Unfortunately, for the most part bankruptcy offers only *individual* means of fighting the creditors. It is hard to imagine how to use the bankruptcy laws in order to organize mass direct action that would seriously disrupt the debt system. In terms of the racist nature of the existing bankruptcy mechanisms, informational campaigns in communities to clear up the myths and disinformation surrounding bankruptcy would be an important first step. And, although not ideal for many, there *are* other options for debtors: debt negotiation or settlement, refusal, living off the grid, leaving the country, etc. One form of collective action is to help each other and build networks of mutual support for those struggling with debt.

With every bankruptcy, a bank or lender loses a certain amount of money—they have rigged the game, so they are probably recovering it in other places. Nonetheless, their books are slightly shaken. One possible action would be a simultaneous mass bankruptcy of those eligible for Chapter 7. This could be organized so that a mass of debtors with debt toward a certain bank declares bankruptcy all at once. We don't know enough about the industry to know what effects this could have. The organizers would need serious legal counseling: bankruptcy laws are laden with fraud protections, which would have to be carefully combed through before taking action. Another possibility would be to organize a critical mass to declare bankruptcy on student loans all at once—knowing they will be dismissed, but defiantly insisting in court that the debts are illegitimate and unpayable. These actions, of course, would need years of planning, preparation, and organization.

RESOURCES
Websites
- Bankruptcy Data (bankruptcydata.com)
- NOLO: Bankruptcy (nolo.com/legal-encyclopedia/bankruptcy)
- American Bankruptcy Institute: Pro Bono Bankruptcy Services Locator (probono.abi.org)

---

[12] "12 Myths about Bankruptcy," *Bankrate.com*, November 4, 2011. http://tinyurl.com/DROMBR.

Articles and Books

- David Cay Johnston, "Five Questions for Elizabeth Warren; Bankruptcy Borne of Misfortune, Not Excess," *New York Times*, September 3, 2000, http://tinyurl.com/DROMJohnston.
- Aparna Mathur, "Medical Debts and Bankruptcy Filings," *American Enterprise Institute for Public Policy Research*, July 28, 2009, http://tinyurl.com/DROMMathur.
- Georgette Miller, *Living Debt Free*, Mentor Equity Press, 2012. (Also available on DVD.)
- Elizabeth Warren, "Feminomics: Women and Bankruptcy," *Huffington Post*, December 17, 2009, http://tinyurl.com/DROMWarren.

REFERENCES

Bankrate. "12 Myths about Bankruptcy." November 4, 2011. http://tinyurl.com/DROMBR.

Bernard, Tara Siegel. "Blacks Face Bias in Bankruptcy, Study Suggests." *New York Times*, January 20, 2012. http://tinyurl.com/DROMBernard.

Dickerson, A. Mechele. "Race Matters in Bankruptcy." *Washington and Lee Law Review* 61, no. 4 (2004): 1725–1776. http://tinyurl.com/DROMDickerson.

Garrett, Thomas A. "The Rise in Personal Bankruptcies: The Eighth Federal Reserve District and Beyond." *Federal Reserve Bank of St. Louis Review*, February 2007. http://tinyurl.com/DROMGarrett.

Khalfani-Cox, Lynnette. "Life after Bankruptcy: 5 Steps to Rebuilding Your Credit, Finances and Emotions." *Daily Finance*, June 3, 2011. http://tinyurl.com/DROMKhalfani2.

Khan, Ajaz Ahmed, and Helen Mould. "Islam and Debt." *Islamic Relief*, April 2008. http://tinyurl.com/DROMKhan.

Li, Wenli. "What Do We Know about Chapter 13 Personal Bankruptcy Filings?" *Federal Reserve Bank of Philadelphia Business Review*, 2007. http://tinyurl.com/DROMLi.

Morgan, Donald P., Benjamin Iverson, and Matthew Botsch. "Subprime Foreclosures and the 2005 Bankruptcy Reform." *Federal Reserve Bank of New York Economic Policy Review*, 2011. http://tinyurl.com/DROMMorgan.

National Foundation for Credit Counseling. "About Bankruptcy." Accessed March 25, 2013. http://tinyurl.com/DROMNFCC.

Peterson, Erin. "Debt-to-Income Ratio Important as Credit Score." *Bankrate*, January 24, 2007. http://tinyurl.com/DROMPeterson.

Smith, Geoff, and Sarah Duda. "Bridging the Gap II: Examining Trends and Patterns of Personal Bankruptcy in Cook County's Communities of Color." *Woodstock Institute*, May 2011. http://tinyurl.com/DROMSmith6.

ELEVEN

STRATEGIES FOR SURVIVAL

LIVING ON THE MARGINS OF THE DEBT SYSTEM

This chapter provides tips for people who, either voluntarily or involuntarily, live at the margins of the credit and banking systems. It gives advice about finding free or cheap meals, renting an apartment with bad credit, and other practical matters. It points to ways we can live, work, and play that are based on principles of solidarity and mutual aid. The information presented here is only the tip of the iceberg—strategies for living off the financial grid could fill an entire manual of its own, and with your help, Strike Debt may produce one in the future. In the meantime, we encourage you to explore the resources listed at the end of this chapter.

Previous chapters have demonstrated how debt works as an engine of inequality and prevents us from depending on each other in healthy ways. In its current form, debt is something like a negative version of solidarity.

Unfortunately, our current economic system leaves very little space for those who don't submit to its predatory logic. Finding ways to live outside of it is an absolute necessity for many, but can also be rewarding and give you a glimpse of what life might be like in a world without debt. That said, have no illusions: it won't be easy. It will require cultivating personal values and taking actions that often stand in stark contrast to the ones our consumer culture promotes so aggressively.

FOOD

According to the Environmental Protection Agency, in 2010, over thirty-three million tons of food were wasted in the United States.[1]

---

[1] "Municipal Solid Waste Generation, Recycling, and Disposal in the United States: Tables and Figures for 2010," *U.S. Environmental Protection Agency*, December 2011. http://tinyurl.com/DROMEPA, 3.

At the same time, over seventeen million households are classified as food insecure and about fifty million individuals in our country use food stamps.[2] The most obvious solution for acquiring food without money is a local food bank or pantry. But even these resources come with restrictions, as some sort of documentation is required to prove eligibility. It is also very unlikely that you can find a truly healthy and well-balanced meal at an emergency food pantry. These types of resources can also be hard to find in rural areas.

While supermarkets are easy to find in most areas, the affordable ones often have poor-quality produce and limited fresh food. Meanwhile, the supermarkets with good produce—piled high in attractive displays—are often expensive, and patronizing them has become a kind of status symbol (think Whole Foods Market). But what happens when these displays of perfectly symmetrical fruit become a tad discolored? What happens to the yogurt after its fateful sell-by date? It goes in the dumpster—and there is where you're likely to find edible items that have been discarded largely for aesthetic reasons. Almost all supermarkets over-purchase—it is better to have too much of a product on hand than not enough. But once space on the shelves runs out, these products mostly move to the garbage. This is incredibly wasteful, yet there is a negative stereotype around people who take food someone else has thrown away. However, as many dumpster divers know, a supermarket dumpster can be a rich source of free, high-quality food. This doesn't mean that all food found in a dumpster is edible. Use your best judgment about anything you find.

To offer one example, Bolthouse Farms—which makes nutritious, delicious, and expensive drinks—is distributed by a company in Brooklyn. Outside the company's office there is a dumpster where you can find perfectly good bottles of juice. It is incredibly exciting to walk away with an armful of beverages for which everyone else pays a pretty penny. And it isn't only food and drink. One person we spoke to once dumpstered an Aerobed from a home goods store. Dumpsters at non-food stores are usually cleaner and less surveilled. While diving itself is not illegal, dumpsters are often on private property, so trespassing can earn you a felony. Trespassing laws when it comes to dumpster diving are not always strictly enforced, but it's best not to take unnecessary risks. You should never risk taking anything from a dumpster marked medical or hazardous waste.

Recovering wasted food works best when it is undertaken as a group activity. Across the country, community groups and charitable organizations are bridging the gap between wasted food and hungry

---

[2] Mark Nord, Margaret Andrews, and Steven Carlson, "Household Food Security in the United States, 2008," *United States Department of Agriculture*, November 2009. http://tinyurl.com/DROMUSDA, 4.

people. A practice known as gleaning has taken off. Large farms and orchards that cannot harvest all of their produce often allow gleaners to collect the extras and bring them to those in need.

The food justice movement Food Not Bombs has a strong chapter in Long Island along with others around the country. Jon Stepanian runs particularly inspiring food shares every single day in different Long Island communities. One Sunday in Hempstead, a group of volunteers recovered and gave away 10,899 pounds of food from fifteen sources. Most of these sources are supermarkets (usually Trader Joe's and Whole Foods), where volunteers pick up boxes of healthy groceries that would have otherwise been tossed. At the food share, people from the community can drop by and take as much as they need. Nobody is turned away. After witnessing thousands of dollars worth of groceries given away at a food share, you will seriously question why people spend so much of their cash on food. You can find a Food Not Bombs collective in just about any large urban area, and many smaller ones too, and you can certainly also start your own.

For more information regarding ways to salvage this "waste" for yourself and distribute it to others, read Jonathan Bloom's *American Wasteland: How America Throws Away Nearly Half of Its Food (and What We Can Do About It)*. Also, look for chapters of Food Not Bombs and Food Recovery Network in your own community. The latter organization takes leftovers from school dining halls and distributes them to people in need.

CLOTHING

With some persistence, it is possible to get most, or even all, of your clothing for free. Many homeless shelters also run clothing drives, although finding them in rural areas can be difficult. Thrift stores can also be useful places to seek inexpensive and sometimes free clothing. The internet can also be a good source of free clothing. Websites like craigslist. org and freecycle.org are good online resources to find people who are looking to get rid of some clothing. Another idea is to organize clothing swaps with friends or in your community. It's important to remember that living off the financial grid can often require forming strong bonds with others. What you offer each other isn't charity, it's mutual aid.

SHELTER
Renting an apartment with bad credit

Among the many hardships capitalism imposes on people with bad credit or no credit, the difficulty of renting an apartment is among the worst. Most landlords and property management companies require prospective renters to undergo a thorough credit check, and the slightest blemish on your credit report can disqualify you immediately. However, there are ways to secure a decent, affordable apartment without ever undergoing a credit check. They sometimes require painstaking work and large investments of time, but bad credit alone won't prevent you from having a roof over your head.[3]

If you're willing to sublet a room in a shared apartment, the odds of avoiding a credit check are greater. By subletting, you rent a room from a tenant on an existing lease, rather than signing a lease of your own. In this way, you avoid dealing directly with a landlord or management company. The tenant you rent from will usually ask for a deposit, but he or she will rarely require a credit check. Many sublets are short term (one to six months), but some last up to a year or more. The best resource for finding sublets is craigslist.org or similar websites, but advertisements can also usually be found in community centers and social gathering points.

Another option involves joining together with a few friends who have decent enough credit to pass a credit check, and who are willing to engage in a little sleight of hand. With two friends, for example, you can search for a three-bedroom apartment. When it comes time to meet the landlord or property manager, you leave while your two friends say they need an apartment with an extra room to use as an office or art studio. Your friends sign the lease but you do not, then you live in the extra room and pay rent directly to your roommates. The odds of getting caught are low, since landlords and property managers rarely visit their tenants' apartment. And even if they do, they must get your consent to enter. That said, the consequence of getting caught can be eviction, so this tactic should be used with precaution.

If you prefer to be on a lease, your best bet is to rent directly from a landlord rather than a management company. A management company will always require a credit check, while some landlords do not. These landlords can be difficult to find, especially in a large city with an active rental market, but it's not impossible. Again, craigslist.org is the best resource. Avoid rental announcements with the shiny logos of management companies; search instead for plain announcements providing basic details. These are more likely to be landlord-rented apartments. Landlords rarely state explicitly in the announcement that they do not require a credit check, but you can call or email them to ask.

If you simply cannot avoid a credit check, then try to provide supplementary information about yourself to the landlord or management company that shows you are financially reliable. Write a letter explaining your financial situation in a sympathetic light. Provide a letter of recommendation from a previous landlord or an employer.

---

[3] Snow Conant, "Rent Apartments with Bad Credit," *My New Place*, August 20, 2008. http://tinyurl.com/DROMConant.

You can also use a cosigner—someone with good credit and a stable income who vouches for your financial solvency and agrees to share the rental liability with you. This person is usually a parent or a friend. Keep in mind, however, that if you slip behind on rent, the landlord can legally go after your cosigner for the money.

Collective housing

Collective housing takes various forms, from condo co-ops, to cohousing facilities, to intentional communities, or communes. If you have poor credit or limited income, the form most relevant to you is probably the rented collective house. This is similar to sharing an apartment as described above, but with a greater emphasis on community. In a rented collective house, residents typically eat meals together, hold weekly house meetings, and engage in group activities. They tend to rent multilevel houses rather than apartments, and they tend to have more residents than in conventional shared apartments. For this reason, rent is usually very affordable. The landlord situation can vary in collective houses; sometimes one person is on the lease, sometimes nobody is. Rarely is everyone on the lease, so collective housing is a good option for people with credit concerns. The Fellowship of Intentional Communities has a great directory for finding collective housing both nationally and internationally.

Squatting

If paying rent is not feasible for you, or if you simply want to save money, squatting—living in an abandoned building—is a widely employed practice with a rich history. By squatting, you not only live rent-free, you also challenge the regime of private property that undergirds capitalism, making it a choice political act for many. Currently in the United States, there are five times as many vacant homes as there are homeless people; in a housing system based on supply and demand, houses remain empty instead of going to the people who need them most.[4] This system can and should be contested. However, squatting comes with definite risks and difficulties that all potential squatters should bear in mind.

If you choose to squat a building with other people, take care in deciding who your co-squatters will be. You will be sharing a living space with them, often under adverse conditions, so it's important that you get along well together. Kicking someone out of a squat—or getting kicked out yourself—can be a painful process, so try to avert this by choosing cohesive housemates at the beginning. Once you choose

---

[4] Tanuka Loha, "Housing: It's a Wonderful Right," *Amnesty International*, December 21, 2011. http://tinyurl.com/DROMLoha.

your housemates, consider drawing up a list of house rules together. These can include "No violence in the squat," "No hard drugs" (hard drugs can give the cops a pretext for evicting everyone), "No stealing from housemates," and other rules that will foster a safe, stable environment. These rules won't necessarily prevent hostile behavior, but they will provide a basis for holding someone accountable if they do something that's harmful to the household.

After you find co-squatters, it's time to select a building to squat. You may want to focus on neighborhoods with buildings that are already squatted, since you're more likely to find other abandoned buildings there, and the neighbors are more likely to be accepting of squatters. Wherever you squat, you should find out if your chosen building is privately owned or if it has been seized by the city government. Your chances of holding the building are greater if it's been seized by the city, while a private owner can evict you fairly easily. You can check on the status of the building by visiting the Register/Recorder of Deeds in your city or county.

Do an inspection of your chosen building before you move in. (You may want to do the inspection at night to avoid detection, but remember to bring a flashlight.) It's easiest to enter a building through a window, but if this doesn't work you may need to get creative. Once inside, inspect the floors, stairs, and roof. If any of these is severely damaged and irreparable, the building is unsafe and you should choose a different building. If you see exposed insulation, which may contain asbestos, choose another building. Inspect the sinks, toilets, and plumbing. If these aren't in working order, getting them to work will be a challenge. If you move into the building, you may have to cart water in from outside. Even if the building is habitable, it is likely to require repairs to be made comfortable.

As much as possible, make your squat look and feel like a genuine home rather than a crash pad. This will not only be more comfortable for you, it will also signal to your neighbors and the authorities that you intend to take care of the property, which can delay or even avert eviction. Laws around squatting vary from country to country, and even in the United States, squatting laws vary from state to state. Check the laws in your state. In some cases, the cops will decide that evicting you is more trouble than it's worth, while in others they will evict you right away. Even if you avoid eviction by the cops, your local housing department may try to evict you, but this entails a long legal process. It's very difficult to avoid eviction entirely (although it's not impossible), but every day you live in the squat is another day with a roof over your head.[5]

[5] "How to Squat a Building," *Freegan.info*, 2008. http://tinyurl.com/DROMFreegan.

With millions of foreclosed properties around the United States, a movement has emerged to move homeless people into vacant houses. One of the organizations doing this is Occupy Our Homes, which has moved people into homes in New York and elsewhere. Take Back the Land, based in Miami, has been reclaiming unused property and defending people against eviction since 2006.

HEALTH AND CARE

Access to health care is a basic human right. Unfortunately for those who are uninsured and living off the financial grid, that access can be hard to come by, especially in rural areas. Taking care of your personal health by exercising, eating well, and washing your hands is important but for many is not enough. If you have a chronic condition or come down with a serious illness that requires medical care, there are some options that won't send you into crushing medical debt. If you're unable to avoid medical debt or already have it, see Chapter Three.

Free clinics

In large cities, free clinics are a great option for non-emergency care, but they have some downsides. A free clinic is often as free as the name suggests, but if you have the resources they will sometimes ask for a small sum of money. However, the bill will be nowhere near the cost of going to an ER or a private doctor without insurance. The biggest problem with free clinics is that they are run almost entirely by volunteers and the demand for these clinics often outweighs the staff resources. If you are going to a free clinic in a city like New York, be prepared to wait for a very long time. You might not even be seen that day. It all depends on the number of doctors working that day and the number of patients that come in. The National Association of Free and Charitable Clinics (nafc clinics.org) can help you find a free clinic in your area, or a clinic that can help with your specific medical concern. Unfortunately, according to the NAFCC there are less than two thousand free or charitable clinics in the United States and most of them are in urban areas.

Convenient care clinics

A "convenient care clinic" is the name given to clinics set up in retail stores like CVS, Target, and Walgreens. These clinics are not free but are usually about half the cost of seeing a doctor without insurance. Generally these clinics are staffed by nurse practitioners or physician assistants. They handle minor health issues like sinus infections and provide preventative care. They cost more than free clinics but you will be seen faster.[6]

---

[6] "Retail Health/Walk-In Clinics: An Overview," *Health Harbor*, 2011. http://tinyurl.com/DROMHH.

Emergency room

No one wants to go to the ER, but do not let fear of medical debt keep you from getting medical help. Not getting medical help when you need it could cost your life. No matter what, ERs have to treat you. While hospitals will slap you with large bills, you can often negotiate down the cost, especially if you are willing to pay cash, as it circumvents dealing with insurance companies, which is something that many doctors like to avoid. Lying to the ER is usually an option as well. This entails giving a fake name and a fake address, so if you're going to do this, make sure you do not bring your ID with you to the ER. Do this at your own risk, as it is illegal and if you are caught you will face legal action, especially if you use a fake name to obtain prescription drugs.

Medicaid

Most people know that if you are sixty-five or older you can get Medicare, but free government health care is available to others as well. Medicaid is a government health care program that serves mostly low-income people. You must make below a certain income level to be eligible for Medicaid, and this level varies from state to state, but it's usually set at or near the poverty line. Medicaid will count money in your bank account as income, so in some cases it's best not to leave a lot of money sitting in the bank. They also count wages, salaries, pensions, veterans' benefits, and Social Security checks as income. However, being poor will not guarantee that you can receive Medicaid if you are under sixty-five. You need to also have a qualified disability. Remember that a disability doesn't just mean a physical disability; certain diseases or conditions, including mental health issues, also count as a disability. Basically, if you have a disease or condition that limits your daily functioning—meaning you have trouble with things like dressing yourself, eating, and moving around—there's a good chance you can receive Medicaid.[7] Another thing to remember if you are disabled and file for Medicaid is that most people have their first request denied. If your request is denied, appeal it and keep appealing it until you're accepted.

Condition-specific institutions

If you do have a chronic condition, it is in your best interest to look for agencies that advocate and offer help to individuals with those conditions. These types of agencies can often help patients find free or low-cost medical care.

---

[7] Peter Crosta, "What Is Medicare/Medicaid?" *Medical News Today.* http://tinyurl.com/DROMCrosta.

Dental and vision care

Many colleges and universities offer free or sliding-scale dental and vision care services. An online search for your area can usually turn up one of these institutions. While this isn't very helpful for most rural residents, it's always worth researching.

FREE SCHOOLS

Until now you've read about how a certain group of people in our society financialize things like housing, health care, and education. But instead of working to guarantee these rights at little or no cost to us, those in power have used our demand for homes, medicine, and schooling to turn a profit.

This is the problem we face: they see our rights as assets. Education to them is another opportunity to generate revenue. Therefore, their interest in it only goes so far as their own financial benefit.

Free education is the opposite. Whereas the financiers offer education for their benefit, we offer education for everyone's benefit. Whereas the financiers ask that you pay dollars, we ask that you pay attention. Whereas financiers capitalize on demand for education, we collectivize it. Whereas the financiers force us into debt bondage, we only ask that you promise to come back next week.

The "free schools" below are only a few of the institutions committed to this kind of education. They're in different places, but their formula is basically the same: *this is our education, right now.*

- The Art School in the Art School (Syracuse, NY): theasintheas.org
- The Center for Popular Economics (Amherst, MA): populareconomics.org
- Knowledge Commons (Washington, DC): knowledgecommonsdc.org
- The Lawn School (New York): lawnschool.net
- The Paul Robeson Freedom School (NYC): freedomschool.tumblr.com
- The Public School (USA): thepublicschool.org
- The Social Science Centre (Lincoln, UK): socialsciencecentre.org.uk
- The Trade School (New York): tradeschool.ourgoods.org
- The Workers' and Punks' University (Slovenia): http://www.culture.si/en/Workers'_Punk_University

As higher education continues to weaken through its own corporatization, some educators have taken to the screens. The websites below and their host institutions sometimes advocate *not* going to college, taking a series of online courses, and spending your time doing something more worthwhile. To compete, major universities have begun offering their own online courses for free. Others are just trying to take advantage of new technologies that disrupt status-quo education models. The education these websites offer is free in the sense that they are free of financial cost and free of the clunky bureaucracies that universities seem to cherish. However, if you believe (like many of us do) that education is more than individualized information delivery through a computer, these may disappoint:

- edX: edx.org
- iTunes U: apple.com/education/itunes-u
- Kahn Academy: khanacademy.org
- MIT OpenCourseware: ocw.mit.edu
- OpenCulture—Free Online Courses: openculture.com/freeonline courses
- UnCollege: uncollege.org

TRANSPORTATION

Walking will always be one of the best and healthiest ways to get around, but it's not always the most practical from the perspective of getting places in a reasonable amount of time. For the able-bodied, bikes are a good way to get around if you lack a car or access to public transit. Unfortunately a good bike can be pricy. A bike share, however, is a program where bikes are placed all around a town for anyone's use (although some of these programs charge a good bit of money and require a credit or debit card). Unfortunately there are only a few major cities in the United States that have bike share programs. It will probably take a while for most of the country to catch on to bike share programs so in the meantime freecycle.org and craigslist.org are good places to look for free bikes.

In an ideal world everyone would be able to get around via bike or merely walking; however, one's degree of physical ability, inclement weather, and sometimes the distance one needs to travel, especially in rural areas, may make these modes of transportation impractical for some. Sadly, sometimes a car is really the best option. Getting rides from friends is a good option but being at the mercy of other people's good graces can be unreliable and unsustainable. Similar to a bike share program, organizations like City CarShare or Zipcar offer members the ability to basically rent a car for a few hours. Members typically log onto the website and claim a car for however long they need one. Many major cities have these programs but they usually require a monthly or annual membership and credit card. Sharing a membership with someone is a good unofficial option. Relayrides.com offers a similar service with some perks. There are no membership fees and you're renting cars from other people in your community.

Unfortunately sometimes renting a car from a major company is your only option, which is pretty hard to do without a credit card. Car rental companies see people who don't have credit cards as risky. Some companies will allow you to use a check or a debit card. If you use a debit card they will most likely charge a security deposit of $200 to $500. Companies may also require you to buy insurance or provide extra proof of identity like utility bills. It's best to call the company and find out what their specific rules are before you go.

If you live in an area with public transit, check to see if you're eligible for any discounts. Many cities offer discount public transit tickets to people with disabilities, seniors, students, and sometimes even teachers.

CASH MONEY
Microcredit

Microcredit tends to sound like a good idea. Maybe you need a little loan, just some seed money, enough to help you to get through a rough patch or to start something new. What if you could borrow the money from a circle of friends, or maybe some kind of nonprofit group? In that case, borrowing the money would be just one part of the deal: the loan would allow you to tap into a support network of people who would help you use the money wisely. Ideally, microcredit would become the gateway to a wide range of services, ranging from language training to legal assistance. In a situation like that, "microcredit" would mean community-based, locally administered, mutually reinforcing networks of generosity and obligation, helping people to leave poverty behind and to achieve some degree of balance and independence.

That is the optimistic view of microcredit programs that has driven their expansion around the world over the past few decades. However, internationally these kinds of programs typically go hand in hand with removing populations from sustainable, non-capitalist ways of living like subsistence farming, and perpetuate a harsh morality of debt. Microcredit programs can begin to resemble banks or worse, charging loan-shark interest rates, narrowing loan criteria, and imposing harsh discipline to ensure repayment. In fact, sometimes programs really are banks: for-profit schemes without any larger social mission.

Do some research, pay attention to the details, don't be seduced by empty rhetoric. Make sure you know about the organization making the loans. Microcredit may offer a valuable boost, but it won't work for long-term needs.

RESOURCES
Websites
General
- Freegan.info (freegan.info)
- Solidarity NYC (solidaritynyc.org)
- Neighborhood Economic Development Advocacy Project (NYC) (nedap.org)

Food
- Food Not Bombs (foodnotbombs.net)
- Food Recovery Network (foodrecoverynetwork.org)
- Long Island Food Not Bombs (lifnb.com)

Shelter
- All Credit Rentals (allcreditrentals.com)
- Craigslist (craigslist.org)
- Occupy Our Homes (occupyourhomes.org)
- Organizing for Occupation (NYC) (o4onyc.org)
- Take Back the Land (takebacktheland.org)

Health and care
- Convenient Care Association (ccaclinics.org)
- National Association of Free and Charitable Clinics (nafcclinics.org)

REFERENCES

Conant, Snow. "Rent Apartments with Bad Credit." *My New Place*, August 20, 2008. http://tinyurl.com/DROMConant.

Crosta, Peter. "What Is Medicare/Medicaid?" *Medical News Today*. Accessed March 25, 2013. http://tinyurl.com/DROMCrosta.

Freegan.info. "How to Squat a Building." Accessed March 25, 2013. http://tinyurl.com/DROMFreegan.

Health Harbor. "Retail Health/Walk-In Clinics: An Overview." Accessed March 25, 2013. http://tinyurl.com/DROMHH.

Loha, Tanuka. "Housing: It's a Wonderful Right." *Amnesty International*, December 21, 2011. http://tinyurl.com/DROMLoha.

Nord, Mark, Margaret Andrews, and Steven Carlson. "Household Food Security in the United States, 2008." *United States Department of Agriculture*, November 2009. http://tinyurl.com/DROMUSDA.

U.S. Environmental Protection Agency. "Municipal Solid Waste Generation, Recycling, and Disposal in the United States: Tables and Figures for 2010." December 2011. http://tinyurl.com/DROMEPA.

TWELVE

MUNICIPAL AND STATE DEBT

CRUSHING DEBT FROM ABOVE

As we've seen in previous chapters, our lives have become increasingly beholden to the logic of debt. It can be hard to tell sometimes whether something as basic as your home is first and foremost a place to live, or a moving piece in a real-estate shell game. And if you're considering pursuing a degree, a debt-benefit analysis might be your first consideration when selecting your area of study: will you be able to find a job in your field that pays well enough for you to survive with the amount of debt you'll need to take on? Though you may not always lose in these risky games we're forced to play, it's always a safe bet that financial institutions will win.

But this new "financialized" way of living doesn't just apply to individuals. Due to significant changes in the way we finance government, the towns, cities, counties, and states we live in are also now run according to the risky logic of debt. Banks are profiting at the expense of state and local governments to the detriment of ordinary residents. Is your city experiencing a budget crisis? Is your state laying off workers and cutting services? Are local hospitals understaffed and underfunded? Do you worry about whether your child's school will have enough money to provide students with a quality education? If this is happening in your community, you are a debtor.

For banks, borrowing money is easy; the federal government will give you as much as you want at a near-zero interest rate. Unfortunately, borrowing money isn't so simple for cities and states. Reduced public funding and shrinking revenues have forced municipalities everywhere to partner with Wall Street investment banks to win access to credit markets, issuing bonds to pay for everything from basic operations, like sewers, to large developments, such as sports arenas. Municipalities guarantee loans by promising that investors will be repaid with tax dollars or revenue generated by the debt-funded project. Wall Street profits from those bonds through fees, interest payments, and "securitization," or the packaging of bonds into debt bundles, which are sold and resold on the global market.

HOW WE GOT HERE

It wasn't always this way. For decades following the Great Depression, the federal government actively invested in social services and infrastructure development, and was regarded as a lender of last resort in a pinch. But when a world recession began in the 1970s, New York City became an involuntary test case for a new way of doing things. Powerful business and real estate interests had already successfully pressured the city to lower their taxes, shrinking revenues significantly. And just as the economy worsened and expenses exploded, the federal government cut support for social services.

When a budget crisis inevitably set in, Washington withheld aid, signaling the beginning of a harsh new era. Other options to help fix New York's budget were available—increasing the city's low property taxes, for example.[1] Instead, an aggressive coalition of city business elites who controlled access to credit forced harsh reforms. Budgets for education, health care, and social services were drastically cut. City workers were laid off or had their wages and benefits slashed. If a crisis arose, the needs of bondholders would be privileged over those of ordinary citizens.

New York quickly became the model for municipal financing everywhere. (It also served as inspiration for the brutal treatment of debtor nations in the global South at the hands of the International Monetary Fund.) From coast to coast, cities and states have become completely beholden to big banks, which have imposed predatory lending practices similar to the ones we experience as individual debtors. The result is shuttered schools and libraries, smaller fire departments, and endless blocks of homes in foreclosure.

The federal bankruptcy code has even been revised to ensure that many municipal bonds will keep paying investors no matter the costs to communities. Bonds are supposed to be bets on the future. In most cases, however, there is no way the lender can lose, but cities can lose a great deal. According to a recent report, of 18,400 municipal bond issuers from 1970 to 2009, only 54 have dared to default.[2]

In 2011, Jefferson County, Alabama, filed the largest bankruptcy in U.S. history to contest a $4 billion debt in the aftermath of a sewer

---

[1] Kim Moody, *From Welfare State to Real Estate: Regime Change in New York City, 1974 to the Present* (New York: The New Press, 2007), 29.

[2] Congressional Budget Office, "Fiscal Stress Faced by Local Governments," *Economic and Budget Issue Brief* (Washington, DC: GPO, 2010). http://tinyurl.com/DROMCBO, 9.

project gone disastrously wrong.[3] Local officials had borrowed vast sums from Wall Street to pay for a treatment plant to stop sewage from flowing into the Cahaba River in a predominantly Black community. The project was never completed because corrupt officials mishandled the funds (seventeen have since been jailed). Lenders demanded repayment anyway, doubling each household's sewer bill in a neighborhood already reeling from poverty. The county's financial trauma has resulted in public service cuts, mass layoffs, and overcrowded prisons.

DEBT DEMOCRACY: STADIUMS VERSUS HOSPITALS

In 1997, the people of Minneapolis passed a referendum specifically requiring a vote before large sums could be spent on sports facilities. Recently, even after hundreds of thousands of dollars of TV ads aired pushing subsidies for a new football stadium there, polls showed only 22% of the public thought any tax dollars should be used to build one. But Minnesota's governor and Minneapolis's mayor sidestepped the people, diverting city tax revenue and creating a new "stadium authority" not subject to referendum law to spend over $300 million in taxpayer money.[4]

At the same time, Ohio's Hamilton County—where one in seven residents now lives in poverty—has slashed education and social service budgets, and is selling off a hospital to make payments on $875 million in bond-financed debt they assumed in the 1990s to build two Cincinnati stadiums.[5] Whose priorities do these development decisions represent?

The large-scale debt-financing of our municipal infrastructure and public institutions provides bankers with hefty profits at citizens' expense and means a smaller voice for the communities that those institutions are meant to serve. Taxpayers are given few opportunities for input as to which bonds are issued and how, and often they find themselves stuck with the tab for debt-funded projects that have no accountability to voters. City officials broker deals with private partners through backdoor channels, zoning off "development districts" or declaring parcels of land "blighted" so they can be seized and sold under eminent domain. Priorities regarding vital public services from schools to hospitals to fire departments are increasingly being made behind closed doors, according to the logic of profits.

---

[3] Steven Church, William Selway, and Dawn McCarty, "Jefferson County Alabama Files Biggest Municipal Bankruptcy," *Bloomberg News*, November 9, 2011. http://tinyurl.com/DROMChurch.

[4] Brian Frederick, "Minnesota Vikings Set to Fleece Unwilling Taxpayers for New Stadium," *ThinkProgress*, February 17, 2012. http://tinyurl.com/DROMFrederick.

[5] Janell Ross, "Ohio County Stadium Debts Force Government to Sell Hospital, Raid Savings," *Huffington Post*, March 16, 2012. http://tinyurl.com/DROMRoss.

In New York, large-scale development financed with public funds and minimal public input is a favorite pastime of billionaire Mayor Bloomberg. In 2004, the rezoning of downtown Brooklyn was approved with virtually no opportunity for direct input from community members. One neighborhood in the crosshairs was the Fulton Street Mall—then the third most profitable retail district in the city and home to a wide array of small businesses, largely owned and frequented for generations by nearby immigrant communities and communities of color.[6] The developer who won the contract to replace the mall with mostly luxury housing and upscale stores received $20 million of federal funds intended to help distressed neighborhoods, as well as additional city subsidies. Meanwhile, hospitals across the city (especially in low-income communities) are closing at an alarming rate.

States everywhere used to finance prison construction either directly through tax revenues or with bonds that could only be issued with direct taxpayer approval. Since the racist war on drugs kicked off in the 1980s, however, prisoner populations across the nation have exploded. The U.S. prison population increased 500% since 1980,[7] and despite the fact that Black and Latino/a crime rates haven't risen for decades, incarceration rates for drug offenses increased 1,311% for Blacks and 1,600% for Latino/as between 1980 and 2000.[8] Legislators have been unable to win citizens' approval to spend massive amounts of taxpayer money on constructing prisons. But with one in a hundred adults in the United States now incarcerated,[9] prison construction and maintenance has become big business.

Encouraged by eager investment bankers and construction companies, state governments have concocted a variety of backdoor schemes, borrowing hundreds of millions of dollars to fund the rapid expansion of prisons with little public oversight. As with sports arenas, a favorite scheme for undemocratically funding prisons is to create separate "bond-issuing authorities" that aren't beholden to voter approval. Though such bonds aren't legally backed with taxpayer money, the state's credit rating is still on the line, and defaulting can have disastrous consequences.

---

[6] "Out of Business: The Crisis of Small Businesses in Rezoned Downtown Brooklyn," *Families United for Racial and Economic Equality* and *The Urban Justice Center*, July 2008. http://tinyurl.com/DROMFUREE, 2.

[7] Kathleen Nolan, *Police in the Hallways: Discipline in an Urban High School* (Minneapolis: University of Minnesota Press, 2011), 22.

[8] Tim Wise, "Racism, White Liberals, and the Limits of Tolerance," *TimWise.org*, December 4, 2000. http://tinyurl.com/DROMWise.

[9] The Pew Center on the States, "One in 100: Behind Bars in America 2008," *The Pew Charitable Trusts*, February 2008. http://tinyurl.com/DROMPew, 5.

When legislators finally decided to close a notoriously abusive and poorly run debt-financed prison in Tallulah, Louisiana, they received a letter from a rating agency notifying them that breaking the prison's lease could damage the state's credit, cutting it off from much-needed funding. Residents demanded the site be turned into a learning center. Instead, Louisiana continued to pay $3.2 million annually, and prisoners continued to suffer more than they might have elsewhere.[10] The perverse incentives of debt have overridden the will of communities time and time again. Many states now spend more on prisons than on higher education. Since 1967, California has reduced funding for higher education by two-thirds while tripling spending on prisons.[11]

Interest rate nightmares

The bonds that municipalities issue require them to make regular payments to bondholders. Often, payment amounts vary based on current interest rates, which can strain municipal budgets when rates suddenly jump up. But sometime in the 1990s, banks came up with a fancy way to convert municipalities' fluctuating interest rates to more predictable fixed rates—all for a fee, of course. These deals were called "interest rate swaps," and they sold like hotcakes—$500 billion worth of hotcakes.

With a swap, the municipality was guaranteed that if interest rates exceeded a fixed percentage, the bank would pay the excess, while if rates dipped below this percentage, the municipality owed the bank. This was all fine when interest rates actually fluctuated, but since the 2008 crash, rates for bonds have remained incredibly low, hovering around 2%. And banks are still demanding that towns, states, school districts, utilities, and other bond issuers pay them back at the much higher rates set by swaps before the crash. The only way out for cities is costly "termination payments." So far, our communities have paid over $4 billion to banks like Citigroup, JP Morgan Chase, Morgan Stanley, and Bank of America to get out of these lousy deals. Not long ago, when these same banks were teetering on the brink, the government bailed them out with taxpayers' money to the tune of over $15 trillion.

Public transit agencies from Boston to Los Angeles have been hit especially hard by poisonous swaps. In NYC, the Metropolitan Transportation Authority (MTA) has so far lost $600 million. Rather than

---

[10] Kevin Pranis, "Doing Borrowed Time: The High Cost of Back-Door Prison Finance," *Justice Strategies*, January 1, 2007. http://tinyurl.com/DROMPranis.

[11] Rachel Meyer, "California's Prison Spending Grows While the State Budget Shrinks," *The WIP*, January 28, 2010. http://tinyurl.com/DROMMeyer.

refuse payment, the MTA has cut service and laid off thousands of workers. Most people who rely on the subway are working class New Yorkers, including many people of color, immigrants, and disabled folks. The MTA passes these illegitimate debts onto riders through recurring fare hikes.[12]

As if all that weren't enough, we've recently learned that many of the world's largest banks have been manipulating a key interest rate known as Libor (the London Interbank Offered Rate). Calculated daily, Libor is based on how much interest banks charge when loaning money to each other. It is then in turn used to set rates for over $800 trillion of investments around the world, including many forms of consumer credit and—you guessed it—municipal interest rate swaps. It turns out banks have been reporting false data, intentionally pushing Libor up or down to capitalize on particular trades. It's anyone's guess as to how many billions of dollars have been stolen, but anyone with a pension or a home or auto loan was likely affected. It's estimated that municipalities in the United States have paid over $6 billion in fraudulent interest and fees due to artificially lowered Libor data, including cities like Baltimore, where more than 80% of school children are poor enough to qualify for free or reduced-price lunch.[13]

Wall Street's criminality reveals that there is no such thing as a free market and never was. In his exposé on municipal bond rigging (which he calls "the scam Wall Street learned from the mafia"), Matt Taibbi explained that Wall Street "skimmed untold billions" from hundreds of municipalities. After they were caught, banks continued investing in city bonds. "Get busted for welfare fraud even once in America, and good luck getting so much as a food stamp ever again," Taibbi wrote. "Get caught rigging interest rates in 50 states, and the government goes right on handing you billions of dollars in public contracts."[14]

HOW CAN WE RESIST MUNICIPAL AND STATE DEBT?

With a problem as structural and deeply ingrained as municipal or state debt, it's hard to imagine changing the system by yourself. The good news is that people across the planet have begun organizing in myriad ways to demand that their towns, cities, and states are no

---

[12] "Riding the Gravy Train: How Wall Street Is Bankrupting Our Public Transit Agencies by Profiteering off of Toxic Swap Deals," *Refund Transit Coalition*, June 2012. http://tinyurl.com/DROMRTC2, 12.

[13] Ann Larson, "Cities in the Red: Austerity Hits America," *Dissent*, November 16, 2012. http://tinyurl.com/DROMLarson.

[14] Matt Taibbi, "The Scam Wall Street Learned from the Mafia," *Rolling Stone*, June 21, 2012. http://tinyurl.com/DROMTaibbi.

longer run according to the logic of debt, but for the benefit of the people who live there. Tactics run the gamut from local direct actions to completely reimagining the banking system. Strike Debt is proud to be part of this global movement.

Just after the financial crisis set in here in New York, a group called the People's Transportation Program, inspired by the community "survival programs" of the Black Panthers, set out to buy subway fare cards in bulk and give away as many free rides as they could swipe through in a day.[15] By their math, for every $75 spent on one-day passes, they could give away over $1,000 worth of rides, keeping money in their communities that might otherwise have gone to banks as payment on MTA debt.[16] Similar actions were planned as MTA rates rose once again in March 2013. In July 2012, Boston activists held subway turnstiles open to protest Wall Street's vise grip on their city's transportation budget.[17] Is the transit system in your community being sucked dry by Wall Street? Maybe a fare strike is in order!

Many communities are organizing lawsuits and legislation to push back against the banks. After their pay was cut to minimum wage, Scranton's municipal unions sued the city, and their wages were restored.[18] Baltimore is suing big banks for manipulating Libor.[19] Oakland, California, is trying to take the dramatic step of severing its relationship with Goldman Sachs for good![20]

Other approaches are aimed at changing the very nature of finance. Many have looked to public banking as a way to fund our municipalities without relying on Wall Street. North Dakota, the only state in the union with a public banking system, has posted budget surpluses every year since the 2008 crisis began and boasts the nation's lowest unemployment rate.[21] Their bank was established in 1919 to empower farmers against big banks and make sure tax revenues were reinvested locally.

---

[15] Julia Dunn, "Pay It Forward: Group Responds to Subway Fare Hike with Free Swipes," *The Indypendent*, June 25, 2009. http://tinyurl.com/DROMDunn.

[16] Block Movement, "Peoples Transportation Program," *YouTube*, March 2009. http://tinyurl.com/DROMPTP.

[17] Jay Jubilee, "Fare Strike Coalition Declares 'Fare-Free Friday,'" *Boston Fare Strike Coalition*, July 30, 2012. http://tinyurl.com/DROMJubilee.

[18] Jim Lockwood and David Singleton, "Scranton, Unions Reach Settlement over Minimum-Wage Back Pay, Motion to Hold Mayor in Contempt," *Scranton Times Tribune*, July 31, 2012. http://tinyurl.com/DROMLockwood.

[19] Michael A. Fletcher, "Baltimore Takes Lead in Suit against Banks over Alleged Libor Manipulation," *Washington Post*, July 11, 2012. http://tinyurl.com/DROMFletcher.

[20] Darwin BondGraham, "Oakland's Toxic Deal with Wall Street," *East Bay Express*, February 15, 2012. http://tinyurl.com/DROMGraham.

[21] Ellen Brown, "North Dakota's Economic Miracle—It's Not Oil," *YES! Magazine*, August 31, 2011. http://tinyurl.com/DROMBrown2.

The idea is relatively simple: All state revenues are deposited in the bank and interest on loans is returned to the community rather than handed to a far-away lender. North Dakota's bank makes stable, low-interest credit available for infrastructure projects and emergency aid, enabling municipalities to avoid the municipal bond trap. It's also further strengthened the local economy by providing credit for small businesses and green energy projects. Bills have been introduced in seventeen states to start public banks, but it's an uphill battle: The banking industry is doing its best to prevent public banking from catching on.[22]

It's certainly possible that different financial and legal structures could help fix our budgets, but the only way to truly defend ourselves against a system that values profits over people is to have real democratic control over our towns, cities, states, and lives. And maybe it's time to start imagining what a world without profits could look like. At the very least, we must insist that banks no longer write the laws dictating how our communities are financed, and that the public has not just a review or an "input," but the power to decide how public resources are used. Over thirty years ago, the city of Porto Allegre in Brazil pioneered a process called "participatory budgeting" that directly involves citizens in determining priorities for municipal spending. It's since been used in over three hundred cities across the world, though only two small districts in New York and Chicago have begun the process here in the United States.[23]

But the idea that some debts can and should be refused is a sentiment that's spreading. In Europe, the rallying cry of the anti-austerity movement has become "we won't pay for your crisis!" Groups from Spain to Tunisia are performing "citizen's audits" of their governments and financial institutions, deciding for themselves which debts are legitimate, and which should be abolished.[24] Have you ever looked at your town budget? Do you know how your elected and non-elected officials fund public works? Who benefits? Who really ends up paying for what? Simply posing these questions in your community is an important first step toward striking debt!

---

[22] Theo Anderson, "The Revolution Will Be Capitalized," *In These Times*, February 4, 2013, http://tinyurl.com/DROMAnderson.

[23] Elizabeth Whitman, "Participatory Budgeting Hits New York City," *The Nation*, April 16, 2012. http://tinyurl.com/DROMWhitman.

[24] Marisa Holmes, "Debt Versus Democracy: A Battle for the Future," *Truthout*, January 2, 2013. http://tinyurl.com/DROMHolmes2.

RESOURCES
Websites
• The Participatory Budgeting Project (participatorybudgeting.org)
• Public Banking Institute (publicbankinginstitute.org)

Articles
• "Citizen Debt Audit Platform: 'We Don't Owe! We Won't Pay!'" *Committee for the Abolition of Third World Debt*, May 14, 2012, http://tinyurl.com/DROMCADTM.
• Amy Goodman, "Matt Taibbi on the Unfolding Libor Scandal and What Senator DeMint's Departure Means for Fractured GOP," *Democracy Now!*, December 13, 2012, http://tinyurl.com/DROMGoodman.
• Jason Hackworth, "Local Autonomy, Bond-Rating Agencies and Neoliberal Urbanism in the United States," *International Journal of Urban and Regional Research* 26, no. 4, 2002, http://tinyurl.com/DROMHackworth.
• "How Cities Can Pursue Responsible Banking: Model Local Responsible Banking Ordinance Creates Community Reinvestment Requirements for Financial Institutions," *National Community Reinvestment Coalition*, July 2012, http://tinyurl.com/DROMNCRC.
• L. Owen Kirkpatrick and Michael Peter Smith, "The Infrastructural Limits to Growth: Rethinking the Urban Growth Machine in Times of Fiscal Crisis," *International Journal of Urban and Regional Research* 35, no. 3, 2011, http://tinyurl.com/DROMKirkpatrick.
• Gretchen Morgenson, "Police Protection, Please, for Municipal Bonds," *New York Times*, August 4, 2012, http://tinyurl.com/DROMMorgenson.
• Observatorio Metropolitano, *Crisis and Revolution in Europe: People of Europe, Rise Up!* (Madrid, 2011) http://tinyurl.com/DROMOM.
• Rachel Weber, "Selling City Futures: The Financialization of Urban Redevelopment Policy," *Economic Geography* 86, no. 3, 2010, http://tinyurl.com/DROMWeber.

REFERENCES
Anderson, Theo. "The Revolution Will Be Capitalized." *In These Times*, February 4, 2013. http://tinyurl.com/DROMAnderson.

Block Movement. "Peoples Transportation Program." *YouTube*, March 2009. http://tinyurl.com/DROMPTP.

BondGraham, Darwin. "Oakland's Toxic Deal with Wall Street." *East Bay Express*, February 15, 2012. http://tinyurl.com/DROMGraham.

Brown, Ellen. "North Dakota's Economic Miracle—It's Not Oil." *YES! Magazine*, August 31, 2011. http://tinyurl.com/DROMBrown2.

Church, Steven, William Selway, and Dawn McCarty. "Jefferson County Alabama Files Biggest Municipal Bankruptcy." *Bloomberg News*, November 9, 2011. http://tinyurl.com/DROMChurch.

Congressional Budget Office. "Fiscal Stress Faced by Local Governments." *Eco-

nomic and Budget Issue Brief. Washington, DC: GPO, 2010. http://tinyurl.com/DROMCBO.

Dunn, Julia. "Pay It Forward: Group Responds to Subway Fare Hike with Free Swipes." *The Indypendent,* June 25, 2009. http://tinyurl.com/DROMDunn.

Families United for Racial and Economic Equality and The Urban Justice Center. "Out of Business: The Crisis of Small Businesses in Rezoned Downtown Brooklyn." July 2008. http://tinyurl.com/DROMFUREE.

Fletcher, Michael A. "Baltimore Takes Lead in Suit against Banks over Alleged Libor Manipulation." *Washington Post,* July 11, 2012. http://tinyurl.com/DROMFletcher.

Frederick, Brian. "Minnesota Vikings Set to Fleece Unwilling Taxpayers for New Stadium." *ThinkProgress,* February 17, 2012. http://tinyurl.com/DROMFrederick.

Holmes, Marisa. "Debt Versus Democracy: A Battle for the Future." *Truthout,* January 2, 2013. http://tinyurl.com/DROMHolmes2.

Jubilee, Jay. "Fare Strike Coalition Declares 'Fare-Free Friday.'" *Boston Fare Strike Coalition,* July 30, 2012. http://tinyurl.com/DROMJubilee.

Larson, Ann. "Cities in the Red: Austerity Hits America." *Dissent,* November 16, 2012. http://tinyurl.com/DROMLarson.

Lockwood, Jim, and David Singleton, "Scranton, Unions Reach Settlement over Minimum-Wage Back Pay, Motion to Hold Mayor in Contempt." *Scranton Times Tribune,* July 31, 2012. http://tinyurl.com/DROMLockwood.

Meyer, Rachel. "California's Prison Spending Grows While the State Budget Shrinks." *The WIP,* January 28, 2010. http://tinyurl.com/DROMMeyer.

Moody, Kim. *From Welfare State to Real Estate: Regime Change in New York City, 1974 to the Present.* New York: The New Press, 2007.

Nolan, Kathleen. *Police in the Hallways: Discipline in an Urban High School.* Minneapolis: University of Minnesota Press, 2011.

The Pew Center on the States. "One in 100: Behind Bars in America 2008." *The Pew Charitable Trusts,* February 2008. http://tinyurl.com/DROMPew.

Pranis, Kevin. "Doing Borrowed Time: The High Cost of Back-Door Prison Finance." *Justice Strategies,* January 1, 2007. http://tinyurl.com/DROMPranis.

Refund Transit Coalition. "Riding the Gravy Train: How Wall Street Is Bankrupting Our Public Transit Agencies by Profiteering off of Toxic Swap Deals." June 2012. http://tinyurl.com/DROMRTC2.

Ross, Janell. "Ohio County Stadium Debts Force Government to Sell Hospital, Raid Savings." *Huffington Post,* March 16, 2012. http://tinyurl.com/DROMRoss.

Taibbi, Matt. "The Scam Wall Street Learned from the Mafia." *Rolling Stone,* June 21, 2012. http://tinyurl.com/DROMTaibbi.

Whitman, Elizabeth. "Participatory Budgeting Hits New York City." *The Nation,* April 16, 2012. http://tinyurl.com/DROMWhitman.

Wise, Tim. "Racism, White Liberals, and the Limits of Tolerance." *TimWise.org,* December 4, 2000. http://tinyurl.com/DROMWise.

THIRTEEN
NATIONAL DEBT

THE POLITICS OF SCARCITY AND CONTROL

WHAT IS NATIONAL DEBT?

In common parlance, when we discuss the national debt of modern nations, we are typically referring to the total amount of money still outstanding that the government has borrowed from any and all sources. The debt may have been taken on to pay for government workers, social programs, infrastructure, research and development, or any expense that could not be paid by the Treasury Department as it came due. A significant portion of the current $16.74 trillion U.S. national debt (as of June 2013) has been taken on to make up for shortfalls caused by tax cuts for the wealthy,[1] or to pay for the war on terrorism and bailouts for banks and corporations. The debt is issued with the promise that by enabling ongoing accumulation and economic expansion, these debts will be paid with taxes collected in the future.

In technical terms, a distinction is often made between national and sovereign debt. Here, the term "national debt" specifically refers to money that is borrowed from sources within the country. Sovereign debt is borrowed from foreign sources like the World Bank, the International Monetary Fund (IMF) or nation-states like China. For our purposes, we will use the term "national debt" when discussing the total U.S. foreign and domestic debt, and will use "sovereign debt" when discussing the debts of other nations.

Government debt is important for us to understand because it profoundly affects the personal, "household" debt that most of the previous chapters have focused on. Government debt is often used as the justification for cutting government spending on subsidies for housing, health care, transportation, nutrition, and education,

---

[1] "The Daily History of the Debt," *Treasury Direct*, June 6, 2013. http://tinyurl.com/DROMTD3.

increasingly shifting the burden onto the shoulders of individuals and families, who often go into debt themselves as a result. The relationship between individual debt and government debt is not only fiscal, it is psychological as well. Citizens of an indebted state are held up as collective objects of shame in the same way that individual debtors are. A clear example of this parallel can be seen in the debt crisis in Greece, where Greek citizens are collectively depicted as being "lazy," "spendthrifts," and "out of control." Similar accusations have been made against people in the global South whose governments have been at a debt impasse since the debt crises of the 1990s. In battles over deficit spending in the United States, whole sectors of populations including the poor, the elderly, immigrants, and the imprisoned are similarly dismissed as parasites.

SCARCITY AND CONTROL

When the international financial system collapsed in 2008, many governments were forced to take on significant amounts of new debt. This was due in large part to severe drops in tax revenues and billions of dollars spent to bail out whole sectors of their economies. Meanwhile, interest rates for borrowing soared for those countries in the most distress. Here in the United States, from December 2007 to January 2009, 3.6 million jobs were lost.[2] The decline in employment resulted in the loss of tax revenue and an increase in government spending through social programs like unemployment compensation. This, in addition to the trillions of dollars spent bailing out banks and corporations, led to a dramatic increase in the national debt. To make matters worse, the national debt was already at record highs after thirty years of tax cuts for the rich and corporations as well as wars for oil in the Middle East. Conservative politicians used the debt they were largely responsible for creating to push even harder for cuts to social programs and the privatization of schools and other public assets. These cuts by the federal government trickled down to the states, counties, cities, towns, and other local municipalities.

Economic readjustments of these kinds are happening around the world. In the European Union (EU), Greece, Spain, Portugal, Ireland, and Italy have been forced by the EU to undergo IMF-like austerity programs that cut government jobs, social services, and privatized government-owned properties and services. These policies have a history.

---

[2] "The Employment Situation—January 2009," *Bureau of Labor Statistics*, January 2009. http://tinyurl.com/DROMBLS4, 1.

Controlling value

After World War II a new constellation of global power emerged in which the United States became increasingly dominant. Though the transfer of power had already happened in regards to both the military and industry, the new financial and monetary framework was negotiated at the Bretton Woods summit of 1944, shortly after which the dollar became the new international reserve currency. Importantly, the summit also produced two powerful new international lending institutions, the International Monetary Fund (IMF) and the World Bank. Both were created with the intention of expanding global trade, working in concert to provide loans to countries in need under the guise of alleviating poverty.

In the 1970s and 1980s, large influxes of capital from oil producing nations began flowing into New York investment banks, creating an urgent need for new profitable investment opportunities at a time of global economic stagnation. The solution was to loan the money at high interest rates to credit-starved governments of the global South. When defaults began to occur, rather than allowing lenders to take a loss, the IMF and World Bank were called on to provide "relief" to distressed debtor nations. They offered to restructure countries' debts but only at a price: governments desperate for relief were forced to implement draconian structural adjustment programs. Large-scale privatization and cuts to social programs and infrastructure projects further impoverished these nations and immiserated their citizens while conveniently opening up sectors of their economies to further exploitative investment.[3] The new loans were themselves often structured in ways that ultimately perpetuated, extended, and increased debt, causing still deeper impoverishment.

These policies and practices reinforced and exacerbated the longstanding patterns of domination and exploitation that were established during the era of colonialism, in effect recolonizing countries that had won sovereignty through anti-colonial struggles. Valiant struggles calling for the abolition of debt in the global South took off in the 1990s and continue today.

The makings of a meltdown

The 2008 international financial crisis was a meltdown of epic proportions. But this was not simply the result of particular abstract economic instruments going awry. A long history of deregulation of the financial industry and Wall Street's subsequent manipulation of derivatives and other financial instruments set the stage for the most

---

[3] David Harvey, *A Brief History of Neoliberalism* (New York: Oxford, 2005).

recent economic crisis.[4] Important regulations put in place after the Great Depression were significantly repealed under Reagan, but the deathblow to the U.S. regulatory structure was delivered under Clinton with the repeal of the Glass-Steagall Act.[5] This law separated traditional banking functions from the risky speculation of stock brokerage houses like Goldman Sachs. Treasury secretary Robert Rubin advised the president to repeal the law, then resigned, and was subsequently paid over $10 million a year by Citigroup, the parent company of Citibank. Alan Greenspan, then chairman of the Federal Reserve and fervent champion of unregulated free markets, also strongly supported the repeal of Glass-Steagall, insisting the banks would regulate themselves because it was in their own best interest.[6]

To fully understand the relationship of national debt to our current economic crisis, we must understand the relationship of the Federal Reserve to the government and the financial industry. In addition to regulating the banking industry, all U.S. paper money is issued by the Federal Reserve. (The words "Federal Reserve Note" are printed on each bill.) When the Federal Reserve creates money, it does so by selling treasury bills to banks and private investors. This means that whenever the Fed creates money, it increases the national debt. One might think that an institution with so much direct influence in creating debt that accrues in our name would necessarily be a fully public institution beholden to thorough democratic oversight. In actuality, the Federal Reserve is better described as a half-public, half-private institution. Although the U.S. president appoints the Fed's chairperson, private bankers are involved in and profit from the operations of the Fed. Private bankers even serve on the Fed's Board of Directors. And, of course, there is the ever-present "revolving door" which allows government officials to rotate with ease between jobs in the private sector and in government service. These practices, which allowed the banking and financial industries to engage in the reckless and fraudulent speculation that led to the 2008 crash, continue to this day.

CONCLUSION

In an article titled "Recovery in U.S. Is Lifting Profits, but Not Adding Jobs," the *New York Times* described our current situation as

---

[4] John Carney, "The Warning: Brooksley Born's Battle with Alan Greenspan, Robert Rubin and Larry Summers," *Business Insider*, October 21, 2009. http://tinyurl.com/DROMCarney.

[5] Board of Governors of the Federal Reserve System, *The Federal Reserve System: Purposes and Functions* (Washington, DC: GPO, 2005). http://tinyurl.com/DROMFed2, 65.

[6] Andrew Clark and Jill Treanor, "Greenspan—I Was Wrong About the Economy. Sort of," *The Guardian*, October 23, 2008. http://tinyurl.com/DROMClark.

the "golden age of corporate profits."[7] This obscene scenario, where "the economy" is taking off but the majority of us are left waving from the runway, is a direct result of over thirty years of neoliberal policy at work. On July 23, 2012, *Forbes* reported, "around the world the extremely wealthy have accumulated at least $21 trillion in secretive offshore accounts. That's a sum equal to the gross domestic products of the United States and Japan added together. The number may sound unbelievable, but the study was conducted by James Henry, former chief economist at the consultancy McKinsey, an expert on tax havens and offshoring."[8] Why is austerity imposed on nations around the world when profits are skyrocketing and untaxed trillions are being hidden in plain sight? Corporations and the elite have abundance while the rest of us are told to make do with less.

Whatever words we use to name our current economic system, it always ends up with economic crisis and austerity. Before the 1929 Stock Market Crash and Great Depression there were similar crashes throughout the nineteenth century. These cycles have repeated throughout history. Indeed, the crash has made visible the otherwise often-obscured nature of capitalism and its political architecture; it is an extremely unequal social system that metes out rewards and punishments through the continuous and violent imposition of discipline and control.

No one knows precisely what a postcapitalist world would look like but we do understand the necessity of working toward a more equitable society and a healthier relationship with the environment. To achieve these goals, the solution must be international. Strike Debt is part of an international debt resisters' movement that demands a global jubilee. Thousands of protesters in Iceland put pressure on the government to refuse to pay its fraudulently imposed national debt. Today, after five years, Iceland has emerged from austerity to economic stability after renegotiating with their foreign creditors.[9] Before them, the people of Argentina were responsible for similar measures in their country, and the resistance continues to be widespread. The Pakistan Debt Cancellation Campaign (PDCC) and other groups staged a number of actions including a three-day hunger strike camp outside the World Bank Islamabad Office in 2010, resulting in the Senate passing a resolution seeking debt relief. PDCC has demanded

---

[7] Nelson D. Schwartz, "Recovery in U.S. Is Lifting Profits, but Not Adding Jobs," *New York Times*, March 3, 2013. http://tinyurl.com/DROMSchwartz.

[8] Frederick E. Allen, "Super Rich Hide $21 Trillion Offshore, Study Says," *Forbes*, July 23, 2012. http://tinyurl.com/DROMAllen.

[9] Simon Bowers, "Iceland Rises from the Ashes of Banking Collapse," *The Guardian*, October 6, 2013. http://tinyurl.com/DROMBowers.

that the government tax the rich and cut military spending as an alternative to accruing further sovereign debt. In El Salvador, people have been calling for an audit of their nation's debt while fighting against the "Public-Private Partnership Law" (P3), the auctioning off of services like education and health care to foreign multinational corporations. And, as the Campaign for Social and Economic Justice (CSEJ) in Jamaica has proclaimed in a leaflet about the debt of their country, "Much of the debt is odious and illegitimate as any debt audit would reveal. We need a moratorium on both local and foreign debt servicing—it is the only way forward."[10]

There have been proposals in the United States, Europe, and countries in the global South to create alternative banking systems based on a local, horizontal, and democratic structures. In the United States, the Public Banking Institute is working to create independent state banks to serve local communities similar to North Dakota's State Bank (*see Chapter Twelve*). Other plans are more inventive and visionary and would challenge the banking system by removing private bankers from national banks.

The struggle against national debts and financial capitalism has been one of the most tenacious in the last few decades. It has often been identified with "The Battle in Seattle" and the other street battles against the IMF, the World Bank, and the World Trade Organization throughout the so-called developed world—in Ottawa, Geneva, Genoa, and other cities. But in fact, that struggle has been expressed in countless demonstrations, general strikes, urban insurrections, and rural guerrilla wars throughout the global South. For example, the Zapatistas rose up in the southernmost province of Mexico, Chiapas, in 1994 to vehemently reject the North American Free Trade Agreement (NAFTA)—a deal that committed their country to further undemocratically implemented, far-reaching structural adjustments, including deep cuts in social spending and mass-privatization of the communal land of over a million indigenous people.

The struggle against debt is not limited to efforts to liberate individuals; the debt bondage of whole societies is also at stake. Much has been gained in these struggles and there is much to learn from their histories. Indeed, many South American nations have been able to escape the control of the IMF and World Bank, but many have died and others are left in poverty due to debt-justified cutbacks and privatizations. The calls for the abolition of personal and government debts are entwined and while the stakes are high, we also find many allies, past and present, who have joined the fight.

---

[10] Cited in Jeremy Dear, Paula Dear, and Tim Jones, "Life and Debt: Global Studies of Debt and Resistance," *Jubilee Debt Campaign*, October 2013. http://tinyurl.com/DROMDear, 22.

RESOURCES

Websites

• Committee for the Abolition of Third World Debt (cadtm.org)

Articles and Books

• Gar Alperovitz, *What Then Must We Do? Straight Talk about the Next American Revolution* (White River Junction, VT: Chelsea Green, 2013).

• Nicholas Bakalar, "Rise in TB Is Linked to Loans from IMF," *New York Times*, July 22, 2008, http://tinyurl.com/DROMBakalar.

• William K. Black, *The Best Way to Rob a Bank Is to Own One: How Corporate Executives and Politicians Looted the S&L Industry* (Austin: University of Texas Press, 2005).

• Eduardo Galeano, *Open Veins of Latin America: Five Centuries of the Pillage of a Continent* (New York: Monthly Review, 1997).

• Michael Hudson, "Why Iceland and Latvia Won't (and Can't) Pay for the Kleptocrats' Ripoffs," *Counterpunch*, August 18, 2009, http://tinyurl.com/DROMHudson2.

• Naomi Klein, *The Shock Doctrine: The Rise of Disaster Capitalism* (New York: Picador, 2011).

• David Levitz, "Icelanders Refuse Bank Debt Payoff to Britain and Netherlands," *Deutsche Welle*, April 10, 2011, http://tinyurl.com/DROMLevitz.

• Steven McCabe, "The Spectacular Rise, Fall and Recovery of Iceland's Economy—Are There Lessons for Us?" *Birmingham Post*, September 19, 2012, http://tinyurl.com/DROMMcCabe.

• Geoff Mann, *Disassembly Required: A Field Guide to Actually Existing Capitalism* (Oakland: AK Press, 2013).

• "The Third World Debt Crisis," *New Internationalist*, March 7, 2000, http://tinyurl.com/DROMNI.

REFERENCES

Allen, Frederick E. "Super Rich Hide $21 Trillion Offshore, Study Says." *Forbes*, July 23, 2012. http://tinyurl.com/DROMAllen.

Board of Governors of the Federal Reserve System. *The Federal Reserve System: Purposes and Functions*. Washington, DC: GPO, 2005. http://tinyurl.com/DROMFed2.

Bowers, Simon. "Iceland Rises from the Ashes of Banking Collapse." *The Guardian*, October 6, 2013. http://tinyurl.com/DROMBowers.

Carney, John. "The Warning: Brooksley Born's Battle with Alan Greenspan, Robert Rubin and Larry Summers." *Business Insider*, October 21, 2009. http://tinyurl.com/DROMCarney.

Clark, Andrew, and Jill Treanor. "Greenspan—I Was Wrong about the Economy. Sort Of." *The Guardian*, October 23, 2008. http://tinyurl.com/DROMClark.

Dear, Jeremy, Paula Dear, and Tim Jones. "Life and Debt: Global Studies of Debt and Resistance." *Jubilee Debt Campaign*, October 2013. http://tinyurl.com/DROMDear.

Harvey, David. *A Brief History of Neoliberalism*. New York: Oxford, 2005.

Schwartz, Nelson D. "Recovery in U.S. Is Lifting Profits, but Not Adding Jobs." *New York Times*, March 3, 2013. http://tinyurl.com/DROMSchwartz.

"The Third World Debt Crisis." *New Internationalist*, March 7, 2000. http://tinyurl.com/DROMNI.

Treasury Direct. "The Daily History of the Debt." June 6, 2013. http://tinyurl.com/DROMTD3.

U.S. Bureau of Labor Statistics. "The Employment Situation—January 2009." February 6, 2009. http://tinyurl.com/DROMBLS4.

FOURTEEN
CLIMATE DEBT

AN OVERDUE BALANCE

WHO'S THE REAL DEBTOR HERE?

Throughout this manual, we've been examining the many ways in which the wealthy and the powerful use claims of debt to steal from and exert control over the vast majority of us. No matter how destructive the results, we are constantly told (and tell ourselves) that such a system is morally just because of a supposedly simple, eternal truth: *Money owed must be repaid.* This deeply entrenched and widely held belief in the black-and-white morality of debt is the linchpin that holds the debt system in place.

But nothing is ever as simple as it seems. At their core, monetary debts are extremely narrow and simplified ways of representing what are often very complicated relationships between creditors and debtors. If we can zoom out from the simple calculation of money owed and look at the broader histories, human relationships, and power dynamics that lie behind a debt, it quickly becomes clear that there are countless ways to imagine who owes what to whom. Seen in this expanded context, a claim that repayment of a debt is morally just can begin to seem absurd. (And yet, despite the often-questionable moral legitimacy of their claims, the harsh truth is that it's usually the ones with the most powers of economic coercion and brute force at their disposal that get to decide which debts are legitimate in the end.)[1]

Nowhere is this dynamic better represented than by the sovereign debts imposed on the people of the global South, as discussed in the previous chapter. For decades, northern banks, the IMF, and the World Bank have demanded that residents of much poorer countries be held responsible for the repayment of loans taken on in their names, often by undemocratic regimes and under outrageous terms that might make a Goldman Sachs banker blush. Under the simple

---

[1] David Graeber, *Debt: The First 5,000 Years* (New York: Melville House, 2011). http://tinyurl.com/DROMGraeber, 14.

logic of debt, the failure to repay such loans has been used to justify the imposition of harsh, undemocratic "reforms" that have caused immense suffering.

But if we pull back and begin to look at the long history of domination, exploitation, and destruction imposed on the people of debtor nations to the benefit of their so-called creditors, it immediately becomes apparent just how questionable the morality of these simple calculations is. For instance, how many dollars should Great Britain pay African nations for the approximately 2.8 million people they abducted into the transatlantic slave trade? What should the annual interest rate be on the debt Spain owes, say, Peru, for the tons of silver it extracted through forced labor, and what should the penalty be for five hundred years of late payment? Though such calculations could never account for the true cost of centuries of suffering and oppression, when confronted with the simple morality that states "all debts must be repaid," it's important to think for a moment about who is really the debtor, and who is the creditor.

Along those lines, as the effects of human-induced climate change have begun to wreak havoc on a global scale, global justice movements have formulated a vitally important question in response: How do the South's monetary debts to foreign creditors compare with the North's liabilities for environmental impacts since the dawn of industrialization? The resulting concept of climate debt, first introduced almost twenty-five years ago, has provoked a powerful ongoing dialogue, elucidating stark disparities in how climate change is caused and experienced around the world.

After over two hundred years of humans spewing massive amounts of carbon dioxide and other greenhouse gases into the earth's atmosphere, the planet is on the verge of an unprecedented ecological catastrophe. We've already seen record-breaking droughts, superstorms, hurricanes, heat waves, and floods. And that's just the tip of the (quickly melting) iceberg. But, historically, people in what have come to be known as "developed nations" are by far the largest emitters of greenhouse gases and have reaped the lion's share of the economic benefits when compared to those of the global South. And although the whole planet is experiencing rising temperatures, the impact is far from equal. Both the IMF and the World Bank have acknowledged that the brunt of the impact will be borne by some of the poorest populations in the world, further immiserating them.[2]

To say nothing of the human misery, suffering, and death wrought by climate change past, present, and future, surely even just the simple monetary costs to the South of repairing damage, adapt-

---

[2] Christine Lagarde, "A New Global Economy for a New Generation," (presented at the World Economic Forum, Davos, Switzerland, January 23, 2013). http://tinyurl.com/DROMLagarde.

ing as possible, and mitigating future damage must be considered a massive debt owed to them by the North. In demanding repayment of this debt, movements for climate justice have done much to highlight the economic forces that compel the destruction of the environment for the benefit of the few at the expense of all—but particularly the world's poorest. To truly understand the nature of the debt that's owed, we'll need to understand the origins of the climate crisis a bit more thoroughly.

Growth, development, and the origins of climate debt

The current vast disparities in wealth, power, and standards of living between the people of developed nations and those of the global South reflect long histories of colonial domination and, later, exploitation through the neoliberal global economic order. In many ways, this centuries-long dynamic has been intensified, shaped, and transformed by industrialized nations' utter addiction to carbon-based fuels.

For most of human history, the naturally renewable energy sources humans used to sustain ourselves were readily found on the earth's surface: firewood, wind, water, animal power, etc. But, at around the turn of the nineteenth century, as the industrial era was dawning, new technologies made it possible to mine massive quantities of carbon-based fuel in the form of coal. Suddenly, people in the industrial centers of northern and central Europe (and soon the United States) were able to tap into extraordinarily potent stores of energy that had accumulated below the earth over millions of years.[3]

The introduction of such an intense productive power into Europe's mix of industrial capitalist and colonial enterprises created enormous amounts of wealth and began a stretch of growth in productive output unparalleled in human history. It also had profound impacts on the way Western societies developed, continually transforming everything from modes of transportation, agriculture, and the organization of cities, to legal systems, forms of government, and the division of labor.[4] Colonies, mobilized to provide critical raw materials for Western industry, were industrialized at a much slower pace and, over time, the disparity in wealth between them and their colonizers increased exponentially.

In various ways, the large-scale transition of Western economies from coal to oil and the emerging global economic order of the mid-twentieth century greatly reduced the political power of labor and increasingly freed capitalist interests from the control of nation states.

---

[3] Timothy Mitchell, *Carbon Democracy: Political Power in the Age of Oil* (New York: Verso, 2011), 15.

[4] David Harvey, *A Companion to Marx's Capital* (New York: Verso, 2010), 203.

With capitalist profit-seeking behavior liberated and further intensified by uninterrupted flows of carbon in the form of oil, it became possible to imagine a global economic system based on growth without limits[5]—though that growth was increasingly concentrated in the hands of the few, at home and abroad.

By the time the era of direct colonialism came to an end in the decades following World War II, carbon-rich industrialization had so thoroughly transformed the entire "Western way of life" that traditional ways of living in far-less industrialized countries of the global South stood in stark contrast. Without irony, industrialized governments seeking to extend their economic and political control pointed to the disparity in wealth between the "developed" North and the "undeveloped" South as justification for the imposition of unsustainable and paternalistic economic development programs through institutions like the IMF.[6] Promising investments and improvements in material conditions, "development experts" were deployed across the global South to push for the top-down implementation of economic, technological, and social changes, dismissing indigenous traditions and worldviews that might conflict with their visions of "progress."

But, to many, it's long been clear that Western-style economic development is as unsustainable as the Western way of life itself. In 1972, the influential Club of Rome think-tank published a groundbreaking and disturbing report titled *The Limits to Growth*, which concluded that the current rates of industrial growth could not be sustained ecologically in the long-term.[7] Subsequent surveys, drawing upon a wider range of experts and a more comprehensive network of scientific data, amplified the 1972 warning about the ruinous impact of unrestrained growth. Thirty years later, the *Limits to Growth* team reprised their study, confirming the original predictions of economic and civilizational collapse in the course of the twenty-first century.[8]

Despite these and many other grave warnings, at this current stage of industrial capitalist development, carbon-enabled growth has become so deeply imbricated in the political, economic, and social operations of everyday life in developed nations that growth is no longer a means to an end, but a necessary end in itself. If capitalism is to continue in anything like its current form, production and consumption must steadily increase whether or not they fulfill a genuine need.

---

[5] Mitchell, *Carbon Democracy*, 15.

[6] Arturo Escobar, *Encountering Development: The Making and Unmaking of the Third World* (Princeton, NJ: Princeton University Press, 1995), 17.

[7] Donella H. Meadows, Dennis L. Meadows, Jørgen Randers, and William W. Behrens III, *The Limits to Growth* (New York: Universe Books, 1972).

[8] Donella H. Meadows, Jørgen Randers, and Dennis L. Meadows, *The Limits to Growth: The 30-Year Update* (White River Junction, VT: Chelsea Green, 2004).

Any slowdown in economic growth (a recession) and the entire system begins to fall apart. Perversely, governments at all levels are tasked first and foremost with ensuring growth—a good quality of life for their citizens is a distant second at best, and the health of the planet that sustains us barely registers.[9]

The crisis is here

Whatever one might make of the decision to organize entire societies around the need for ever-increasing profits, the fact of the matter is that such a choice is no longer an option—at least when it comes to profits enabled by carbon-based fuels. For one thing, the earth's supply of carbon-based energy is limited, and we're starting to bump up against that limit. Extracting fossil fuels has become an increasingly costly and energy-intensive enterprise, and while we may be able to prolong the inevitable with new, environmentally destructive technologies like fracking and deep-sea drilling, it won't be long before the costs and energy required to extract carbon from the earth outweigh the benefits.

But more importantly, the burning of fossil fuels, deforestation, and other destruction of plant life through capitalist activity has lead to a massive buildup of carbon dioxide and other gases in the earth's atmosphere. Before industrialization, carbon absorbed by plants and the oceans more or less balanced emissions from volcanoes and other sources. But over the last two centuries of carbon-fueled capitalist growth, a dramatic rise in greenhouse gases has begun to increase the amount of heat retained on the planet, causing wild fluctuations in global temperatures and destabilizing the balance that made settled human life possible for the past twelve thousand years.

Scientists calculate the amount of carbon dioxide in the atmosphere in measurements of parts per million (PPM). Historically, carbon dioxide was about 275 PPM. NASA scientist James Hansen has calculated that the highest level of carbon dioxide and its equivalents that the atmosphere can safely contain is about 350 PPM.[10] Currently, we're at 394 PPM and rising rapidly. The average global temperature has already increased by one degree Celsius and predictions consistent with current observations suggest that the temperature will rise by six to eight degrees Celsius by 2100 unless dramatic measures are taken soon. All the ruinous impacts we have seen so far are just the beginning. We're quickly approaching a point of no return.

The development-inclined World Bank concludes in a recent report that even if countries adhere to UN-brokered emissions-reduc-

[9] Harvey, *A Companion to Marx's Capital*, 259.

[10] James Hansen et al., "Target Atmospheric CO_2: Where Should Humanity Aim?" *The Open Atmospheric Science Journal* 2, 2008. http://tinyurl.com/DROMHansen, 226.

tion pledges—and they haven't been thus far—we're likely to see a 3.5 to 4 degree Celsius increase this century. The report warns that such an increase will result in unprecedented heat waves, water scarcity, food shortages, droughts, increasingly powerful hurricanes, inundation of coastal cities, and severe impacts on ecosystems. Ominously, it continues, "a 4°C [warmer] world is so different from the current one that it comes with high uncertainty and new risks that threaten our ability to anticipate and plan for future adaptation needs."[11]

Some see global crisis on an unprecedented scale unfolding in as little as a few years. Guy McPherson, an ecologist who has been studying climate change for twenty-five years, estimates that we'll cross the threshold of 400 PPM in the next couple of years. "At that time," he says, "we'll also see the loss of Arctic ice in the summers." Loss of Arctic ice means solar radiation that would otherwise have been reflected back out of the atmosphere will now be absorbed by the ocean, causing a significant intensification in warming and unleashing a host of unpredictable repercussions for global weather patterns. He warns, "The implications are truly dire and profound for our species and the rest of the living planet."[12]

Calculating the debt

The concept of ecological debt was first introduced by Chile's Instituto de Ecología Política in the lead-up to the 1992 Earth Summit in Rio de Janeiro—the first major international climate summit, involving representatives and heads of state from 172 governments. Ecological debt was explicitly presented as a framework for discussing how much of their sovereign debts countries in the South should pay in light of the historical legacy of resource exploitation, loss of biodiversity, pollution, and outright destruction they've suffered at the hands of the North. Many argued that the obligation to repay the more recent high-interest loans had to be balanced against moral and economic liabilities from the more distant past.[13]

But, as with any monetary debt, the full dimensions of ecological debt did not readily lend themselves to quantification. (How do you calculate the dollar value of a traditional way of living that's no longer possible?) Still, carbon emissions can be reliably measured and certainly represent a quantifiable economic benefit to those who emit

[11] Potsdam Institute for Climate Impact Research and Climate Analytics, "Turn Down the Heat: Why a 4°C Warmer World Must Be Avoided," *The World Bank*, November 2012. http://tinyurl.com/DROMWB, ix.

[12] Cited in Dahr Jamail, "Are We Falling off the Climate Precipice? Scientists Consider Extinction," *TomDispatch.com*, December 17, 2013. http://tinyurl.com/DROMJamail.

[13] Andrew Ross, "Climate Debt Denial," *Dissent*, Summer 2013. http://tinyurl.com/DROMRoss3.

them, alongside a neatly correlating negative impact on the climate we all share. As the impacts of global climate change came more clearly into view, this portion of the ecological obligation, appraised on the basis of atmospheric emissions estimates by nation, emerged as the main vehicle for demanding repayment, and subsequently came to be known as climate debt.

A brief look at the breakdown of carbon emissions by nation over time quickly confirms what we already know: the lion's share of the greenhouse gases that are now wreaking ecological havoc were emitted to benefit industrial economies, profit-seeking enterprises, and the attendant consumer culture rooted in countries of the North. To give one quick example of the disparities the data reveals, the average Briton emits about as much carbon dioxide in one day as a Kenyan will in an entire year.[14]

Though the profits of climate destruction tend to accrue to those who've caused it, it so happens that the world's poorest people, largely in nations of the global South, experience the destructive effects in extreme disproportion. One reason for this disparity is geographical: increase in sea levels, desertification, and storms all tend to occur with the most intensity nearer to the equator, around which many of the world's poorest nations are arrayed. Additionally, many inhabitants of the South live and sustain themselves in traditional ways that are often intimately reliant on their specific local environments. When those environments change dramatically, or are no longer inhabitable, the challenge of adapting is far greater than it is for the larger propor- tion of people in industrialized nations whose climate-change-inducing consumption and production processes are less specifically local.

Poorer nations also simply lack the money needed to mitigate, adapt to, or repair the destruction that's being visited upon them. The impact of recovery and cleanup is eating into a significant percentage of the GDP of nations that are already struggling to maintain a foothold in a global economy stacked against them. In 2012, record-breaking Typhoon Bopha slammed into the Philippines, causing then-unprec- edented death and destruction. Describing his country's predicament at the time, a Filipino UN negotiator explained, "We have never had a typhoon like Bopha. . . . Each destructive typhoon season costs us 2% of our GDP, and the reconstruction costs a further 2%, which means we lose nearly 5% of our economy every year to storms. . . . We have not seen any money from the rich countries to help us to adapt. . . . We cannot go on like this."[15]

---

[14] Rachel Oliver, "Rich, Poor and Climate Change," *CNN.com*, February 18, 2008. http://tinyurl. com/DROMOliver.

[15] Cited in John Vidal, "Will Philippines Negotiator's Tears Change Our Course on Climate

The following year, the Philippines were hit again. Typhoon Haiyan, the strongest cyclone to make landfall in recorded history, killed over six thousand people, displaced millions more, and caused billions of dollars of damage. Such events will undoubtedly continue with increasing frequency and intensity thanks to the greenhouse-gas-induced warming of the ocean. Why should Filipinos, who on average emit 0.9 metric tons of carbon annually, pay for the destruction wrought by people in nations like the United States, who emit 17.6?[16]

And yet, despite the outsized role the United States plays in perpetuating the climate crisis, it's important not to close our eyes to the deep disparities in experiences of climate change that exist even within the wealthier countries where it's produced. Although U.S. residents are the global leaders in carbon use, members of the wealthiest 1% in the United States use ten thousand times more carbon than the average U.S. resident.[17] And climate-induced disasters on the scale of Hurricane Katrina and Superstorm Sandy readily exposed the uneven pattern of impacts within cities, where communities of color and poor populations were often devastated and the wealthy often left relatively unscathed.

Climate debt in default

Though, crucially, the '92 Earth Summit in Rio failed to set clear, enforceable goals for the reduction of carbon emissions, 154 governments did ratify the United Nations Framework Convention on Climate Change (UNFCCC), which created a formal international process for negotiating coordinated global action in response to the climate crisis. (Forty more countries have since signed on.) Since then, climate justice activists and governments of the world's least developed countries have been elaborating the concept of climate debt and pushing the cause for repayment at major UNFCCC conferences. Results have often been slow in coming. Tellingly, despite the intense ongoing UNFCCC negotiations held since '92, the amount of carbon pumped into the atmosphere annually has nearly doubled.

After 2009's Copenhagen summit once again failed to produce meaningful, legally binding commitments from industrialized nations for compensation and emissions reductions, over thirty thousand grassroots activists from 140 countries came together in Cochabamba, Bolivia to consolidate their demands. Organized around principles of participatory democracy, the 2010 World People's Conference on Cli-

Change?" *The Guardian*, December 6, 2012. http://tinyurl.com/DROMVidal.

[16] Annie Lowrey, "The Inequality of Climate Change," *New York Times*, November 12, 2013. http://tinyurl.com/DROMLowrey.

[17] Wolfgang Gruener, "Bill Gates Uses 10,000 Times the Energy of the Average American, MIT Says," *TG Daily*, April 28, 2008. http://tinyurl.com/DROMGruener.

mate Change produced a detailed People's Accord, which outlined a legal framework for how the North can be held accountable for their outsized role in the destruction of the climate.[18]

Among other things, the document calls on the North to "decolonize the atmosphere" by reducing and absorbing their emissions; to guarantee the human rights of the hundreds of millions forced to migrate by eliminating restrictive immigration policies; to monetarily compensate the South for the "loss of development opportunities due to living in a restricted atmospheric space"; to pay the costs of mitigation and adaptation; and to finance and share clean technologies.[19] Bolivia submitted a proposal to the UNFCCC based on the Cochabamba accords shortly thereafter.

But they're up against an array of powerful interests. Governments of wealthy nations—particularly the United States—have obstructed climate justice proposals at virtually every turn. With a little digging, behind these government officials' and diplomats' intransigence, you can usually find the influence of a sophisticated network of ultra-rich individuals who benefit from the climate crisis through crisscrossing networks of trade, finance, and carbon-rich industry. An eye-opening 2011 report from the International Forum on Globalization maps how these "carbon billionaires" use their personal wealth to exert a tremendous amount of influence, playing governments off of each other and holding climate negotiations hostage to ensure they can continue reaping profits without being held accountable for the environmental costs.[20]

BEYOND GROWTH AND DEBT

Within our current nation-state-based global political framework, calculating climate debts by country may be the most practical way to account for the history of Northern-imposed capitalist industrial development and the disparities in wealth and mass-destruction it continues to cause. Those of us who live in wealthy nations, to the extent that we engage with or agitate against the governments that claim to represent us, must demand that reparations are made for the environmental damage caused by over two hundred years of intense exploitation of the earth's natural resources at the expense of the world's poorest.

---

[18] Nicole Fabricant and Kathryn Hicks, "Bolivia vs. the Billionaires: Limitations of the 'Climate Justice Movement' in International Negotiations," *North American Congress on Latin America*, Spring 2013. http://tinyurl.com/DROMFabricant.

[19] "Peoples Agreement," *World People's Conference on Climate Change and the Rights of Mother Earth*, April 22, 2010. http://tinyurl.com/DROMPWCCC.

[20] "Outing the Oligarchy: Billionaires Who Benefit from Today's Climate Crisis," *International Forum on Globalization*, December 2011. http://tinyurl.com/DROMIFG.

But in the same way that calculations of monetary loans simplify complicated relationships, calculating climate debt by nation-states' emissions can obscure important exploitive power dynamics that exist at every level in a globalized neoliberal economy. Ultimately, beyond the billionaires and intransigent governments that perpetuate climate change lies the compelling force of the global capitalist economy itself, the very existence of which hinges on the ability to burn and emit carbon without acknowledging the costs. Its logic is integrated into our very way of life. As such, paying back the climate debt owed must be seen as just the first step towards setting aside our collective obsession with growth.

This is the fundamental challenge of climate change. If we're going to avert complete destruction of the environment, what's really needed is a radical shift in the values that guide us, along with a transformation of the way we organize our lives and our communities. A global economic system that relies on never-ending economic growth inevitably means more carbon emissions and greater climate change. To those of us who've lived our entire lives in such a world, it's difficult to know how to begin imagining new ways of living together prosperously, with respect for each other and our shared climate. There are no simple answers.

But traditional cultures that have been resisting the imposition of Western-style economic development for decades may be able to provide some clues in the search for alternatives. In Andean regions of Latin America for example, over decades of common struggle against the destructive effects of development projects, a rich discourse around concepts of *vivir bien* has emerged among diverse communities of indigenous people, peasant groups, and the urban poor. Though a simple translation of the Spanish words "vivir bien" would be something like "to live well," the term refers to a confluence of rich political and philosophical concepts of "harmonious living" emerging from Aymara, Quechua, Kichwa, Guarani, and other regional traditions.[21]

As these traditions largely lack notions of linear progress, their concepts don't lend themselves to simple translation, but provide valuable counterpoints to Western worldviews. Though different cultures emphasize different aspects, concepts of vivir bien generally address issues Westerners might group under the term "quality of life," but with the understanding that true well-being can only occur in a community. Importantly, nature is considered to be part of the community rather than simply a setting or a resource to be exploited. Though concepts

---

[21] Eduardo Gudynas, "Buen Vivir: Today's Tomorrow," *Development* 54, no. 4, 2011. http://tiny url.com/DROMGudynas.

of vivir bien have been enshrined in the constitutions of both Bolivia and Ecuador, it doesn't represent a fixed set of principles. It continues to evolve in response to technocratic, commodifying, growth-focused development ideologies, yet draws in other facets of Western thought when useful as well. As Western cultures begin to imagine what life after the past two hundred years of carbon-fueled growth might look like, we might do well to draw in aspects of vivir bien in return.

RESOURCES
Articles and books

- Anthony Costello, Mustafa Abbas, Adriana Allen, Sarah Ball, Richard Bellamy, Sharon Friel, Nora Groce, Anne Johnson, Maria Kett, Maria Lee, Caren Levy, Mark Maslin, David McCoy, Bill McGuire, Hugh Montgomery, David Napier, Christina Pagel, Jinesh Patel, Jose Antonio, Puppim de Oliveira, Nanneke Redclift, Hannah Rees, Daniel Rogger, Joanne Scott, Judith Stephenson, John Twigg, Jonathan Wolff, and Craig Patterson. "Managing the Health Effects of Climate Change," *The Lancet* 373 (2009): 1693–1733. http://tinyurl.com/DROMCostello.
- "Each Country's Share of CO_2 Emissions," *Union of Concerned Scientists*, August 20, 2010. http://tinyurl.com/DROMUCS.
- International Climate Justice Network, "Bali Principles of Climate Justice," *World Summit on Sustainable Development*, August 2002. http://tinyurl.com/DROMICJN2.
- Tim Jackson, "Prosperity without Growth? The Transition to a Sustainable Economy," *Sustainable Development Commission*, March 2009. http://tinyurl.com/DROMJackson.
- Cedric Johnson, *The Neoliberal Deluge: Hurricane Katrina, Late Capitalism, and the Remaking of New Orleans* (Minneapolis: University of Minnesota Press, 2011).
- Naomi Klein, *The Shock Doctrine: The Rise of Disaster Capitalism* (New York: Picador, 2011).
- Austin Ramzy, "After Protests, Chinese City Halts Chemical Plant Expansion," *Time*, October 20, 2012. http://tinyurl.com/DROMRamzy.
- "Shouldering the Costs: Who Pays in the Aftermath of Hurricane Sandy?" *Strike Debt*, December 2, 2012. http://tinyurl.com/DROMSD.

REFERENCES

Escobar, Arturo. *Encountering Development: The Making and Unmaking of the Third World*. Princeton, NJ: Princeton University Press, 1995.

Fabricant, Nicole, and Kathryn Hicks. "Bolivia vs. the Billionaires: Limitations of the 'Climate Justice Movement' in International Negotiations." *North American Congress on Latin America*, Spring 2013. http://tinyurl.com/DROMFabricant.

Graeber, David. *Debt: The First 5,000 Years*. New York: Melville House, 2011. http://tinyurl.com/DROMGraeber.

Gruener, Wolfgang. "Bill Gates Uses 10,000 Times the Energy of the Average American, MIT Says." *TG Daily*, April 28, 2008. http://tinyurl.com/DROMGruener.

Gudynas, Eduardo. "Buen Vivir: Today's Tomorrow." *Development* 54, no. 4 (2011): 441–447. http://tinyurl.com/DROMGudynas.

Hansen, James, Makiko Sato, Pushker Kharecha, David Beerling, Robert Berner, Valerie Masson-Delmotte, Mark Pagani, Maureen Raymo, Dana L. Royer, and James C. Zachos. "Target Atmospheric CO_2: Where Should Humanity Aim?" *The Open Atmospheric Science Journal* 2 (2008): 217–231. http://tinyurl.com/DROMHansen.

Harvey, David. *A Companion to Marx's Capital*. New York: Verso, 2010.

International Forum on Globalization. "Outing the Oligarchy: Billionaires Who Benefit from Today's Climate Crisis." December 2011. http://tinyurl.com/DROMIFG.

Jamail, Dahr. "Are We Falling off the Climate Precipice? Scientists Consider Extinction." *TomDispatch.com*, December 17, 2013. http://tinyurl.com/DROMJamail.

Lagarde, Christine. "A New Global Economy for a New Generation." Presented at the World Economic Forum, Davos, Switzerland, January 23, 2013. http://tinyurl.com/DROMLagarde.

Lowrey, Annie. "The Inequality of Climate Change." *New York Times*, November 12, 2013. tinyurl.com/DROMLowrey.

Meadows, Donella H., Dennis L. Meadows, Jørgen Randers, and William W. Behrens III. *The Limits to Growth*. New York: Universe Books, 1972.

Meadows, Donella H., Jørgen Randers, and Dennis L. Meadows. *The Limits to Growth: The 30-Year Update*. White River Junction, VT: Chelsea Green, 2004.

Mitchell, Timothy. *Carbon Democracy: Political Power in the Age of Oil*. New York: Verso, 2011.

Oliver, Rachel. "Rich, Poor and Climate Change." *CNN.com*, February 18, 2008. tinyurl.com/DROMOliver.

Potsdam Institute for Climate Impact Research and Climate Analytics. "Turn Down the Heat: Why a 4°C Warmer World Must Be Avoided." *The World Bank*, November 2012. http://tinyurl.com/DROMWB.

Ross, Andrew. "Climate Debt Denial." *Dissent*, Summer 2013. http://tinyurl.com/DROMRoss3.

Vidal, John. "Will Philippines Negotiator's Tears Change Our Course on Climate Change?" *The Guardian*, December 6, 2012. http://tinyurl.com/DROMVidal.

World People's Conference on Climate Change and the Rights of Mother Earth. "Peoples Agreement." April 22, 2010. http://tinyurl.com/DROMPWCCC.

FIFTEEN

PROSPECTS FOR CHANGE

JOIN THE RESISTANCE!

The chapters of this manual highlight the inherent injustice of the kinds of debt that afflict most people living in the United States and around the world today, and provide some advice about what to do about them. If anything should be clear by now, it's that all of these forms of debt are connected. They didn't all just somehow happen. This is a system that's been built to keep money flowing from our pockets into those of Wall Street, corporations, and creditors, with the hope that we won't do anything about it.

Being in debt can be isolating and demoralizing. Understanding the debt system holistically is just the first step toward collectively envisioning and enacting its abolition. The reason you have tens of thousands of dollars in medical bills is that we don't provide medical care to everyone. The reason you have tens of thousands of dollars of student loans is because the government, banks, and university administrators have contrived to cut government subsidies that support education while driving college costs through the roof. Unlike fifty years ago, it's simply impossible for all but the wealthiest to attend college without them. Bubbles drive housing and food prices up, wages are kept artificially low so that they don't keep up with inflation, and more and more of us rely on proliferating forms of "casual," "flexible," and part-time employment.

The moment we can make these connections in our own lives, we can stop being ashamed and start getting angry—and most of all, we can turn our outrage into action. Any way that you are able to fight back is important. But what those running and benefitting from the debt system are really afraid of is that a large number of us might start to join together. That's why it's so important to them that debtors feel ashamed and alone. Because they know that by keeping us isolated, we have no power. They also know that the moment large numbers of debtors start talking to each other, joining forces, and fighting back—they're in big trouble. The whole system is built on the assumption that we won't.

There is strength in numbers. Individually our debts overwhelm us; collectively a debt resistance movement can overwhelm the system. We are not looking for debt "forgiveness" because we didn't do anything wrong. We seek the abolition of debt profiteering, the creation of a new financial system, a new economy, and a new way of life based on justice, self-determination, and concern for the common good.

LOOKING BACKWARD

Movements for debt resistance have a very long history. From ancient times, people have challenged the harsh penalties visited on defaulters, including branding, torture, imprisonment, and even slavery. In ancient Athens, the first known democratic constitution came about largely as a result of an outright rebellion of debtors (who at that time were primarily male heads of household) outraged at seeing their wives and children seized and carried off in chains to slavery.

As for the United States, imprisonment for debt was common here well after the War of Independence (two signers of the Declaration of Independence themselves later ended up imprisoned for debt!). The 1780s saw a huge wave of foreclosures and debt imprisonments. There were various forms of debt resistance at this time, with the most dramatic being Shays's Rebellion, a group of veterans who banded together to stop foreclosures. It took many campaigns and mobilizations throughout the first half of the nineteenth century to abolish debtors' prisons (though people are still incarcerated because of debt—see *Chapter Nine*). After the Civil War, there were outright insurrections waged by small farmers being foreclosed upon against the "trusts" that were the ancestors of giant U.S. corporations.

During the 1920s there was an expansion of credit and rampant speculation that led to the 1929 Stock Market Crash. The ensuing Great Depression made the consequences of extreme inequality and unchecked capitalist exploitation clear. The limits of capitalism and the possibilities for alternative ways of organizing society were deeply felt. People banded together to block home evictions and farm foreclosures, workers organized their own credit and mutual aid associations, labor unions were a force to be reckoned with, and the Communist Party couldn't be denied as a genuine political presence. As a desperate move to shore up faltering confidence in a capitalist system, politicians brokered a compromise between an insurgent left and a nervous capitalist class in the form of the New Deal. The new rights and services established under this compromise provided a baseline of respect for human life and some modicum of dignity for many Americans, but they were systematically denied to Black people, who were not considered to be among those worthy of receiving them. The state and the banks largely took over the job of organizing pensions (Social Security), mortgages (Fannie Mae), university education (the GI Bill) and, in the 1960s, health care (Medicare).

During a series of financial crises in the 1970s, business and financial interests took advantage of workers' weakened position to reassert their power and begin a decades-long walk-back of this postwar compromise. Overall, the defunding of government programs and the long decline of labor unions resulted in a massive increase of debt and suffering, and economic inequality has once again returned to the extraordinary heights of pre-Depression days. And yet, despite the capitalist classes' shredding of this tacit social contract, we're just now seeing the first glimmers of a people's movement here in the United States that demands the space to imagine and experiment with postcapitalist ways of life and rejects the debt system that disciplines us. Thankfully, there's much inspiration to be found in movements for economic justice across the world.

Debt resistance movements have cropped up just about everywhere across the planet. The Global Justice Movement that emerged in much of the global South in the 1980s, 1990s, and early 2000s was a broad constellation of social struggles against paying "odious" national debts (that is, debt for things no person or country should have had to pay for to begin with) to international banks. In many ways, it was brilliantly successful, forcing banks—both private lenders and institutions like the World Bank and International Monetary Fund—to renegotiate the loans by cutting their interest rates, reducing the principal, and in some cases simply canceling loans outright.

There have also been some remarkable struggles against personal debt during those same years, like the movement of El Barzón in Mexico. In 1994, the Mexican peso dramatically lost value compared to the U.S. dollar, which set off a steep inflation that increased the interest on variable-rate loans and often made loans, including mortgages, that were denominated in U.S. dollars ten times larger. This brought nearly 30% of the people indebted to banks into default.[1] The El Barzón movement began by claiming that the loan repayment conditions after the collapse of the peso were the fault of the government and the banks, and that it would be unfair to hold the debtor responsible. Their slogan was, "*Debo, no niego, pago lo justo*" ("I owe, I don't deny it, I'll pay what is fair"). The movement grew rapidly across the country and was known both for its

---

[1] Heather Williams, *Planting Trouble: The Barzón Debtors' Movement in Mexico* (San Diego: Center for U.S.-Mexican Studies, 1996).

practical approach (by setting up legal consultation services for debtors) and its riveting tactics. It forced the government to come to the aid of the embattled debtors and had a definitive, positive impact on their situation.

Still, the battle is far from being won. In 2008, the world's poorest countries were paying $23 million a day in interest payments to the rich industrial world, for loans where the original principal had often already been paid back several times over.[2] For much of the 1990s and '00s, one of the most popular refrains was that the real solution for "Third World poverty" was not less debt, but more. Hence the craze for "microfinance," the practice of making small cash loans without collateral to rural women as well as the urban poor. For a while, this new model swept the world, as it seemed to provide a magic bullet out of poverty. But as time went on, it became clear these microcredit banks weren't charities; they charged interest and were followed by other banks charging even higher rates of interest. Intense shaming and repossessions began, and in recent years, India and Bangladesh have seen a mass wave of suicides of "beneficiaries" of microcredit loans unable to face the disgrace of inability to pay. There have been popular movements that have risen up to fight microcredit; Mujeres Creando (Women Creating) is a Bolivian anarcha-feminist collective that participates in a range of anti-poverty work, including propaganda, street theater, publishing, radio programming, and direct action. In 2001, they occupied the Bolivian Banking Supervisory Agency on behalf of people indebted to microcredit agencies.

The Mujeres also helped a group called Deudora (Debtor)—made up largely of poor women from the barrios—infiltrate a special luncheon attended by the Banking Supervisory Agency's Superintendent and microcredit lenders. They took the opportunity to sing and shout about their suffering and denounce the bankers in front of several television cameras. After three and a half months of near-daily protests, the Mujeres and the Deudora managed to sit down with the large banking and financial associations and reach an agreement whereby the debtors whose houses were being auctioned would have their debts excused.[3]

THE RESISTANCE IS GROWING

Changing the financial system may seem wildly ambitious, but in fact, financial systems change all the time. The question is whether it will change for the better.

---

[2] "Our Campaign for Climate Justice," *World Development Movement*, accessed May 17, 2013. http://tinyurl.com/DROMWDM.

[3] Juventudes Libertarias de Bolivia, "With Dynamite and Molotovs, Anarchists Occupy Government Buildings," trans. Robby Barnes and Sylvie Kashdan, *A-Infos*, July 2, 2001. http://tinyurl.com/DROMJLB.

Anti-debt movements exist and they're growing stronger. Around the world, popular movements are beginning to rattle the chains, seeing debt for what it is—a form of domination and exploitation—and collectively rising up against it. From Chile to Québec, students have challenged the bondage of educational debt traceable to cutbacks and privatization and scored major victories. In Greece, Spain, and now Italy, we're seeing veritable uprisings against governments demanding austerity so that tax money can flow exclusively to foreign bondholders. These movements are growing ever more effective. And governments have been forced to backtrack.

It's important to note that when these movements win, it's almost never by lobbying the politicians or playing the games of the creditor class. We'll never win so long as those in power make up the rules and so long as we concede to them. The aim is not just to cancel debts but to fight the conditions and values that got us into debt in the first place. And increasingly, people are starting to realize that the way to do that is not to ask for anything, but to start creating new institutions of our own by which we can collectively provide for our needs. Bankers and politicians are frightened by direct challenges to power that would render them irrelevant.

As our movement gets stronger, we can be sure the politicians will make concessions that undermine substantial change. We've already seen a little of this in the United States. The Obama administration has set up the Consumer Financial Protection Bureau and has begun talking about tinkering with the student loan system. But— inadequate as these measures may be—the Obama administration never would have done any of this were it not for the growing wave of defaults and increasing signs of organized debt resistance. In the end, as was the case with the New Deal, the aim of reform is not primarily to help people, but to preserve the existing structure of power. This doesn't mean that we shouldn't fight the government on its own terms (for example, by opposing cuts to social programs or further tax cuts for the rich). But we've seen over and over again that the only way to make the government and the elite take notice is to set our own terms, by being clear about what values matter to us—health, housing, education, our environment, and our relationships.

HOW DO WE STRIKE DEBT?

Strike Debt, an offshoot of Occupy Wall Street, emerged out of a series of open assemblies in the spring of 2012 with the aim of sparking conversations about debt as a global system of domination and exploitation. Debt resistance can take many forms and Strike Debt is developing tactics, resources, and frameworks for generalizing the fight against the debt system. Underlying all of Strike Debt's projects—from this manual to the Rolling Jubilee to various direct actions and examples of mutual aid—is support for a jubilee: a full cancellation of all debts. The cancellation of debts is not a new notion, but rather one that is deeply rooted in many faith traditions including Judaism, Christianity, and Islam. Historically, civilization after civilization has recognized that when debt gets unmanageable, it must be cancelled. And jubilees still work today. For example, there was a kind of jubilee in Iceland after the 2008 economic crisis: instead of bailing out their banks, Iceland canceled a percentage of mortgage debt (*see Chapter Thirteen*).

To promote this concept and raise awareness about how the wealthy profit from our indebtedness, Strike Debt launched the Rolling Jubilee in November of 2012, and it has been our most visible project so far. Strike Debt raised over $600,000 from thousands of individual donors, many deeply indebted themselves, to purchase defaulted debt for pennies on the dollar and keep it out of the hands of collectors. We have entered this market not to make a profit but to help people by abolishing $15 million worth of debt all over the country to date, while highlighting how the debt system preys on our families and communities.

Like the manual you are reading, the Rolling Jubilee was designed to expose and undermine the ways that debt works. Few people realize that their debts are sold on shadowy markets to speculators hoping to cash in on suffering and misfortune. The Rolling Jubilee effort was never intended to be a solution to the debt crisis. Strike Debt recognizes that the impact of debt cancellation, even on a mass scale, would be negligible unless it was coupled with a far deeper restructuring of our economic system. We need a jubilee *and* a total transformation of the current financial paradigm. We need a final jubilee to end the need for jubilees.

Debt resistance is not the final goal of the movement; it is just a beginning. We must ensure that these new structures sustain the environment that has always sustained us. What will these structures look like? How will we build them? We do not have all the answers, but the questions have to be asked. Traditionally, alternative economies have focused on local forms of mutual aid that operate under and within capitalism. While these models are desirable, it will be important for us to increase their breadth and scale if we are to challenge and eventually replace our failed economic system. Our values will serve as our North Star: putting people and nature before profits; meeting need and not greed; empowering all and not just a few; becoming less alienated from our work and from each other; and creating more leisure time to spend with our loved ones. As the content of this manual has demonstrated, another world is both possible and necessary.

Small-scale examples already abound. Community-supported agriculture is a growing alternative to the industrial food system. Community land trusts offer a model of affordable housing that prevents foreclosures of homes and property speculation. "Really, Really Free Markets" based on fair trade are dedicated to sharing resources on the basis of a gift economy in which the exchange of used furniture and clothing, childcare, and skilled labor are just a few examples. Employee-owned companies and worker-controlled, democratically run cooperatives are flourishing. To support these endeavors we need a new banking system that offers non-exploitative forms of credit and that is run for the benefit of all, not just the lenders who extract income from loans, investments, and rent. We must remember that as part of the ongoing bailout of the financial sector, billions if not trillions of dollars of loans were handed out at 0% interest, millions of dollars of which ended up as Wall Street bonuses. One of many possible solutions worth investigating is public banking (*see Chapter Twelve*), where states, cities and local communities finance individual initiatives and communal enterprises.

What other forms can debt resistance take? That is something we need to figure out together. We must work to understand the intricacies of our debt-driven economy. We also need to listen to and learn from the people around us so we can understand how debt affects our lives in both similar and uneven ways, paying keen attention to the ways that it intersects with factors like race, gender, age, ability, nationality, and so on. As we have seen, predatory lending, from subprime mortgages to payday loans to for-profit colleges, disproportionately impact low-income communities and communities of color. The issue of debt also affects us as workers, connecting this movement to fights for higher wages and better benefits. Debt resistance also dovetails with broader struggles for racial equality and economic justice, and we need to make these connections more visible and powerful.

For now, there are countless ways to "strike" debt: demanding a people's bailout and an end to corporate welfare; collectively refusing to pay illegitimate loans; targeting and shutting down collections agencies, payday lenders, or for-profit colleges; regulating loan speculators out of business; reinstating limits on usurious interest rates; defending foreclosed homes; fighting tuition hikes and school budget cuts; resisting austerity policies; fighting militarism, which accounts for half of our nation's discretionary spending; organizing debtors' associations and unions; and more. On the constructive side, building an alternative economy run for mutual benefit is a long-term goal. To get there we must experiment with everything from education, counseling, direct action, financial civil disobedience, and, importantly,

building relationships among ourselves to create broad social movements. Debt resistance needs to spread far and wide and be adapted
to different contexts and communities.

In contrast to the recklessness and manipulation by the individuals who sit atop our financial system, those of us who advocate debt
resistance take our collective responsibility very seriously. By dissolv-
ing the bonds that bind us to corporations, financial institutions, and
governments all over the world, we seek to forge new bonds with one
another based on equitable and sustainable forms of exchange.

At the time of this writing, examples of financial manipulation
continue to arise. Matt Taibbi recently wrote an article revealing
another scandal equal to or greater than Libor. It is titled, "Everything
Is Rigged: The Biggest Price-Fixing Scandal Ever."[4] The subtitle goes
on to report, "The second huge financial scandal of the year reveals the
real international conspiracy: There's no price the big banks can't fix."
But this is no aberration of capitalism; this is its essence.

Remember: we don't owe Wall Street anything, we owe each other
everything. The possibilities of organizing around debt resistance are
only beginning to be realized. Strike Debt, like Occupy Wall Street,
hopes to inspire both autonomous action and collective resistance.

RESOURCES
Articles and Books

• William K. Black, *The Best Way to Rob a Bank Is to Own One: How Corporate Executives and Politicians Looted the S&L Industry* (Austin: University of Texas Press, 2005).
• George Caffentzis, "University Struggles at the End of the Edu-Deal," *Mute Magazine*, April 15, 2010, http://tinyurl.com/DROMCaffentzis1.
• George Caffentzis, "Workers against Debt Slavery and Torture: An Ancient Tale with a Modern Moral," *Edu-Factory*, July 2007, http://tinyurl.com/DROMCaffentzis4.
• Harry Cleaver Jr., "Notes on the Origin of the Debt Crisis," *Midnight Notes*, 1990, http://tinyurl.com/DROMCleaver.
• Silvia Federici, "African Roots of U.S. University Struggles: From the Occupy Movement to the Anti-Student-Debt Campaign," *unsettling knowledges*, January 2012, http://tinyurl.com/DROMFederici1.
• Silvia Federici, "The Debt Crisis, Africa and the New Enclosures," *Midnight Notes*, 1990, http://tinyurl.com/DROMFederici2.
• María Galindo, "The Creative Force of Bolivian Debtors," in *Quiet Rumours: An Anarcha-Feminist Reader* (3rd edition), ed. Dark Star Collective (Oakland: AK Press, 2012), 128–29.

[4] Matt Taibbi, "Everything Is Rigged: The Biggest Price-Fixing Scandal Ever," *Rolling Stone*, April 25, 2013. http://tinyurl.com/DROMTaibbi2.

- Clifford Geertz, *The Rotating Credit Association: A Middle Rung in Development* (Cambridge, MA: Massachusetts Institute of Technology, Center for International Studies, 1956).
- David Graeber, *Debt: The First 5,000 Years* (New York: Melville House, 2011), http://tinyurl.com/DROMGraeber.
- Lamia Karim, *Microfinance and Its Discontents: Women in Debt in Bangladesh* (Minneapolis: University of Minnesota, 2011).
- Midnight Notes Collective and Friends, *Promissory Notes: From Crisis to Commons*, 2009, http://tinyurl.com/DROMMidnight.
- Scott Pierpont, "Disobeying the Banks: An Interview with Enric Duran," *Institute for Anarchist Studies*, December 2009, http://tinyurl.com/DROMPierpont2.

REFERENCES

Juventudes Libertarias de Bolivia. "With Dynamite and Molotovs, Anarchists Occupy Government Buildings." Translated by Robby Barnes and Sylvie Kashdan. *A-Infos*, July 2, 2001. http://tinyurl.com/DROMJLB.

Taibbi, Matt. "Everything Is Rigged: The Biggest Price-Fixing Scandal Ever." *Rolling Stone*, April 25, 2013. http://tinyurl.com/DROMTaibbi2.

Williams, Heather. *Planting Trouble: The Barzón Debtors' Movement in Mexico*. San Diego: Center for U.S.-Mexican Studies, 1996.

World Development Movement. "Our Campaign for Climate Justice." Accessed May 17, 2013. http://tinyurl.com/DROMWDM.

APPENDIX A:
SAMPLE LETTERS TO CREDIT
REPORTING AGENCIES

This content is slightly modified from Carreon and Associates (carreonandassociates.com). See *Chapter One* for information about credit reporting agencies.

Request for investigation of credit report

Dispute letter to credit bureau

"Intent to sue" letter to credit bureau

Reply to a CRA accusing you of credit repair

Send your letters to the address of the appropriate agency:

Experian	TransUnion Consumer Relations
P.O. Box 9556	P.O. Box 2000
Allen, TX 75013	Chester, PA 19022-2000

Equifax
P.O. Box 740241
Atlanta, GA 30374-0241

1. REQUEST FOR INVESTIGATION OF CREDIT REPORT

[Your Name]
[Your Address]
[Experian, Equifax or TransUnion address]
[Date]
Attn.: Consumer Relations

Consumer Relations Dept.:

I am requesting with this written notice that the following inaccurate items be removed from my credit report. The items are not correct and are causing me financial distress because of their derogatory information. The items are as follows:

[Creditor]
[Account number]
[Rating (e.g., curr was 30, charge off, 90 days, etc.)]
[Reason why it should be removed: i.e., not mine, never late, disputed before yet still remains, incorrect information like payment history, date opened or balance owed.]

I understand you are required to notify me of your investigation results within 30 days.

My contact information is as follows:

> [Your name, not signed]
> DOB: [Date of birth]
> SSN: [Social Security number]
> [Address]

Sincerely,

[Your name, signed]

2. DISPUTE LETTER TO CREDIT BUREAU

Provide any proof you have with this dispute.

> [Your Name]
> [Your Address]
> [Experian, Equifax or TransUnion address]
> [Date]

To whom it may concern:

In reviewing my credit report, I realized there are several inaccurate listings. These accounts are incorrect and several are outdated. The following accounts need to be investigated immediately to reflect my true credit history:

> Acct: [-xxxx-xxx:]

This account is listed as being 60 days late. I have never been late on this account.

> Acct: [-xxxx-xxx:]

This account is listed as being 30 days late. This account does not belong to me.

> Acct: [-xxxx-xxx:]

This account is listed as being 60 days late. The creditor lost my check and agreed to correct the late notation. (Enclosed is a copy of their letter stating such).

Additionally, you are reporting several other accounts as delinquent that are past the seven-year reporting time as allowed under the Fair Credit Reporting Act. The following accounts should be deleted immediately:

> Acct: [-xxx:] over seven years old
> Acct: [-xxx:] over eight years old
> Acct: [-xxx:] over seven years and four months old

Please forward an updated copy to me at your earliest convenience with the above noted corrections. My current address is listed above.

Sincerely,

[Your signature]

[Your printed name]

3. "INTENT TO SUE" LETTER TO CREDIT BUREAU

Send this letter to the CRA if you intend on suing them. You can sue them in your county for damages and subsequently send a copy of that to them, offering to settle or appear. If you sue them, be sure you have a case.

[Your Name]
[Your Address]
[Experian, Equifax or TransUnion address]
[Date]

To Whom It May Concern:
REF: Intent to file suit: violation of the FCRA

I have sent [#] previous letters to you, all by certified mail (copies of receipts enclosed) requesting that you remove inaccurate information from my file and you have failed to do so.

Accordingly, I can show a judge that these accounts are inaccurate and that you violated the Fair Credit Reporting Act by ignoring my requests to investigate the items. My previous letters—all sent certified mail—stated my reasons for an investigation and these reasons were not frivolous in any way.

If this final request does not prompt you to conduct a proper investigation of the accounts in question, and send proof to me of said investigation, I will file a civil suit in [name of your county, state] for damages. I take my credit very seriously and your lack of professionalism and assistance is unacceptable. I am well aware of my rights under the FCRA and intend to pursue them to the maximum.

I anticipate your response.

Sincerely,

[Your signature]

[Your printed name]

4. REPLY TO A CRA ACCUSING YOU
OF CREDIT REPAIR

Use this letter to demand that a credit bureau continue to investigate items you have initiated a dispute on. Often a CRA will accuse you of using a credit repair company, which by the way is your right! Here is a letter to put them in their place and to avoid slowing your disputes.

> [Your name]
> [Your address]
> [Experian, Equifax or TransUnion address]
> [Date]

To whom it may concern:

RE: Credit Repair Accusation

Please be advised that I have received your computer generated letter stating that you have ceased investigation of my credit reports because, in your opinion, you believe that I have used a third party credit repair agency. Not only do I believe this to be a stall tactic on your part to grant you an additional 30 days to comply with my original request, but I believe it to be a blatant violation of the FCRA.

You were advised by me on [insert date] by certified mail (copy enclosed) that I questioned the accuracy of a few items on my credit reports. That request was written by me and mailed by me—not a third party agency. It appears obvious to me that you are abusing your power under the FCRA to escape a complete investigation.

Additionally there is no law that states a consumer cannot use a third party, so using that as your excuse is a moot point. As a matter of fact, Congress has found the whole process so overwhelming that they afford consumers the right to use a third party on their behalf if the consumer so chooses. This is why your statement is so outrageous.

I reserve the right to sue your credit bureau for violations of the FCRA and I believe I can prove that you did not use reasonable measures to insure the accuracy of my credit reports and now you are stalling the process further.

Please take notice that this letter dated [insert today's date] is formal notice to you that I am requesting that you continue forward with my original investigation request and send the results to me within 15 days. I therefore legally and lawfully refuse your "form letter," thus giving you only 15 days, not 30 more.

I am outraged at your accusation and I have fully researched my rights in regards to my credit file. I look forward to your expediting my original request immediately.

Sincerely,

[Your signature]

[Your printed name]

APPENDIX B:
SAMPLE LETTERS TO CONSUMER
REPORTING AGENCIES FOR
CHECKING ACCOUNTS

All five sample letters have been modified from those made available on Chex-Systems Victims (chexsystemsvictims.com). See *Chapter One* for information about consumer reporting agencies for checking accounts.

ChexSystems/TeleCheck Letters:

> Initial dispute

> Demand for removal to reporting agency

> Procedural request

Financial Institution Letters:

> Demand for removal to financial institution (abuse/fraud)

> Demand for removal to financial institution (non-sufficient funds)

Send your letters to the address of the appropriate agency:

> ChexSystems Consumer Relations
> 7805 Hudson Road
> Suite 100
> Woodbury, MN 55125

> TeleCheck Services, Inc.
> Attention: Consumer Resolutions-FA
> P.O. Box 4514
> Houston, TX 77210

1. INITIAL DISPUTE

> [Your name]
> [Your address]
> [ChexSystems or TeleCheck address]
> [Date]

RE: Consumer ID # [Your Consumer ID #]

Consumer Relations Dept.:

I have recently been informed that there is negative information reported by [name of bank] in the file [ChexSystems/TeleCheck] maintains under my Social

Security number. Upon ordering a copy of the report, I see an entry from this bank listing a "[condition, e.g., NSF, overdraft, account abuse]" in [month] [year].

I am unaware of ever having a "[same condition]" from this bank. Please validate this information with [name of bank] and provide me with copies of any documentation associated with this "[same condition]" bearing my signature. In the absence of any such documentation, I ask that this information be immediately deleted from the file you maintain under my Social Security number.

You have 30 days to verify this information and to provide me with a document bearing my original signature. If you cannot, I am demanding removal under the Fair Credit Reporting Act.

This report is *severely* restricting my banking abilities.

My contact information is as follows:

> [Your name, not signed]
> [Social Security number]
> [Address]
> Cc: [Lawyer's name]

Sincerely,

[Your name, signed]

2. DEMAND FOR REMOVAL TO REPORTING AGENCY

> [Your name]
> [Your address]
> [ChexSystems or TeleCheck address]
> [Date]

RE: Consumer ID # [Your Consumer ID #]

Consumer Relations Dept.:

This letter is in response to your recent claim that [name of bank] has verified this account to be mine. Yet again, you have failed to provide me with a copy of any viable evidence submitted by [name of bank]. Be advised that the description of the procedure used to determine the accuracy and completeness of the information is hereby requested, to be provided within fifteen (15) days of the completion of your reinvestigation.

Additionally, please provide the name, address, and telephone number of each person contacted at [name of bank] regarding this alleged account. I am formally requesting a copy of any documents provided by [name of bank]. If [name of bank] does not validate the debt, it is a violation of the FCRA [611 [15 U.S.C. § 1681i] a 6 B iii:

"a notice that, if requested by the consumer, a description of the procedure used to determine the accuracy and completeness of the information shall be provided to the consumer by the agency, including the business name and address of any furnisher of information contacted in connection with such information and the telephone number of such furnisher, if reasonably available."

The listed item is entirely inaccurate and incomplete, and represents a very serious error in your reporting.

Failure to comply with federal regulations by credit reporting agencies is investigated by the Federal Trade Commission (see 15 U.S.C. § 41). I am maintaining a careful record of my communications with you for the purpose of filing a complaint with the FTC and the State Attorney General's office, should you continue in your noncompliance.

My contact information is as follows:

[Same as sample letter #1]

3. PROCEDURAL REQUEST

> [Your name]
> [Your address]
> [ChexSystems or TeleCheck address]
> [Date]

RE: Consumer ID # [Your Consumer ID #]

Consumer Relations Dept.:

As I have not heard back from you in over [15/30/45] days regarding my notice of dispute dated [date letter was sent], I must presume that no proof in fact exists.

You are currently in violation of the Fair Credit Reporting Act.

Your failure to respond, in writing, hand signed, and in a timely manner, will work as a waiver to any and all of your claims in this matter, and will entitle me to presume that you are reporting my name and Social Security number in error, and that this matter is permanently closed. Remove me from your records immediately.

Failure to respond within 30 days of receipt of this certified letter will result in a small claims action against your company. I will be seeking a minimum of $5,000 in damages for:

> Defamation
>
> Negligent enablement of identity fraud
>
> Violation of the Fair Credit Reporting Act

For the purposes of 15 U.S.C. § 1692 et seq., this notice has the same effect as a dispute to the validity of the alleged debt and a dispute to the validity of your claims. This notice is an attempt to correct your records, and any information received from you will be collected as evidence should any further action be necessary. This is a request for information only, and is not a statement, election, or waiver of status.

My contact information is as follows:

[Same as sample letter #1]

4. DEMAND FOR REMOVAL TO FINANCIAL INSTITUTION (ABUSE/FRAUD)

> [Your name]
> [Your address]
> [Name and address of original bank]
> [Date]

RE: Acct # [Your account #]

To whom it may concern:

This is a formal notice of dispute regarding information that [name of bank] sent to [ChexSystems/TeleCheck], a consumer reporting agency.

The following false information was sent to [ChexSystems/TeleCheck]:

> [List the information the way it is shown in the report]

This information was disputed with [ChexSystems/TeleCheck] on [date]; however, [Name of bank] verified the information as accurate. This falsely reported information damages my financial reputation and should be removed immediately.

[Name of bank] reported [account abuse/suspected fraud/fraud] when in fact, no [abuse/fraud] took place. There was no illegal activity on the account.

[Only include these two sentences if no money is owed to the reporting bank]: [Name of bank] did not experience any financial loss and no money is owed on this account. There was no violation of the account agreement that governed the account.

Under my rights under the Fair and Accurate Credit Transactions Act, I am asking for an investigation of this reported information, and removal of the false information reported to [ChexSystems/TeleCheck].

Sincerely,

[Your name]

cc: [Bank branch where account was opened]

5. DEMAND FOR REMOVAL TO FINANCIAL INSTITUTION (NON-SUFFICIENT FUNDS)

> [Your name]
> [Your address]
> [Name and address of original bank]
> [Date]

RE: Acct # [Your account #]

To whom it may concern:

This letter is regarding account # [xxxx-xxx], which you claim [condition, e.g., "I owe $100.00"]. This is a formal notice that your claim is disputed.

I am requesting validation, made pursuant to the Fair Debt Collection Practices Act. Please note that I am requesting "validation"; that is, competent evidence bearing my signature, showing that I have, or ever had, some contractual obligation to pay you.

Please also be aware that any negative mark found on my credit reports, including [ChexSystems/TeleCheck], from your company or any company that you represent for a debt that I do not owe is a violation of the Fair Credit Reporting Act. Therefore if you cannot validate the debt, you must request that all credit reporting agencies delete the entry.

Pending the outcome of my investigation of any evidence that you submit, you are instructed to take no action that could be detrimental to any of my credit reports.

Failure to respond within 30 days of receipt of this certified letter will result in legal action against your company. I will be seeking a minimum of $5,000 in damages for:

> Defamation

> Negligent enablement of identity fraud

> Violation of the Fair Credit Reporting Act

For the purposes of 15 U.S.C. § 1692 et seq., this notice has the same effect as a dispute to the validity of the alleged debt and a dispute to the validity of your claims. This notice is an attempt to correct your records, and any information received from you will be collected as evidence should any further action be necessary. This is a request for information only, and is not a statement, election, or waiver of status.

My contact information is as follows:

[Same as sample letter #1]

APPENDIX C:
SAMPLE LETTER TO COLLECTION AGENCIES REGARDING (ALLEGED) MEDICAL DEBT

This content is slightly modified from Carreon and Associates (carreonandassociates.com). See *Chapter Three* for information about medical debt.

Request to Validate Medical Debt

[Your name]	[Your address]
[Address of collection agency]	[Date]
Amount of debt: [ ]	Date of Service: [ ]
Provider of Service: [ ]	

Dear collection agent,

I received a bill from you on [date] and as allowed under the Fair Debt Collections Practices Act (FDCPA), I am requesting that you allow me to validate the alleged debt. I am aware that there is a debt from [name of hospital/doctor], but I am unaware of the amount due and your bill does not include a breakdown of any fees.

Additionally, I am allowed under the Health Insurance Portability and Accountability Act (HIPAA) to protect my privacy and medical records from third parties. I do not recall giving permission to [name of provider] for them to release my medical information to a third party. I am aware that the HIPAA does allow for limited information about me but anything more is to only be revealed with the patient's authorization. Therefore my request is twofold—validation of debt and HIPAA authorization.

Please provide breakdown of fees including any collection costs and medical charges.

Provide a copy of my signature with the provider of service to release my medical information to you.

Cease any credit bureau reporting until the debt has been validated by me.

Please send this information to my address listed above and accept this letter, sent certified mail, as my formal debt validation request, which I am allowed under the FDCPA. Please note that withholding the information you received from any medical provider in an attempt to be HIPAA compliant can be a violation of the FDCPA because you will be deceiving me after my written request. I request full documentation of what you received from the provider of service in connection with this alleged debt.

Additionally, any reporting of this debt to the credit bureaus prior to allowing me to validate it may be a violation of the Fair Credit Reporting Act, which can allow me to seek damages from a collection agent. I will await your reply with above requested proof. Upon receiving it, I will correspond back by certified mail.

Sincerely,

[Your Signature]

[Your Printed Name]   Certified mail No: [ ]

APPENDIX D:
SAMPLE LETTERS TO
COLLECTION AGENCIES

Both sample letters have been modified from those made available on Debt Consolidation Care (debtconsolidationcare.com/letters). See *Chapter Nine* for information about debt collection.

> Dispute letter
>
> Cease and desist letter

1. DISPUTE LETTER
> [Your name]
> [Your address]
> [Collection agency's address]
> [Date]

Dear [name of collection agency]:

I am writing in response to your [letter or phone call] dated [insert date], (copy enclosed) because I am disputing the alleged debt.

Before you contact me again, please provide me with the following documentation:

> proof that you own the debt or are authorized to collect on this debt on behalf of the current owner;
>
> proof that the debt was actually incurred by me with respect to the original creditor;
>
> a copy of any judgment (if applicable);
>
> proof that you are licensed to collect debts in [insert name of your state]

Be advised that I have documented all correspondence with respect to this debt and will not hesitate to report any violations of the law to my State Attorney General, the Federal Trade Commission, and the Better Business Bureau.

Finally, if you are not authorized to collect this debt thereon, I demand that you immediately forward this dispute letter to the original creditor to inform them of my dispute.

Sincerely,

[Your signature]

[Your printed name]

2. CEASE AND DESIST LETTER

[Your name]

[Your address]

[Collection agency's address]

[Date]

Dear [name of collection agency]:

This letter comes in response to your repeated attempts to contact me regarding an alleged debt, which I am contesting.

I demand that you cease and desist from any further attempt to contact me at work or by phone.

Please be aware that I will continue to document all attempts to communicate with me with respect to the alleged debt, and that any further such attempts may constitute a violation of the Fair Debt Collection Practices Act (FDCPA). I will not hesitate to report violations of the law to my State Attorney General, the Federal Trade Commission, and the national Better Business Bureau.

Sincerely,

[Your signature]

[Your printed name]

INDEX

See also payday loans; prepaid cards; subprime loans; transaction costs

G

Gates, Kelly, 6
gender, 5–6, 8, 10, 12, 112, 158–159, 210, 213
See also transgender people
general purpose reloadable (GPR) cards, 117–118
See also prepaid cards
"Get Checking" course, 36
GI Bill, 67, 71–72, 83, 209
See also ownership society
Ginnie Mae (Government National Mortgage Association), 82
Glass-Steagall Act, 190
gleaning, 167
Global Justice Movement, 196, 209
See also debt resistance, history of
global South, 1, 9, 101, 178, 188–189, 192, 195–198, 200–201, 203, 209–210
globalization. *See* neoliberalism
Goldman Sachs, 183, 190, 195
government debt. *See* municipal debt; national debt; state debt
grants, 67
Great Depression, 81, 83, 178, 190, 191, 208
infrastructure development, 178
Great Recession. *See* financial crisis of 2008
Greece, 188, 211
greenhouse gases, 196, 199, 201–202
See also carbon emissions
GreenPath, 160
Greenspan, Alan, 190
gross domestic product (GDP), 57, 201
growth, unlimited, 197–199, 203–205

H

Hamilton County, Ohio, 179
health care
condition-specific institutions, 172
convenient care clinics, 171
denial of treatment, 61
dental and vision care, 173
emergency room (ER), 61, 143, 172
for-profit, 56–58, 62
free care, 12, 61, 171
free clinics, 61, 171
in the United States, 56–58
medical loss ratio, 57
nonprofit, 62
public hospitals *vs.* private hospitals, 61
single-payer, 62
spending, 57–58
urgent care, 61
universal, 57, 62–63
See also medical debt
health insurance
bankruptcy, 55, 57–58, 154, 158
coverage, 57–61
premiums, 55
private insurance bills, 59

See also medical debt
Health Insurance Portability and Accountability Act of 1996 (HIPAA), 60
Healthcare for the 99%, 62
Healthcare-NOW!, 62
Henry, James, 191
Higgins, Jim, 114
Himmelstein, David, 56
homelessness, 5, 92, 110, 167, 169, 171
LGBTQ people and, 5
homeownership, 2, 72, 81–86, 89–94
household debt, 2–4, 41
See also consumer debt
housework, 7
housing debt. *See* mortgage debt
human rights, 171, 203
Hurricane Katrina, 202

I

Iceland, 191, 212
immigrants, 29, 102, 110–112, 114–115, 129, 133, 180, 182, 188, 203
criminalization of, 112
incarceration. *See* criminal justice system
income
difficulty for unbanked people to prove, 112
seasonal, 111
income inequality
corporate profits, 8, 20, 30, 57, 65, 69–70, 109–110, 120, 138, 178–179, 182, 191, 207, 213
LGBTQ people and, 5
people of color and, 2, 5–7, 56, 84–85, 111, 213
people with disabilities and, 5–6
transgender people and, 5
United States compared to peer countries, 6
women and, 5–8
Income-Based Repayment Plan (IBR), 72
indigenous people, 192, 198, 204
Individual Tax Identity Number (ITIN), as substitute for Social Security Number (SSN), 115
industrialization, 196–203
Innovis, 21
inquiries, credit scoring and, 23, 24, 29
Institute on Assets and Social Policy (IASP), 7
Institute on Taxation and Economic Policy (ITEP), 98
interest rates, 10, 23, 27, 31, 40–44, 42, 47–48, 69, 71–72, 74, 77, 82, 85, 99, 103, 110, 116, 125–126, 128–131
See also annual percentage rate (APR)
International Forum on Globalization, 203
International Monetary Fund (IMF), 9, 187–189, 192, 195, 196, 198, 209,
See also structural adjustment programs
interest rate swaps, 181–182
Ireland, 19, 188
IRS (Internal Revenue Service), 15, 97, 99, 100, 102–106
Islam, 154, 212
Italy, 188, 211

ABOUT STRIKE DEBT

The Debt Resisters' Operations Manual is a project of Strike Debt. Strike Debt is building a movement of debt resistance and liberation based on principles of anti-oppression, autonomy, democratic decision-making and direct action. Debt resistance can take many forms and Strike Debt is developing tactics, resources, and frameworks for expanding the fight against the debt system while developing alternative systems of mutual aid for the common good.

Strike Debt emerged out of thematic assemblies held in May 2012 in solidarity with the student strikes in Montreal. Occupy Theory, Occupy Student Debt Campaign, and Free University collaborated to hold an assembly on Education and Debt. Several weeks later, the group continued to meet under the name "Strike Debt." Strike Debt quickly realized that organizing around all forms of debt provided much-needed energy and systematic analysis to the movement.

In addition to this manual, Strike Debt initiatives include launching the "Rolling Jubilee," a mutual-aid project that buys debt at steeply discounted prices and then abolishes it; hosting debtors' assemblies; and planning direct actions across the country, ranging from debt burnings to targeted shutdowns of predatory lenders. Each project is seen as a strike against the predatory debt system.

To contact Strike Debt, please email **INFO@STRIKEDEBT.ORG** or visit **STRIKEDEBT.ORG**.

ABOUT PM PRESS

PM Press was founded at the end of 2007 by a small collection of folks with decades of publishing, media, and organizing experience.

We seek to create radical and stimulating media to entertain, educate, and inspire. We aim to distribute these through every available channel with every available technology, whether that means you are seeing anarchist classics at our bookfair stalls; reading our latest vegan cookbook at the café; downloading geeky fiction e-books; or digging new music and timely videos from our website.

Contact us for direct ordering and questions about all PM Press releases, as well as manuscript submissions, review copy requests, foreign rights sales, author interviews, to book an author for an event, and to have PM Press attend your bookfair:

PM Press • PO Box 23912 • Oakland, CA 94623
510-658-3906 • info@pmpress.org • www.pmpress.org

FOPM: MONTHLY SUBSCRIPTION PROGRAM

Friends of PM allows you to directly help impact, amplify, and revitalize the discourse and actions of radical writers and artists. It provides us with a stable foundation to build upon our early successes and provides a much-needed subsidy for the materials that can't necessarily pay their own way. You can help make that happen—and receive every new title automatically delivered to your door once a month. And, we'll throw in a free T-shirt when you sign up.

Here are your options:

- **$30 a month**: Get all books and pamphlets plus 50% discount on all webstore purchases
- **$40 a month**: Get all PM Press releases (including CDs and DVDs) plus 50% discount on all webstore purchases
- **$100 a month**: Superstar—Everything plus PM merchandise, free downloads, and 50% discount on all webstore purchases

For those who can't afford $30 or more a month, we have Sustainer Rates at $15, $10 and $5. Sustainers get a free PM Press T-shirt and a 50% discount on all purchases from our website.

Your Visa or Mastercard will be billed once a month, until you tell us to stop. Or until our efforts succeed in bringing the revolution around. Or the financial meltdown of Capital makes plastic redundant. Whichever comes first.

MORE FROM
COMMON NOTIONS

*Sex, Race, and Class—The Perspective of
Winning: A Selection of Writings 1952–2011*
by Selma James
ISBN: 978-1-60486-454-0
$20.00

"In this incisive and necessary collection of essays and
talks spanning over five decades, Selma James reminds
us that liberation cannot be handed down from above.
This is a feminism that truly matters."
—Dr. Alissa Trotz, Associate Professor of Women
and Gender Studies, Director of Caribbean Studies,
University of Toronto

---

*Revolution at Point Zero:
Housework, Reproduction,
and Feminist Struggle*
by Silvia Federici
ISBN: 978-1-60486-333-8
$15.95

"This timely collection of Federici's essays reminds us that
the shape and form of any revolution are decided in the
daily realities and social construction of sex, care, food,
love, and health. Women's struggle to take control of this
labor is everybody's struggle, just as capital's commodification of their demands is everybody's commodification."
—Massimo De Angelis, author of *The Beginning of History:
Values, Struggles, and Global Capital*

*In Letters of Blood and Fire: Work, Machines,
and the Crisis of Capitalism*
by George Caffentzis
ISBN: 978-1-60486-335-2
$19.95

"A historian of our own times, Caffentzis carries
the political wisdom of the twentieth century
into the twenty-first. Here is capitalist critique and
proletarian reasoning fit for our time."
—Peter Linebaugh, author of *The Magna Carta Manifesto:
Liberties and Commons for All*